AMERICAN SAINT

ALSO BY JOAN BARTHEL

A Death in Canaan
A Death in California
Love or Honor
Girl Singer

AMERICAN SAINT

THE LIFE *of* ELIZABETH SETON

❧

JOAN BARTHEL

THOMAS DUNNE BOOKS
ST. MARTIN'S PRESS ☙ NEW YORK

THOMAS DUNNE BOOKS.
An imprint of St. Martin's Press.

AMERICAN SAINT. Copyright © 2014 by Joan Barthel. Foreword copyright © 2014 by Maya Angelou. All rights reserved. Printed in the United States of America. For information, address St. Martin's Press, 175 Fifth Avenue, New York, N.Y. 10010.

www.thomasdunnebooks.com
www.stmartins.com

Designed by Anna Gorovoy

Library of Congress Cataloging-in-Publication Data

Barthel, Joan.
    American saint : the life of Elizabeth Seton / Joan Barthel. — First edition.
       pages cm
    Includes bibliographical references and index.
    ISBN 978-0-312-57162-7 (hardcover)
    ISBN 978-1-250-03715-2 (e-book)
    1. Seton, Elizabeth Ann, Saint, 1774–1821.   2. Christian saints—
United States—Biography.   I. Title.
    BX4700.S4B36 2014
    271'.9102—dc23
    [B]
                                                          2013030995

St. Martin's Press books may be purchased for educational,
business, or promotional use. For information on bulk purchases, please contact
Macmillan Corporate and Premium Sales Department at 1-800-221-7945,
extension 5442, or write specialmarkets@macmillan.com.

First Edition: March 2014

10 9 8 7 6 5 4 3 2 1

To Irene Fugazy
Sister of Charity of New York
and all women religious
the honor and the hope of the Church

But who can search the Secret Soul
and turn the rooted Sorrow . . .

—FROM A LETTER OF ELIZABETH SETON
TO HER FATHER, DR. RICHARD BAYLEY,
THURSDAY, FEBRUARY 20, 1800

FOREWORD

※

by Maya Angelou

Elizabeth Ann Seton lived many important lives and died before she was fifty. She lived a life as a wife, as a mother of five children, and as a widow. She became interested in the Catholic Church. It gave her a direct and fundamental entrance to God. She founded the first Catholic school in the United States and the first order of active American nuns. Seton's life and achievements are proof that courage is the most important of all the virtues.

As both a Protestant and a Catholic, she was a religious woman who loved the Christian way and dared to support her conscience. Even today, many American nuns are rebuked by the Vatican for following the dictates of their conscience. I can only imagine how a principled Catholic woman of God survived more than two hundred years ago in a climate that had few precedents of female religious leadership.

American Saint: The Life of Elizabeth Seton is a map that allows us to follow the journey of this remarkable woman. We are able to examine each stop she made along the way, and we are amazed at her courage to get up and start her journey again, against visible and tangible odds.

The reader is engrossed and inspired by the telling of Elizabeth Ann Seton's life. She took her family motto from the twelfth-century coat of arms, "At whatever risk, yet go forward," as her command to live her life and her conscience for the glory of God and the benefit of human beings.

the women were held in more than fifty cities across the country. Petitions were signed. Letters poured in. A resolution on their behalf was proposed in the U.S. House of Representatives. An editorial in *The New York Times* said, "It would be a tragedy, far beyond the church, if their fine work and their courageous voices were constrained."

On June 18, 2012, because the Vatican document complained that nuns spend too much time on social justice issues and not enough on promoting Church doctrine, some nuns set out to illustrate their work with the poor and powerless. "Nuns on the Bus" traveled across nine states, stopping at homeless shelters, food pantries, schools, and health-care facilities run by nuns, protesting budget cuts in programs for the poor. At the end of the tour, in Washington, D.C., Dr. Sayyid Sayeed, the national interfaith director of the Islamic Society of North America, said, "Nuns on the bus speak for not just Catholics, not for Christians only, not for Jews. They speak for all of us."

In August 2012, some nine hundred members of the LCWR gathered in St. Louis for their annual assembly. "Be truthful, but gentle and absolutely fearless," Franciscan Sister Pat Farrell, the LCWR president, told the women, as for three days they discussed the Vatican document. Was this doctrinal process an expression of concern or an attempt to control? Does the institutional legitimacy of canonical recognition allow them the freedom to question with informed consciences?

On the last night of the assembly, the group gave its highest honor, the Outstanding Leadership Award, to Immaculate Heart of Mary Sister Sandra Schneiders, who has written about feminism and the church, citing "the sins of patriarchy, notably sexism, clericalism and racism." The Vatican protested the award.

In April 2013, the new pope, Francis, reaffirmed the doctrinal assessment of the Leadership Council of Women Religious. In August, Archbishop Peter Sartain of Seattle, head of the three-bishop team in charge of the process, spoke at the group's annual assembly in Orlando. He did not specify how the investigation was proceeding, and he did not explain what the Vatican means by "radical feminist themes." Pat

INTRODUCTION

❧

"O ver the pope as expression of the binding claim of ecclesiastical authority, there stands one's own conscience, which must be obeyed before all else, even if necessary against the requirement of ecclesiastical authority."

Father Joseph Ratzinger wrote that at the time of the Second Vatican Council. Then, as Pope Benedict XVI, he authorized a crackdown on American nuns who are obeying their consciences above all else.

On April 18, 2012, the Vatican accused the Leadership Conference of Women Religious, which represents 80 percent of American nuns, of promoting "radical feminist themes incompatible with the Catholic faith" and "corporate dissent" against Church teachings, especially those on women's ordination, contraception, and homosexuality. Three bishops were appointed to revise the LCWR's statutes, to approve speakers at its assemblies, to review its plans and programs, and to launch a plan of reform that the Vatican called "a doctrinal assessment" and that on National Public Radio Maureen Fiedler, a Sister of Loretto, called "a hostile takeover."

Most Americans have never met a Vatican official, but they have met nuns. In the wake of the harsh rebuke, vigils and rallies supporting

McDermott, a Sister of Mercy, says that to have bishops review and oversee the organization's statutes, plans, and programs, and approve its speakers, is "unacceptable."

The doctrinal assessment of the Leadership Conference of Women Religious will take five years, and no one knows what will happen at the end.

But Elizabeth Seton was there at the beginning.

She knew that officially it was a lazaretto, named for Lazarus, the leper in the New Testament whom everyone shunned for fear of contagion. But throughout her detailed journal, she determinedly called it a prison, where they were "bolted in and barred with as much ceremony as any monster of mischief might be—a single window double grated with iron thro' which, if I should want anything, I am to call a centinel, with a fierce cocked hat and long riffle gun, that is that he may not receive the dreadful infection we are supposed to have brought with us from New York."

These predawn bells were announcing prayer, she knew. At home, Elizabeth began each day with a heartfelt greeting to God; in this alien place, she was stunned into silence. "The Matins Bells awakened my Soul to its most painful regrets and filled it with an agony of sorrow which could not at first find relief even in prayer."

She had not listened—had *chosen* not to listen—to concerned people who had advised against this trip, even when one dear friend had pronounced it "next to madness."

She had left four young children behind, whom she'd watched from the ship's railing until they were out of sight. They were crying. She had left them behind, even knowing that thirteen-month-old Rebecca, newly weaned and sickly, might die.

She had come with her oldest child, even though an eight-year-old might have been better left at home with her brothers and sisters.

She had come in the hope that the warmer climate of Italy, where Will had friends, would ease his tuberculosis and he would get well.

She had come with the near-certainty that he would not get well.

Yet she had come.

————

ONE

Elizabeth woke in darkness, to the ringing of church bells.

A wind gusted through crevices in the brick wall; the room was clenched in cold. Waves crashed on the rocks below as white foam splashed high and hard against the little barred window, blotting out the moonlight.

Will and Anna were still asleep on the cold brick floor. There was no fire, but Elizabeth's eyes burned from fatigue, from yesterday's stinging wind on the open boat that had brought them, an hour over pitching waves, to this despairing place.

"Prison" is the word Elizabeth used in the journal she'd begun to keep on board the *Shepherdess* during the seven-week crossing from New York to Italy. Because yellow fever was rampant in New York, and the ship had come without medical clearance—a Bill of Health—the Setons were not allowed on shore at Leghorn; instead, while a band on the quay played "Hail Columbia" in honor of the arriving Americans, they were rowed to quarantine in a dungeonlike building at the water's edge. A guard pointed their way with his bayonet: up twenty twisting stone steps to Room #6, "naked walls, brick floor and a jug of water," where for forty days Elizabeth and her husband and their daughter would be confined.

Elizabeth Bayley Seton was twenty-nine years old—dark-haired, dark-eyed, a beautiful woman barely five feet tall, brimming with energy and confidence. While other passengers on the long voyage had been seasick, Elizabeth had kept well. "I have not the least disposition to sickness," she wrote airily.

Until Elizabeth went to Italy, she had traveled outside New York only to see friends in Pennsylvania. In the lazaretto at Leghorn, she was setting out on an unpredictable path that would take her to a place unknown and unimagined, where who she was and what she did would reshape the American world.

But on this Sunday, November 20, 1803, she did not know that.

Church bells rang again. "At no loss to know the hours," she wrote wryly. "Night and day four Bells strike every hour and ring every quarter."

The bells rang at the Church of St. James, in the shadow of the lazaretto. Later, Elizabeth would kneel in its ancient nave, but only as a curious Protestant who had never been inside a Catholic church, who had been brought up to regard Catholics with disdain.

Elizabeth was an Episcopalian—born into, married into, and well settled into the religion of the social and political elite. Her maternal grandfather was an Anglican priest, ordained in London. The first Episcopal bishop of New York presided at her wedding.

In the Episcopal tradition, Elizabeth approached God through her Bible, which she had brought with her to Italy, along with the Book of Common Prayer, the Psalms with commentaries, and a sewn-together booklet of sermons of Rev. Henry Hobart at Trinity, her church in New York. On her first day in the lazaretto, she turned to them all.

"Retrospections bring anguish," she decided. "In the little closet from whence there is a view of the Open Sea . . . I first came to my senses and reflected that I was offending my only Friend and resource in my misery and voluntarily shutting out from my Soul the only consolation it could receive—pleading for Mercy and Strength brought peace—and with a cheerful countenance I asked Wm what we should do for Breakfast."

The officer in charge of the lazaretto—the *capitano*—had sent warm eggs and wine. A bottle of milk was set down at the door. Will's friends the Filicchis sent dinner, along with one of their servants, a lively little gray-haired man named Louis who would live in a connecting room throughout the Setons' stay.

But Will was too weak for breakfast; terribly chilled, sweating with fever, he could not even sit up. He'd improved noticeably on the ship, where he'd eaten and slept well. "My Seton is daily getting better," Elizabeth had written in a letter carried home by a passing vessel. Now she was so stricken at his condition—"My Husband on the cold bricks without fire, shivering and groaning"—that when Louis tried to serve her, she refused to eat. "My face was covered with a handkerchief when he came in and tired of the sight of men with cocked hats, cockades and bayonets, I did not look up."

By evening, with Will asleep and Anna jumping rope, Elizabeth was calm again. "Opening my Prayer Book and bending my knees was the Signal for my Soul to find rest . . . after Prayers, read my little book of dear H's sermons—and became far more happy than I had been wretched."

That first day in the lazaretto set the pattern for the days ahead: prayer and comfort, then tears and anguish, refuge in prayer again— alone or with Anna, with Will when he was able. "We pray and cry together, till fatigue overpowers him, and then he says he is willing to go—cheering up is useless, he seems easier after venting his sorrow and always gets quiet sleep after his struggles."

On Monday the *capitano* came with his guards to set up a bed with curtains for Will and bedding for the benches that Elizabeth and Anna would sleep on. He took down their names: Signor Guillielmo, Signora Elizabeth, Signorina Anna Maria. His voice was sympathetic, so Elizabeth looked up at him. "His great cocked hat being off I found it hid grey hairs and a kind and affectionate countenance." Shaking his head sadly, the *capitano* pointed upward, reminding her that all was in the hands of "le Bon Dieu."

Will knew the Filicchi brothers, Antonio and Filippo, from having worked in their shipping firm. On Tuesday, when they brought their personal physician, Dr. Tutilli, Will was better, and so encouraged by the visit that he was able to get down the twenty steps to the gate and talk with his friends. But the next day he was too weak to make the descent. When the men came up to the grilled window, Will was so eager to talk that he stood too close, and the *capitano* held him back with a stick. "It reminded me of going to see the Lions."

Friday, November 25, was their son William's birthday. He would be seven. Will wept so inconsolably that Elizabeth's anguish at their situation turned into anger. "Consider—my Husband who left his all to seek a milder climate confined to this place of high and damp walls exposed to cold and wind which penetrates to the very bones, without fire except the kitchen charcoal which oppresses his Breast so much as to nearly convulse him—no little syrup nor softener of the cough . . . milk, bitter tea, and opium pills which he takes quietly as a duty without seeming even to hope is all I can offer him from day to day—when Nature fails, and I can no longer look up with cheerfulness, I hide my head on the chair by his bedside and he thinks I am praying—and pray I do, for prayer is all my comfort, without which I should be of little service to him . . . if we did not now know and love God—if we did not feel the consolations and embrace the cheering Hope he has set before us, and find our delight in the study of his blessed word and truth, what would become of us?"

⟨⟨✦⟩⟩

What would become of us?

That question had been a plaintive echo in Elizabeth's mind and heart for most of her life. Before she could walk and talk, she was moving from place to place in a precarious pattern of living that would influence her shifting moods, from laughter and peaceful contemplation to thoughts of suicide.

Even before she was born, the pattern of uncertainty, of absence and longing, had been set. Her father, Dr. Richard Bayley, was a restless, impatient man, resolute in his determination to become a skilled, respected doctor at a time when butchers and barbers dominated the medical field. Of the more than 3,500 practicing physicians in the colonies before the Revolutionary War, only about 400 had degrees from a medical school. "Quacks abound like locusts in Egypt," one observer noted. "No candidates are either examined or licensed, or even sworn to a fair practice." Blistering was used as a remedy for almost any ailment. An irritating agent, such as a mustard plaster, was applied to the skin, so that blisters formed. When the blister was drained, it presumably drew out the infection or inflammation. Tuberculosis was commonly attributed to drinking too much hot tea or sleeping in feather ticks, and medical treatment often boiled down to "Keep the head cool, the feet warm, and the bowels open."

The first medical school in New York City—King's College, later Columbia—had just opened in 1767 when Richard Bayley managed to get a meeting there with Dr. John Charlton, who had been a surgeon at the court of George III. When Dr. Charlton accepted Richard Bayley as student and assistant, he introduced him to the world of medical royalty, and to his sister Catherine.

Catherine was the daughter of Mary Bayeux, a descendant of French Huguenot settlers in New Rochelle, New York, and Rev. Richard Charlton. A devout Irish Protestant, her father had graduated from Trinity College in Dublin and been ordained an Anglican priest in London before being assigned to New York as a missionary. As rector of St. Andrew's Church on Staten Island, he included "Negroes" in his catechism classes, an eyebrow-raising step in the 1770s and a very early example for a very young Elizabeth of the command of conscience.

When Catherine and Richard were married on January 9, 1769, at St. John's Episcopal Church in Elizabethtown, New Jersey, Dr. Thomas B. Chandler presiding, they entered a world of privilege. Doctors belonged to the first class of society, along with lawyers, rich merchants, and government officials, and Dr. Bayley was especially well connected. His mentor, Dr. Charlton, was a stout, florid man who liked to display his wealth, "quite ready to parade himself and his horse for the benefit of inquisitive folk." Charlton and his wife, Mary, heiress to the de Peyster family fortune, lived at 100 Broadway, the widest and grandest street, with so many prominent residents that its lower end, at the Bowling Green, was known as the "court" section of town. The Bayleys were entertained at dinner parties, card parties, and balls in rooms bright with crystal, the floors covered with "Turkey worked" carpets. Josiah Wedgwood sold "creamware," a rich glazed pottery, and advertised black pottery that made ladies' hands look whiter. Shops at Hanover Square catered to first-class tastes, with dry goods and laces, pictures and pipes, coffee and cutlery, and furniture from the London cabinetmaker Thomas Chippendale. Women retailers, the "She-Merchants," handled olive oil, Canary wine, and imported glassware. At her cosmetics shop, Mrs. Edwards sold "An Admirable Beautifying Wash for Hands Face and Neck, it makes the Skin soft, smooth and plump, it likewise takes away Redness, Freckles, Sun-Burnings or Pimples."

But with some twenty thousand people crowded into an area less than one mile square, only the rich had elbow room. The "inferior orders of people" lived on narrow, twisting lanes often deep with mud, where feral hogs rooted through garbage, where women washed clothes in a pond "foul with excrement, frog-spawn and reptiles . . . dead dogs, cats." During one bleak winter, when the East River became a block of solid ice, more than four hundred men, women, and children crammed into the municipal poorhouse. To ease the overcrowding, the Common Council found funds to move poor vagrants someplace else—anyplace else—outside the city. Whale-oil lamps flickered at some street corners, but since they were smoky, not much brighter than lightning bugs, the new lamps were small deterrent to thieves, called "footpads." Women turned to crime—two were hanged as pickpockets in 1771—and prostitution. A visiting Scotsman counted "above 500 ladies of pleasure" lodged so close to St. Paul's Chapel that their red-light district was called the "Holy Ground." Working men who wore trousers and caps, not knee breeches and tall hats, whose houses lacked multiple fireplaces and multiple servants to fetch firewood, began to deride the upper class as "silk stocking" and "big wig."

When Richard and Catherine married, rumblings of revolution were being heard throughout the city. The Sons of Liberty had organized to protest regulations from London, particularly burdensome taxes, but Richard was unconcerned. Taxes had been a fact of colonial life since Willem Kieft, an early director-general of New Amsterdam, had tried to tax the Indians. Like other Loyalists, Richard Bayley relied on George III to maintain the colonies as his peaceable kingdom. Six months after his marriage, he sailed for London to study with the renowned Dr. William Hunter, leaving behind a pregnant wife.

While he was away, redcoats opened fire on a crowd in Boston, killing five people in what was called "the Boston Massacre." The first serious clash of the Revolution in New York, the Battle of Golden Hill, was fought on a wheat field at the crest of John Street, the street where Elizabeth would, at an especially melancholy time in her life, find shelter.

And Richard's first child, Mary Magdalen, was born. She was a quiet girl who grew up to be a woman as deliberately quiet as her sister, Elizabeth, would be volatile. Mary once described herself as a woman who had "an irresistible impulse to steer clear of people and things, as much as I can, so as to avoid interfering with their interests or plans, be they what they may." In contrast, Elizabeth would refer to herself as "the Mad Enthusiast" and had such a boundless imagination that she once thought of "running away, over the seas . . . in disguise, working for a living."

Mary Bayley was more than a year old when her father came home. He stayed home for nearly three years, the happiest time—and the longest time—that he and his young wife would be together.

It was an opulent time for educated doctors, who dressed like nobility and were treated royally. Dr. John Bard, the oldest doctor in the city, was known for the snuff-colored suit he wore on weekdays and the scarlet one on Sundays. Lace ruffles on shirts, silk stockings, and silver shoe buckles were part of an eminent physician's uniform, and his fees were equally impressive: $25 for a tonsillectomy, $50 to $100 for the amputation of a limb, $125 for cataract removal by pressing the eyeball with the thumb. Dr. Bayley and Dr. Charlton were the first physicians in the city to make house calls by carriage, charging a hefty $5 for a visit with a single dose of medicine plus "verbal advice." The fees doubled in stormy weather.

It was a threatening time. By springtime of 1774, revolution was no longer a possibility to be talked about in coffeehouses and taverns but a looming reality to be faced. Following the lead of patriots in Boston, some Sons of Liberty boarded a British vessel, the *London,* anchored in New York Harbor. Dressed as Mohawk Indians, they climbed down into the hold of the ship, brought up eighteen crates of tea, slashed them open, and threw the tea over the side. In early September, the First Continental Congress, stepping-stone to war, convened in Philadelphia.

Elizabeth Ann Bayley was born on August 28, 1774, as the delegates from Massachusetts were passing through New York City on their way to Philadelphia. Samuel Adams, resplendent in a new red coat and cocked hat, led the group, which included his cousin John. The men admired the city's grand houses and its many well-laid-out streets, and enjoyed a lavish breakfast at the country estate of the patriot John Morin Scott, whose son Lewis would one day marry Elizabeth's best friend. But John Adams was less impressed with New Yorkers. "They talk very loud, very fast and altogether," he complained. "If they ask you a question, before you can utter three words of your answer, they will break out upon you again—and talk away." He was as glad to leave the city as Elizabeth, even when she had become a scorned and hated woman, would be saddened.

By early 1775, revolution seemed inevitable. The king's reaction to the unrest had blared across the ocean: "The colonists must be reduced to absolute obedience, if need be, by the ruthless use of force." Richard Bayley had a wife and two young daughters, but a few months after Elizabeth was born, he sailed to London again, to study at Dr. Hunter's new school of anatomy on Great Windmill Street.

Elizabeth was a nursing infant on the April day in 1775 when a rider galloped down the Post Road to tell of bloodshed at Lexington, Massachusetts. The Sons of Liberty paraded down Broadway with fireworks, bells, and cheers. General George Washington—erect, grave, at six feet three inches the very portrait of a commander— arrived in the city in June; more bells, more cheers.

By Elizabeth's first birthday in August, when the cheering stopped, Loyalists were fleeing to safe havens: Nova Scotia, the Bahamas, the West Indies, England itself. Patriots were sending their families to the country, then joining the rebel army. The city began to shut down. Coffeehouses and taverns boarded up. With shipping trade suspended, food was scarce. At the end of the year, with winter taking hold and firewood hard to come by, even at black market prices, the city's population dropped from twenty thousand to five thousand. Streets were torn up to make trenches, cannon hauled to positions at waterside.

Catherine Bayley and her two little girls began moving from place to place—to her father's house on Staten Island, to other relatives there, to her brother's country house on Long Island—wherever safe shelter could be found in a world of gunfire and threat.

What would become of us?

<hr />

The tavern on the Post Road in New Rochelle, New York, with decent food and soft-enough beds for travelers between New York and Boston, was so respectable that for years it served as meeting place for the town's elders, various city functions, even as City Hall. Unlike some rowdy saloons in the city—the Dish of Fry'd Oysters, the Dog's Head in the Porridge—this spare, unpretentious stone building was simply LeConte's, established in the late 1600s, later managed by Guillaume LeConte, Richard Bayley's grandfather. When Richard and his brother William were boys in New Rochelle, they regularly headed for the tavern after school, where they squatted outside until their grandfather appeared to take them to his house, to tell them stories they could not hear often enough about the LeConte history and the splendid sword—jeweled hilt, gold braid on the scabbard—that had belonged to a noble ancestor and now hung against a length of rich red velvet in a place of honor over the fireplace.

The LeContes of New Rochelle were descendants of the early Protestants—the Huguenots—who had fled persecution in Catholic France and named their New World haven after their beloved La Rochelle in Normandy. Mary Bayeux, Elizabeth's grandmother, had been a Huguenot descendant, too; the thread of oppression, rebellion, flight, and exile was woven early into Elizabeth's life narrative.

The Bayleys came from Hoddesdon, a village in Hertfordshire, England, where the church displayed a monument in honor of the respected Bayley family. William Bayley Sr. emigrated to the colony of Fairfield, Connecticut, so like the grassy shires of his rural homeland that it had become the destination of choice for many English immigrants, with thriving farms and an energetic social life. He became close friends with Thomas Pell, another Englishman from Hertfordshire, who'd married an Indian princess. At a ball on their spacious estate, Pelham Manor, William met Suzanne LeConte; she was seventeen and he twice her age when they married.

After Richard was born in 1744, the little family moved to New Rochelle, where William Jr. was born a year later. The boys grew up on a farm at the edge of tangled woods, where they learned to track a bear, to trap a muskrat, to handle a shotgun. From their Huguenot mother they learned Norman French. They had their formal education at the Trinity Church School in town, where their classmates included John Jay, destined to be the first chief justice of the United States. It was a carefree childhood. Their great-aunt Hester, who made what people claimed were the best spice cakes in the county, teased them: "Bayleys they might be, but they had the LeConte trick of always turning up when something good was on hand."

When Grandfather LeConte died, their aunt Ann, Suzanne's sister, summoned them to the parlor, where she read from his will: "I leave to my two grandsons, William and Richard Bayley, 20 pounds . . .

and my gun, sword and watch . . ." Richard intended to be a doctor, so he took the big gold watch, wound with a key; William took the short musket with a flaring muzzle and the prized sword.

Four years later, when their father had died and their mother remarried, both Bayleys set out from New Rochelle to seek their fortunes in New York City. While Richard was absorbed in medicine, William opened a hardware store on one of the handsome Hanover Square streets, so successfully that he soon opened another at the Fly Market on the riverfront, where New Yorkers bought beef and mutton, fruit and vegetables from country farms, blackfish and flounder and salted cod. With this expansion, he became prosperous enough to advertise:

> William Bayley has imported . . . a New and general
> assortment of hard ware, toys and trinkets; plated, japan'd and
> brown tea urns and coffee pots of the newest fashion; a large
> assortment of paper hangings of the newest patterns; a great
> variety of portable printing presses, from 10s each to 51s each;
> gentleman's tool chests of various prices, with a number of
> other articles too tedious to mention . . . Ready money for
> bees-wax and old brass.

William was twenty when he left New Rochelle. Ten years later, he would return to marry Sarah Pell, Thomas Pell's granddaughter, and to serve for years as Elizabeth's substitute father.

Richard was twenty-one and would never go back.

❦

Elizabeth was almost surely baptized at Trinity Church, although church records were lost in the blaze of 1776, when the church burned and its steeple crashed to the ground. For most of her life, she was listed as a communicant at Trinity, open only to the baptized. She was always exacting that her children be baptized there. Her wealthy godmother, Sarah Startin, was a member of Trinity.

Sixteen religious houses were open in the city when Elizabeth was born. The Congregationalists and the Lutherans each had a church; the Presbyterians had three. The Methodists worshipped in a simple church, forty by sixty feet, with a whitewashed interior, white sand on the floor, and backless benches, but without bells, steeple, or organ, which were considered "unnecessary adornment." Quakers had a meetinghouse. The synagogue on Mill Street could be traced back to 1654, when a Rosh Hashanah service had been held there, genesis of Congregation Shearith Israel, the oldest in North America. There were churches for Baptists, Anabaptists, Moravians, and Reformed Dutch.

The Anglican Church reigned, the enclave of the elite, as it had been since early in the century when Edward Lord Cornbury, the cross-dressing English governor—lip color, hoop skirts—had given a sizable chunk of Manhattan real estate to Trinity Church, then persuaded the Assembly to raise taxes in order to give its rector a higher salary. In midcentury, King's College had opened in a vestry room at Trinity, with a student body of eight young men and a faculty of one Anglican priest. After the Revolution, the Anglican Church in the new republic became "the Protestant Episcopal Church, an American corporation, a unit, not of the English church but of the church in America, in communion with the Church of England." Still, religion and politics remained entwined: President George Washington had his own named pews at Trinity and its chapel, St. Paul's.

There was no Catholic church. When Elizabeth was born, Catholic worship was illegal in most of the colonies, an enforcement of the penal laws laid down in England two centuries earlier, which excluded Catholics from all public activities, including voting, serving on juries, and holding hands. Catholic priests who ventured into the city were liable to arrest and life in prison; attempted escape meant the gallows. Anyone who knowingly harbored a Catholic priest was fined two hundred pounds—half to be paid to the government, half to the informer who'd turned in the priest's host—and further punished with three days in the pillory.

Persecution in the name of the Lord had always proved the ecumenical nature of religious intolerance. In this country, faith had been recognized as a handy weapon since Puritans in Massachusetts banished nonconformists and hanged some Quakers who dared to return. Peter Stuyvesant had vigorously harassed Jews settling in New Amsterdam. Catholics in England had been beheaded, while in Catholic France one of Elizabeth's Huguenot ancestors had been dragged by her hair to a bloody death in the streets of Paris.

In New York City, though, discrimination against Catholics was based not only on historical precedent but also on contemporary social reality. Except for a handful of the affluent, mostly French aristocrats and representatives of the Spanish crown, Catholics in Elizabeth's city were the persistently poor: immigrants who poured from the reeking holds of ships, exchanging poverty and hunger in the Old World for disease-plagued squalor in the New. Mostly Irish, mostly uneducated and unskilled, they settled in slums along the East River, where privies overflowed, where polluted alleys were deep with garbage and an occasional animal carcass, where after ten o'clock at night tubs of human waste were dumped into the river, with stinking overflow onto the wharf. The immigrants were considered "a public nuisance" and "the off-scourings of the people" as they crammed into small, fetid spaces with no access to clean water. Catholics smelled bad.

Elizabeth would dance at the exclusive City Assemblies, open to "none but the first class of society." For someone of that class to consider becoming a Catholic was unthinkable, and for most of her life Elizabeth didn't think about it. Although as a girl she liked Methodist hymns and daydreamed about becoming a Quaker "because they wear such pretty plain hats," she was an unquestioning Episcopalian who cherished the Bible and quoted the Psalms and attended Trinity and St. Paul's with a religious attitude that was blithe, untroubled, and, considering how organized religion would splinter her life, heartbreaking. In a letter to a friend, Elizabeth wrote, "The first point of religion is cheerfulness and harmony."

TWO

◦❧◦

Richard Bayley returned to New York on July 12, 1776, in the uniform of a lieutenant in His Majesty's Troops.

In Philadelphia, the Continental Congress had voted to "dissolve the connection between Great Britain and the American colonies." When the news reached New York, the Declaration of Independence was read aloud on the Commons; the enormous statue of George III on the Bowling Green was toppled from its fifteen-foot-high marble pedestal, the head hacked off and stuck on a spike at the Blue Bell Tavern. From the roof of his City Hall headquarters, General Washington had watched thousands of enemy troops—British in red coats, Hessians in blue—disembark onto Staten Island and Long Island.

Dr. Bayley was home for just a few weeks, long enough for Elizabeth to realize that this handsome dark-eyed stranger was her father and for Catherine to become pregnant. Then he left town again, involuntarily this time, assigned to Newport, Rhode Island, with the fleet of Admiral Lord Richard "Black Dick" Howe.

Elizabeth had her second birthday on August 28 in the middle of the two-day Battle of Long Island that was less a battle than a slaughter. When an army of five thousand Hessians surrounded eight hundred Americans, some patriot soldiers were shot as they bogged down in muddy marshes, some "pierced with the bayonet to trees." On September 12, Washington accepted his officers' advice to abandon the city that the British would hold for seven years. When some of them urged that they burn down the city before they left, Congress rejected the idea.

Just after midnight on September 21, a fire broke out in the Fighting Cocks Tavern on the wharf. As flames swept uptown, choking smoke and fiery red wind-borne flakes of burning shingles filled the air. General Washington watched the blaze from his retreat in Harlem Heights. "Providence, or some good honest fellow, has done more for us than we were disposed to do for ourselves," he said. Among the two hundred men and women rounded up for questioning was a twenty-one-year-old American officer, Nathan Hale, who did not admit to a role in the fire but did admit to being a spy, and was immediately hanged. Although the rebels were generally blamed for the fire, no one could be sure. All people really knew was that a quarter of their city was gone. Among the five hundred houses and shops consumed by the flames were the hardware stores of Elizabeth's uncle William Bayley, who retired to New Rochelle and the life of a country squire, leaving as a memento of his mercantile career only a clapboard sign—WM. BAYLEY, TINSMAN—flapping in the wind.

Curled up in her mother's lap, Elizabeth listened to her read the story of "Goody Two-Shoes," about a poor orphan girl—Margery Meanwell—with just one shoe who is so thankful for the gift of another shoe that she grows up to become a teacher and helps other people, then marries a rich man, virtue rewarded. Elizabeth nestled in the softness of her mother's voice, the warmth of her closeness, the fragrance of soap and clean linen.

For a few months in the winter of 1776 into the early spring of 1777, Elizabeth was living safely with her mother and her sister Mary at the Long Island house of her uncle John Charlton.

Then, suddenly, her father was back, and her mother was gone.

In Newport, Dr. Bayley had asked repeatedly for leave to visit his pregnant wife and been repeatedly refused. When he had an urgent message from home and was again denied leave, he resigned his commission, forfeiting all salary for the year and a half he'd served, and rushed back to his family. Catherine Charlton Bayley died on May 8, 1777, giving birth to a daughter whom Dr. Bayley named Catherine.

Then, just as suddenly it seemed, Elizabeth had a new mother.

When his wife died, Richard Bayley had a busy practice, along with his medical research and teaching, and three young daughters, one a sickly infant. As soon as the prescribed year of mourning was complete, he married Charlotte Amelia Barclay, a granddaughter of Jacobus Roosevelt, founder of the Hyde Park branch of that family dynasty.

Elizabeth had only that sweet, shadowy memory of her mother reading the nursery story. But when her little sister died a year and a half later, the memory was clear and would remain with her. Years later, she recalled the autumn day in 1778 when baby Catherine lay in the darkened parlor, dressed in a long white gown. Elizabeth had stepped outdoors into the daylight when some sympathetic ladies approached.

> At four years of age sitting alone on a step of the door while
> my little sister Catherine lay in her coffin they asked me did I
> not cry when little Kitty was dead No because Kitty is gone
> up to heaven I wish I could go too with Mamma.

Charlotte Bayley was not the wicked stepmother of the storybooks, but she was never a loving presence to Richard's daughters. The woman whom four-year-old Elizabeth called "Mrs. Bayley" was just eighteen when she became the instant mother of three daughters while promptly beginning to have children of her own: two in the first three years of a marriage shaky from the start.

In this bewildering new household, Elizabeth's longing persisted.

> At six taking my little sister Emma up to the garret showing
> her the setting sun told her God lived up in heaven and good
> children would go there—teaching her her prayers.

At home, Elizabeth stayed as close to her father as she possibly could. At school, she learned to recite her lessons quickly, so she could rush down to the street to see him on his medical rounds, embrace him, and scurry back to the classroom before the teacher noticed. For Richard Bayley, education was essential. Both Elizabeth and Mary attended Mama Pompelion's, a small school where girls learned reading and writing, some arithmetic and geography, and grammar. Along with academic subjects, Elizabeth learned the piano, at her father's insistence. "Music and French must have their hours," he told her. Throughout her life, music would be for her both pleasure and consolation.

In the occupied city, the privileged, especially the British officers, lived gaily, with balls and formal dinners, fox hunting and golf, and saltwater bathing parties. Pictures of the king and queen in burnished gold frames were sold at the stationery shop of James Rivington, the Tory publisher who would later become one of George Washington's most reliable spies. A new bakery shop in Hanover Square offered "all sorts of Pastry Cakes Sweet-Meats and Jellies."

Like other well-to-do civilian families, the Bayleys were comfortable, able to afford food and firewood. But the fire of 1776 had left destitute refugees with no place to live except "Canvas Town," a collection of flimsy tents made from the sails of rotting ships. When snow fell nearly every day from November 1779 to March 1780, piling on the rooftops and banking against the doorways of the expensive shops where milliners, dressmakers, and wigmakers served His Majesty's officers and their wives, some residents of Canvas Town quietly froze to death.

Military rule was imposed in an atmosphere of chilling cruelty: a British commander took revenge on the Sons of Liberty by murdering some two hundred American prisoners, either by starving them or by poisoning their flour rations with arsenic. Even Richard Bayley, the Loyalist doctor, was affected. When he saw a drunken soldier thrown from his cart and run over by a careless driver, he got down from his chaise, administered first aid, and notified the hospital. For his act of conscience he spent a day in jail. He considered leaving the city, but conditions improved when his friend Sir Guy Carleton took command, and in the end, his medical work, especially his ongoing investigation into the causes of epidemics, kept him in New York.

Elizabeth once remembered that her stepmother was often "in great affliction." In 1781, when Charlotte Bayley was expecting another child—her third in four years—Elizabeth and Mary were sent to their uncle William in New Rochelle.

Even after the Declaration of Independence had been adopted, William Bayley had signed a petition to the British commander, General William Howe, urging negotiation that would "restore the colonies to the peaceful protection of His Majesty." Nevertheless, the patriot council that controlled confiscated Tory property allowed him to buy a 250-acre waterfront estate in New Rochelle, largely because his wife, the former Sarah Pell, was a granddaughter of the Indian princess whose people had originally granted the land.

Elizabeth's new home was a cheerful, rambling Colonial house overlooking Long Island Sound. A wide center hall ran from front to back on the main floor, with a broad staircase rising to bedrooms upstairs. A fireplace brightened the formal dining room; the parlor was lined with shelves of books. Porches in both front and back opened onto a grassy lawn with a large, ridged boulder just made for climbing and a terraced slope running down to the beach.

Uncle William and Aunt Sarah welcomed Elizabeth and Mary into their large, lively family, where someone was always playing the piano, or climbing the boulder, or reading aloud from a schoolbook. At eight and twelve, the girls fit well into their lineup of cousins: William Jr., ten; Susannah, eight; Joseph, five; and Richard, three. The newest Bayley cousin, Anne, was born the year Elizabeth arrived; in Elizabeth's four years there, she particularly enjoyed helping with the baby, holding her as she took her first wobbly steps. Their childhood friendship would continue until they were grown women, when it would shatter in theological disagreement.

Besides her Bayley cousins, Elizabeth had a flock of LeConte cousins, the children of the cousins her father had known in New Rochelle. And they all had friends around the house. For the first time in her life, Elizabeth was part of a household brimming with laughter and conversation and children's squabbles, much of it in French. Uncle William liked to sit on the porch, whittling toys, telling stories of the days when he and Elizabeth's father had roamed the woods and looked for bear tracks and never missed Great-Aunt Hester's baking day.

But his warm, fatherly presence could not eradicate—could only emphasize—the sadness she felt at her own father's absence. She often slipped away, down the sloping front lawn to the sandy shore of Long Island Sound.

> Delight to sit alone by the waterside—wandering hours on
> the shore humming and gathering shells—every little leaf and
> flower, animal, insect, shades of clouds or waving trees,
> objects of vague unconnected thoughts of God and heaven.

For a child of four or six or eight to talk of God and heaven might suggest that Elizabeth was "born holy."

She wasn't. She was born into a family and a social context framed by such sturdy religious belief that her beginning spirituality was an unconscious imperative. She'd lived at St. Andrew's parish house with her grandfather the priest, with the Bible as primer; even her overwhelmed young stepmother had taken time to teach her the Psalm "The Lord is my Shepherd . . ." Elizabeth Bayley was a natural child who grew to be a natural woman with the usual assortment of natural needs and desires, attitudes, and questions. That early sense of the spiritual, so spontaneously expressed, seems largely intuitive, based on her intensely human need for love and comfort. She prayed before she was four years old, long before she had a belief system to give her prayers context. She prayed when "God" and "heaven" were only words, but words that made her feel, in a way both elusive and sure, that she was loved and held dear and would never be abandoned. She prayed when she couldn't explain what prayer meant; she prayed by simply thinking about God, without yet realizing that turning the mind and heart to God is the essence of prayer.

Still, there was a breath of mystery about a child who kept looking for God, to whom "every little leaf and flower" was a reminder of the divine. Plenty of people, not a mystic among them, like to say they can pray more easily in a forest or a garden than in a church. But Elizabeth was eight. Clearly she was aware, very early, of the hand of God in all created things, in all forms of life. "Vague and unconnected thoughts," of course; the connection would not be made until God's existence in all reality blended with her own.

Elizabeth was twelve when she and Mary came back to New York City, to their father's house on Smith Street. Their stepmother now had six children, from seven years to a newborn, and Elizabeth was thrilled. "Home again at my Father's—pleasure in reading prayers— love to nurse the children and sing little hymns over the cradle."

After seven years of occupation, the British had finally left the city, taking their time about it. "The town now swarms with Americans, and their insolence is not to be borne," a Briton in New York wrote to a London newspaper in the spring of 1783. On May 6 of that year, General Washington met with Sir Guy Carleton to plan an orderly evacuation. Still, the king's birthday on June 4 was celebrated with fireworks and a royal salute. On Thursday, November 16, 1783, Washington proclaimed a "Day of Public Thanksgiving for the final establishment of American Independence." November 25 was celebrated as "Evacuation Day," followed by a week of banquets and galas, including Governor DeWitt Clinton's dinner, where 120 guests drank 135 bottles of Madeira, 36 bottles of port, 60 bottles of English beer, and 30 bowls of punch and broke 60 wineglasses and 8 cut-glass decanters. On December 4, Washington said a tearful good-bye to his troops and was ceremoniously escorted out of town, even while some British ships still lay at anchor in New York Harbor. The last of the king's men finally sailed on December 6, with a letter from Washington to Carleton wishing that "your

Excellency, with the troops under your orders, may have a safe and pleasant passage."

Many civilian Tories had evacuated as well, and their properties had been confiscated. Some particularly unwelcome Tories not speedy enough or smart enough to get out on their own had been tarred and feathered. Though Richard Bayley had been not merely a Loyalist but a British military officer, he was not pressured to leave; Alexander Hamilton pointed out in a series of pamphlets that successful men of ability were urgently needed in the city's recovery. In 1786, the year Elizabeth returned to New York, Tories not banished by name were restored to full citizenship while often retaining close friendships with those on the wrong side of the war: Dr. Bayley named his son born that year Guy Carleton Bayley.

For Elizabeth, "home again at my Father's" meant far more than location. It meant being with him every morning at breakfast, at 3:00 P.M. dinner if he could get away, perhaps an evening supper. It meant the loving closeness she'd yearned for. It meant listening to him talk about his work, about his concern with public health, especially as it affected the poor. It meant reading with him by the fireside—Dr. Bayley had studied Shakespeare in school; Elizabeth would inherit his love of language and lace it throughout her letters. ("Oh where are all my dreams and Fancies fled . . .") It meant hearing him discuss the events of the day, with Congress setting up shop in the city and the thrilling prospect of Elizabeth's hometown being the first capital of the United States of America. It meant absorbing and treasuring her father's occasional pieces of advice: "Never dwell on trifles, be mistress of yourself, then I am convinced you will always have the credit of acting well."

At forty-four, Dr. Bayley had reached the top tier of prominent surgeons. He was the first to amputate an arm at the shoulder and had taken on his own students, including David Hosack, an eighteen-year-old apprentice whose reputation would eventually rival his teacher's. Bayley was teaching anatomy in a room at New York Hospital when John Hicks, one of his students, waved a severed limb out the window, toward a boy peering in: "See, here is your mother's hand that has cuffed your ears many a time!" By terrible coincidence, the boy's mother had recently died; his father and a group of friends went to the graveyard and by even worse coincidence found her coffin empty.

Medical students were known to have stolen corpses from the Negro Burial Ground in the fields behind the Commons, with no repercussions. But snatching the body of a white woman from Trinity's churchyard brought on the "Doctors' Riot" of April 1788.

Some five thousand angry men stormed the hospital, the medical school at Columbia College, and doctors' homes, shouting, "Kill the doctors!" Most of the students, including John Hicks, and the doctors had fled, but Dr. Wright Post, who would become Elizabeth's brother-in-law—an elegant figure in velvet coat, ruffles, and knee britches—stayed in the dissecting room to guard the anatomical specimens. The mob smashed the place apart, carrying what they could, including partially dismembered corpses, to make a bonfire outside. The sheriff and Mayor James Duane arrived in time to take Dr. Post to safety in jail.

That night, Dr. Bayley was also taken into protective custody. Governor Clinton rushed to the scene, along with some city fathers; as the rioters threw stones and bricks, John Jay was struck, suffering "two large holes in his forehead," and carried home unconscious. Three rioters were shot dead. Elizabeth remembered "a night passed in sweat of terror saying all the while OUR FATHER."

Dr. Bayley published an affidavit in the newspapers, swearing that he had never taken bodies from graves "in any churchyard or cemetery." But the city remained on edge. He drew up his will, leaving all his property and possessions to his mother in Westchester County and to his wife, Charlotte, and the children he had with her. Then he went back to England; Elizabeth and Mary went back to New Rochelle.

When the girls had first been sent to New Rochelle, they had at least known that their father was in New York. Elizabeth had felt sure that he would call for them to come home one day, and that had happened. Now he was truly gone, across the ocean. When would he come back? He was still regarded with some suspicion in the city, and

Elizabeth and Mary were old enough to recognize that his marriage was not happy.

Would he ever come back?

What would become of us?

In New Rochelle, Elizabeth spent most of her time reading, playing the piano, or taking solitary walks.

There had been no word from her father in a year:

Walks among cedars singing hymns—joy in God that he
was my father—insisting that he should not forsake me—my
Father away, perhaps dead—but God was my Father and I
quite independent of what might happen.

Insisting.

Not wishing, not hoping, not even asking, but insisting: a growing spiritual awareness, the determination that she could demand of God what God might demand of her. No longer looking for God in the clouds, somewhere up in the sunset sky; Elizabeth needed a nearby God, in a secure place in her life, in her real world.

❦

In the lazaretto, Anna was beginning to cough, with pain in her chest.

A large crowd of men—thirty or forty, Elizabeth thought—had been crammed into a nearby room. Cold, hungry, survivors of a ship-wreck, they quarreled and yelled and cursed day and night.

Will's fever sometimes ran so high that the bed shook with his breathing. When he wept and said he knew he was dying; when a heavy storm crashed against the window; when Anna coughed in the night and said she was going to die, too: "If I could forget my God one moment at these times I should go mad."

That she could not forget was largely due to the influence of Rev.

Henry Hobart, the young curate at Trinity who'd become her spiritual counselor and friend. He'd written to her as soon as she sailed for Italy. "My heart has accompanied you across the ocean. I have felt its boisterous storms. My prayers have ascended to heaven for your safety . . . I miss you and the family at church, but wherever you are, God will hear and receive your prayer."

Elizabeth believed that. Her prayers flowed from years of immersion in the Bible: not self-centered but God-centered prayers of praise and thanksgiving from both the Hebrew and the Christian scriptures that she threaded through her Italian journal. With the Book of Samuel, her soul did "rejoice indeed in the Lord and Triumph in the God of its salvation." With the Gospel of Matthew, she did "love the Lord your God with all your Soul." On October 6, the day the *Shepherdess* left New York, she'd begun reading the New Testament through, as she had done for years, then started again with the Old. She prayed Psalm 118 every day: "Give thanks to the Lord for he is good, his mercy endures forever."

She prayed in petition, too. While Will prayed for a cure—"oh the promises he makes if it pleases God to spare him"—Elizabeth prayed that Will's desperation would bring him closer to God.

She prayed for herself, that she might maintain her strength and confidence in God throughout this trial.

She prayed that she would keep praying.

On the tenth day in quarantine, she was graced with an afternoon of contemplative prayer.

She awoke before dawn. At ten o'clock she read and prayed with Will and Anna. By noon, Will was asleep, Anna playing in the adjoining room where Louis cooked for them. When Elizabeth was "alone to all the World, one of those sweet pauses in spirit when the Body seems to be forgotten came over me."

She laid her head on the table and closed her eyes, remembering.

In the year 1789 when my Father was in England I jumped
in the wagon that was driving to the woods for brush about a

mile from Home. The Boy who drove it began to cut and I set
off in the woods—soon found an outlet in a Meadow and a
chestnut tree with several young ones growing around it
attracted my attention as a seat—but when I came to it found
rich moss under it and a warm sun—here then was a sweet
bed, the air still a clear blue vault above, the numberless
Sounds of spring melody and joy—the sweet clovers and
wildflowers I had got by the way, and a heart as innocent as a
human heart could be filled with even enthusiastic love to God
and admiration of his works—still I can feel every sensation
that passed thro' my Soul—and I thought at that time my
Father did not care for me—well God was my Father—my All.
I prayed—sung hymns—cryed—laughed in talking to myself
of how far He could place me above all Sorrow—then layed
still to enjoy the Heavenly Peace that came over my Soul; and
I am sure in the two hours so enjoyed grew ten years in my
spiritual life—told cousin Joe to go Home with his wood, not
to mind me and walked a mile round . . . then sung all the way
Home—with a good appetite for the Samp and fat pork.

On Monday, December 5, Will woke early, in great pain. Elizabeth
sent for Dr. Tutilli, who came, looked at Will, then told her he could
do nothing. She must send for the British chaplain, "for Him who
would minister to his Soul."

Will heard the doctor. He drew himself toward his wife and murmured, "I breathe out my Soul to you." He lay back and closed his eyes.

The *capitano* arrived, shocked because the doctor had told him the
patient might be gone in a few hours. Dismayed that Elizabeth was
alone, he urged her to let him bring someone to stay with her. "Oh
no, what had I to fear?" and again, as though to convince herself,
"what had I to fear?"

All night she sat close to Will, listening for his breathing. Once, in
the blackness, she kissed his face to see if it was cold.

She would not write in her journal for a week.

THREE

Elizabeth was sixteen when she met Will at a ball. She was a dark-eyed beauty, supple and petite, her black hair piled in waves, with ringlets around the neck. Will was twenty-two—tall, fair, and handsome. As they danced, they made such a striking pair and were so absorbed in one another that people noticed.

He called her Eliza.

Will had just come back from Europe, where he'd spent two years learning business methods and working with the Filicchi shipping firm in Leghorn as preparation for joining his father's firm in New York. Elizabeth had just come back to the city, too, after two years at her uncle William's house in New Rochelle.

They danced and they talked. Will could describe the European cities he'd known—Florence, Pisa, and Leghorn, the port city where ships arrived from New York. In Leghorn he'd intended to have his portrait done but found no one who could take it properly; one artist had told him that his face was very difficult to take and he would not attempt it, lest he lose his reputation. Will had traveled to the industrial cities of Sheffield, Manchester, and Birmingham, then to Madrid, which he'd found an expensive place to live, and to Genoa, which he considered handsome and stylish, with many more fine buildings than

Barcelona. He'd become fluent in Italian and was able to converse with local ladies, who he said "were extremely well dressed, but not nearly as beautiful as ladies in America."

Elizabeth had longed to travel; growing up, she had "a reigning passion in my breast to see the world, and Europeans in particular." She was interested in stories of Europe, and she was interested in the gentleman telling them.

The gentleman, William Magee Seton, was descended from Scottish nobility; one unlucky ancestor, Mary Seton, had been lady-in-waiting to Mary Queen of Scots. His father, William Seton, was born in Scotland and had grown up in England; at sixteen he emigrated to New York to seek his fortune in the beckoning New World.

He found it quickly. Within a few years he was part-owner of an ironworks in New Jersey and had bought property in Nova Scotia and in the interior of New York known as "the Mohawk lands." By the time he was twenty-two, he had helped found the New York Chamber of Commerce, had set up the shipping firm of Seton and Curson, and had married his partner's daughter Rebecca.

Since his early success, Seton had urged his widowed mother in England to come to New York to live. Instead, she sent a wedding gift of a silver tea set inscribed with the family coat of arms—a shield with three crescents, framed with trailing ivy, topped with a fire-breathing dragon—and the family motto: *At Whatever Risk, Yet Go Forward*. And she kept up a steady flow of advice in her letters. "I have heard, my dear William, that you take too much snuff. For God's sake, take as little as possible, for nothing hurts the health so much and generally makes one look quite stupified."

Seton was so determined to have his mother meet his bride that he and Rebecca made the crossing a few months after their marriage. They were on their way back to New York when their first child, William Magee—named for his father and a wealthy family friend— was born on board the *Edward* on April 20, 1768, as the ship was nearing Norfolk, Virginia.

Will was baptized as soon as the Setons reached New York, on

May 8, at Trinity Church. Yet he'd grown up as a cultural Christian only, not a churchgoer; Elizabeth could not talk about God and faith with him any more than she could with her father. But at sixteen, her faith was still private, her God largely confined to the pages of her Bible and the Book of Psalms. Although she would come to be concerned about Will's lack of interest in the spiritual, she had neither inclination nor reason, in the early days of their relationship, to bring God into the conversation.

Like most sons of the upper class in the colonies, Will had been sent to school in England. His grandmother there reported to his father that she had met Mr. Rose, Will's teacher, and that the boy was studying Roman history, Goldsmith's *The History of England,* French spelling, French tables, and French grammar. She found her grandson to be "a sweet-tempered boy and I hope will turn out to your satisfaction. Mr. Rose says he is doing very well . . . I see him almost every day but I don't spoil him. Indeed, the child is so good-tempered that I never have cause to find fault with him." While the Revolutionary War was raging in America, twelve-year-old Will had visited London, where he'd not only heard the king speak but had followed him into the robing room and watched him take off his crown. He'd seen Lord North, the stout, round-shouldered prime minister who thought that the Americans would surrender, and who Will thought was "the shabbiest of the Lords, wearing a nasty old brown coat."

William and Rebecca had three sons after Will: James, John, and Henry. Rebecca died giving birth to her fifth child, her only daughter, Anna Maria, named for Rebecca's sister. The girl grew to be a celebrated beauty; at fifteen, she married John Middleton Vining, a member of the House of Representatives from Delaware, later a United States senator.

When Elizabeth and Will met, he had come back to New York for his sister's wedding in the autumn of 1790, to the delight of his grandmother. "Nothing could have been duller than the weddings I have seen in this family . . . I tell them all that if they want a merry wedding, they must go to America."

———

The city itself was merry, with William Seton playing a major part in its postwar revival.

Throughout the Revolution and the occupation, he'd been loyal to the British crown, as manager of the vigorous Port of New York, with some five hundred vessels, both merchant and warships. One British captain whom he had entertained wrote that Seton was "liked and esteemed by everyone and not spending less than six guineas a day." After the war, Seton, like Richard Bayley, remained welcome. When the French journalist and revolutionary Brissot de Warville visited New York, he found William Seton as respected as a citizen of the new republic as he had been as a Tory. "What will give you a good idea of his integrity," de Warville wrote, "is that he was chosen to an important place notwithstanding his known attachment to the British cause."

That place was cashier of the Bank of New York, the first bank in the city, an appointment arranged by Alexander Hamilton, who knew the urgent need for experienced, knowledgeable businessmen. Until the Bank of New York was chartered, most states issued their own paper money; coins were not minted until 1792, in Philadelphia. A dollar became the basic unit because both the Americans and the British called the Spanish piece of eight, with its sound basis in Europe, a "dollar" (and a quarter of it was "two bits" of the eight).

Will had worked under his father as clerk of discount at the bank for two years, from 1786 to 1788, before going to Europe to study finance. Elizabeth was living in New York in those same two years, but a young girl would never have walked into a bank. Except for the handful of "She-Merchants," banking was exclusively a man's prerogative, though Elizabeth would one day defy gender boundaries and claim it as hers, too.

Under William Seton's management, the bank made its first loan to the federal government in 1789: $200,000 at 6 percent interest. As the new government was forming, Congress leased space at Fraunces Tavern, famous for its house drink—rum punch with nutmeg—and for its history: The first chamber of commerce was founded there by farsighted businessmen, including Seton, and the Sons of Liberty had gathered in the elegant three-story building to plan the New York Tea Party. City Hall became Federal Hall, with an immense eagle emblazoned above the front portico, and the ceiling in the Senate chamber patterned with thirteen stars and suns. On April 30, 1789, Seton watched as George Washington, wearing a brown broadcloth suit, white silk stockings, shoes with silver buckles, and his dress sword, stood in the sunshine on the second-floor balcony and took the oath of office as the first president of the United States.

Most of the leaders in the new government lived in the city, always the center of political, commercial, and social life in all its permutations. The red-light district, populated during the British occupation by ladies from Liverpool, now with mostly homegrown talent including "many fine, well-dressed women," continued to thrive in its familiar location, the "Holy Ground" just west of St. Paul's Chapel. Secretary of State Jefferson, accustomed to his spacious Monticello, rented a house on Maiden Lane and, even though New York was only the temporary capital, promptly began extensive renovations. Hamilton lived on Wall Street. Only Vice President John Adams, who couldn't afford Manhattan, rented a country house, Richmond Hill, a one-mile commute by chaise to his job in Federal Hall.

Washington was not a flamboyant man; elaborate titles that were suggested for him, including "Excellency," "His Majesty the President," and "His Highness the President of the United States of America and Protector of the Rights of the Same," gave way to a simple "Mr. President." For all his personal modesty and precarious financial status—he'd needed a bank loan to pay for his travel to New York—he always felt that a leader should set a stylish example. His first New York residence as president was a fine three-story house on Cherry Street, with seven fireplaces and a large garden. But its ceilings were so low that one evening a lady's ostrich-feather headdress caught fire from the candles of a chandelier. Halfway through his term, he moved to the former home of the minister of France, a Broadway mansion that required a head steward to supervise a household staff of twenty maids, housekeepers, and cooks. Coachmen drove Washington around town in a yellow coach decorated with cupids and flowers, drawn by four—sometimes six—white horses. The New Year's party there to welcome 1790 was so grand that Abigail Adams compared it to galas she'd attended at the Court of St. James in London, when her husband was diplomatic minister there. Ladies in New York dressed so luxuriously and wore such opulent jewelry that Brissot de Warville thought men would be deterred from marrying. "Luxury is already breeding in this city a most dangerous class of men—bachelors. They are afraid to marry because it is so expensive to keep a wife."

New Yorkers reveled in the glitter and pushed hard for their city to remain the capital until it would move to its permanent location on the Potomac River, not far from Washington's Mount Vernon. Philadelphia lobbied to be the temporary capital, too. When the Senate vote was a tie, thirteen to thirteen, John Adams cast the deciding vote in favor of Philadelphia, which, given his opinion of New York when he first visited the city, the week Elizabeth was born, could have come as no surprise.

So the government moved, but the music played on. Elizabeth and Will saw one another often, at parties and dances where upper-class New Yorkers met and mingled. In a letter to his brother James, who was working in the West Indies, Will mentioned three ladies who sent their love, including "Miss Bayley." But other young ladies—and their mothers—had their eyes on this extremely eligible young bachelor, who was well educated and well traveled as well as rich, and it was Mary Hoffman with whom eager gossip had him linked. "It is currently reported and generally believed that I am to marry [her]," Will wrote. "But I should think twice before I committed that *faux pas* . . . I must confess that I admire her mental accomplishments very much and was I inclined to matrimony not all impossible what I might fall in love with her and have no doubt she will make an excellent wife and happy the man who gets her."

When Elizabeth came back from New Rochelle, her father was back from England, where he'd fled after the Doctors' Riot. He was living with his wife at 49 Smith Street, where their seventh child was born that year, 1790.

But Elizabeth wasn't coming home. She was not welcome in the house. She never knew the specific reason; in her recollections, she wrote only of "a family disagreement—could not guess why when I spoke kindly to relations they did not speak to me—could not even guess how anyone could be an enemy to another." Later, when Richard and Charlotte Bayley finally separated and he moved out permanently, he forbade Elizabeth ever to seek reconciliation with her stepmother.

Too old to be her uncle's responsibility any longer, Elizabeth lived sometimes with relatives on Staten Island, who had sheltered her and her mother in the desperate days when "What would become of us?" had first sounded in her life. Most of the time she lived with her sister in the city. Mary had married Dr. Wright Post, one of their father's most promising medical students; the newlyweds were living on John Street, near the theater. Although Elizabeth was welcomed there, the inescapable truth was that although she had a room of her own, she had no true home.

But she had Will. In the icy winter of 1791, there were skating parties on the Fresh Water Pond, meetings in the homes of mutual friends, tea and conversation around the fire. Springtime was for strolling, in groups or with a married friend, on the new paved paths called "foot-walks" and along the city's showcase street, Broadway, lined with elegant shops. New York was considered "the gayest place in America." A circus came to town, with a clown and a rider who, standing on a galloping horse, threw an orange into the air and caught it on the tines of a fork. In a popular magic show, "A Natural Philosophical Experiment," a person could write a question on a slip of paper, put it into a loaded pistol, and fire it. Without the performer seeing the question, a dove would appear with the answer in its bill. The old Fort George on the harbor was dismantled, its stones used to pave the Battery, the elm-shaded promenade that Elizabeth loved, which Washington Irving would describe, using the Algonquin Indian name, as "the pride and bulwark . . . of the beauteous island of Manna-hata."

The more Elizabeth and Will were together, the more they found in common: history, literature, poetry. Elizabeth could recite lines from James Thomson's *The Seasons,* a lengthy poem with lush passages that appealed to her love of nature ("Welcome, ye shades! Ye bowery thickets, hail! Ye lofty pines! Ye venerable oaks!"). They shared their pleasure in the cadence of the French language and a passion for music. Thanks to her father's insistence, Elizabeth had become a fine pianist. Will played the violin so well that he'd once considered a career as a concert violinist. He delighted in opera; the first opera in the city, *Le Tonnelier,* was presented at the City Tavern in 1790. In Florence, Will had been thrilled by an operatic tenor, Giacomo Davide, and he told Elizabeth that one day she must hear him, too.

Sixteen was a marriageable age at a time when girls put their hair up and were fitted for ball gowns at fourteen, and Elizabeth was prepared, with "fine plans of a little country home, to gather all the little children round, and teach them their prayers and keep them clean and teach them to be good." Even if "a little country home" was unrealistic, since Will was headed for a career in his father's business, her love for him—and his for her, she believed—was very real.

Then, in July, shortly before Elizabeth's seventeenth birthday, Will booked passage on the *Eagle* and went back to Europe.

She would always remember her emptiness then.

Folly, folly—sorrow, romance—
how silly to love anything in this world

Julia Sitgreaves Scott, Elizabeth's best friend, was a beautiful, vivacious member of New York society; Elizabeth nicknamed her "Gloriana" from Spenser's fantasy, *The Faerie Queene.* They visited constantly—a walk, a ride, tea and conversation. Sometimes they even dressed alike. They'd met through Dr. Bayley's friendship with Julia's husband, Lewis Allaire Scott, a leading lawyer in the city; his father, John Morin Scott, had been John Adams's host at breakfast. But their female friendship was intensely personal. When Will sailed, Julia was visiting family in Easton, Pennsylvania, so Elizabeth went to Easton. She needed Julia.

Because men ruled the world, both individually and collectively, the alliances of women were generally disregarded. Why would women need other women? Women needed men. In the late eighteenth century, though, long before the bonds of sisterhood were recognized in the women's movement, Elizabeth and her women friends relished that bond. Males and females were emotionally segregated, but women could be sustenance for one another. In their talks and letters, they could share intimately and be deeply affectionate and supportive. Knowing that the other cared for them affirmed their caring about themselves.

"There is not an hour of my Life in which I do not want either the advice or soothings of Friendship," Elizabeth wrote to Eliza Sadler, whom she'd met through her father's connection with Eliza's husband, Henry, and who, like Julia, had become a beloved friend, "my Sad." Elizabeth and her friends shared hopes and longings and fears, offering advice and suggestions whether asked for or not, never concerned with caution. "One of the pleasures of my attachment to you," Elizabeth wrote to Julia, "has always been that I might speak my mind to you with freedom."

Elizabeth brought to these friendships her customary wholehearted commitment. In her letters, she was thinking out loud, whether it was a serious thought ("What I most desire and wish for you now is peace, that first and most perfect of all earthly attainments") or a flippant one, as when a troublesome mutual acquaintance was visiting Julia—"I wish you joy of Miss Chippy. Pray get her a husband if you can." Elizabeth took her friendships so seriously that at one point in her life she was writing to Julia at eleven o'clock at night when she had to stop in midsentence, to give birth. That child, along with Elizabeth's other children, belonged to her friends, as theirs belonged to her. Children, especially daughters, were an important extension of women's attachments. To Elizabeth's children, Eliza was "Aunt Sadler," Julia was "Aunt Scott." Sad told Elizabeth to "keep in your children's minds their mother's friend."

Throughout her life, Elizabeth honored friendship as "one of the great spiritual resources of human existence."

After her visit with Julia, Elizabeth settled into her sister's household as gracefully as she could. The women were very different, and not as intimately attached as Elizabeth was to her women friends. Mary sometimes seemed to resent Elizabeth's friendships; she could criticize Eliza Sadler for her frequent jaunts to Europe. Mary had chosen the life of a quiet homebody, a woman who tried "to circumscribe my wishes within the bounds of prudence and propriety, and to act upon that conviction." Although Elizabeth was prudent and proper enough, she saw no particular need to circumscribe her wishes; the women could easily get on one another's nerves.

But the city was bursting with too much energy for Elizabeth to remain isolated. When the first federal census was taken in 1790, the population of New York City was 33,131, triple the number seven years earlier, when the British had finally gone home. City records listed 330 licensed drinking places, half of them grog shops and gin mills, but the other half respectable taverns, suitable for dinners and meetings, with accommodations for ladies in private rooms. The City Tavern offered subscription concerts. General Washington did not say good-bye to his troops in a government building or in a church but in the Long Room at Fraunces Tavern.

The first public library in the city, the New York Society Library, closed during the Revolution, had reopened with a large stash of books that had been hidden in the undercroft of St. Paul's, and new shipments arrived regularly from Europe. Even women were allowed to subscribe, with an initial fee of five pounds and dues thereafter of ten shillings a year. President Washington was never fined for overdue books, although other government officials were, including Chief Justice John Jay, who read—or at least checked out—three books a week. In a new republic that valued literacy, the library took pains to protect its treasures: "No person has a right to insert any comments, however correct, in the margin or other parts of a book, either with a pen or pencil."

Along with religious books, poetry, history, and mythology, Elizabeth loved to read romantic novels. Nearly two hundred novels, mostly British and European, were printed in America in the 1790s, with sex and violence as thematic as they are today. *Charlotte Temple,* the story of an innocent fifteen-year-old schoolgirl seduced by a dashing British naval officer, set in Revolutionary New York, typified the bestsellers of the time. The fiction section in the New York Society Library continued to expand, even though a published essay declared that because the themes of novels were "the passions of love, jealousy, hope, fear, remorse, revenge, rapture and despair," reading them was "one of the standard causes of insanity."

On Sundays Elizabeth went with the Posts to St. Paul's, the chapel of Trinity Church, which had been saved from the fire of 1776 because people were able to stand on its flat roof and douse the flakes of burning shingles that flew through the air. St. Paul's was a graceful little church with Doric columns and fourteen cut-glass chandeliers in the nave.

When she turned eighteen on August 28, 1792, she was still rootless and, one desolate day, hopeless.

> *Alas alas alas! Tears of blood! My God—*
> *horrid subversion of every good promise of God*
> *in the boldest presumption—God had created me—*
> *I was very miserable, he was too good to condemn*
> *a poor creature made of dust driven by misery,*
> *this the wretched reasoning—Laudanum—*
> *the praise and thanks of excessive joy*
> *not to have done the horrid deed—*
> *the thousand promises of ETERNAL GRATITUDE.*

Suicide by overdose—such a terrifying thought that it's tempting to dismiss that journal entry as the momentary, meaningless outburst of an impulsive young heart.

Certainly Elizabeth was emotional, inclined to dramatics; the "Mad Enthusiast." Her father had admonished her in a letter: "Calm that glowing of your soul, that warm emanation of your chest, for a more temperate climate."

But Elizabeth was a grown woman, not a moody teenager, when she wrote that anguished cry. She did not keep a daily journal in the usual eighteenth-century style, as George Washington meticulously recorded his everyday routine, from attendance at St. Paul's on the first Thanksgiving Day (it rained; few people showed up) to a terrible toothache ("swelled and inflamed gum") on March 18, 1790, a Monday. Not until years later, when she thought she was about to die, did Elizabeth record what she considered the significant episodes in her life, beginning when her mother had died, when Elizabeth was four. The memory of her emotional turmoil at eighteen had stayed with her for years, still searing when she wrote her remembrances. And a family memoir written by her grandson Robert Seton bears out her stark intention: "She occasionally had her fits of melancholy and one in particular, when about eighteen she so far forgot herself at a time of unusual despondency as to entertain the wicked purpose of self-destruction."

Elizabeth herself once confirmed it in a letter to her brother-in-law Henry Seton. He had survived a shipwreck and confessed in a letter to her that he wished he had not; feeling forsaken, he wanted to die. In her reply, she recalled "the moment twenty years ago in which I asked the same question—forsaken by all, you say, left to God alone—I have been so too, dear Henry."

God alone. In the depths of despair, a critical moment of awareness, a long step from the flower beds of her childhood into the jagged pathways of adult life. Trust in God alone: a defining phase in her emotional and moral and psychological development, stretching toward an authentic spirituality in which prayer was not mere piety and her Bible was not simply reading, even careful and devout reading, but "lamentation and longing and wondering (sometimes hopeful) about what God has in mind."

Will's brother James had studied in England, as Will had, and had been appraised by their grandmother as "one of those agreeable creatures, there is no depending on him when out of your sight." He'd worked in the West Indies, as preparation for a business career; in 1792, he came back to New York and married Mary Hoffman, whom Will had predicted would make "an excellent wife," and who would in time become Elizabeth's bitter enemy.

And Will came back from Italy.

He had stayed in Europe less than a year, almost a turnaround trip at a time when a transatlantic crossing took nearly two months. But that year of his brother's wedding was also the year his stepmother died. After Will's mother's death, William Seton had married her sister, Anna Maria Curson, and fathered more children. Many more. When Anna Maria had her eighth child, Seton's mother in England had written to him with her customary directness: "I congratulate you, my dearest William, on the recovery of your beloved wife and with the addition to your already large family, the number of which might frighten some people."

Will had always been as close to his stepmother, whom he called "My Dear Mom," as Elizabeth had been remote from hers, always "Mrs. Bayley." And he was as devoted to his father as Elizabeth was distanced from hers. Back in the big Seton house on Stone Street, Will could be emotional support for his father and the children. He could help his father prepare to set up his new shipping firm, scheduled to open when Seton resigned as cashier at the Bank of New York. He could rejoin the world of New York society, where people met at teas, at an evening of music, at a party or a dance, which meant that he would see Elizabeth again.

Will's cousin Mary Seton was married to John Wilkes, a nephew of the famous liberal member of the British Parliament who had once been assailed for his pro-American views. John and his brother Charles had come to New York with letters of introduction to William Seton, who had set them up in business. Dr. Bayley and the Posts, along with Elizabeth, were friends of the Wilkeses, so it was not long before Elizabeth and Will would meet in a private setting.

When they did, it was music that underscored their renewed

friendship. On the violin he had bought in Cremona, the first known Stradivarius in this country, Will played French ballads, melodies from the American Revolution, Vivaldi's violin concertos, and sometimes, to Elizabeth's delight, a duet with her at the piano.

Will no longer seemed wary of marrying. In Leghorn, he'd seen that marriages were often arranged for reasons of finance and fortune; he'd met a young woman, newly married, who'd told him that if she had known as much about her husband before they married as she did now, she never would have had him.

Will now had determined to marry for love. Elizabeth always had. They continued to meet, into the winter and spring of 1793, both at public events and in private—chaperoned—at the home of a married friend. Soon he was no longer just "Will" in the notes Elizabeth began sending him by houseboy.

My dearest Will—
I have resolved to do my duty and go and see Mrs. Dwight this afternoon and if the weather remains clear it is my intention to pass an hour with Mrs. Wilkes in the evening where you may have the honor of seeing me if you please—

Your EB

Mrs. Sadler is not going to the concert this evening and wishes very much to see us there this evening—do not be too late—

Yours EB

Whenever Will did not come as expected, Elizabeth took the initiative.

Your Eliza is well and would be perfectly happy if she could enjoy the society of her friend. I have wished very much to see you and know that indisposition alone could have prevented my wish— tomorrow I will wait in anxious expectation

Believe me your own

By the autumn of 1793, Elizabeth was as sure of Will's love as she had long been of her own.

> Your Eliza's eye is very ugly but not very painful but it
> will prevent the possibility of my going out therefore
> you must devote a great deal of your time to me—
> come as early as possible—we shall dine at one today
> as Post is going out of town—
>
> > Yours EB

Finally, a crucial appointment.

> My father dined with us and has gone I don't know where—
> I don't think you will meet him until the evening—
> Your apology is already made for one who is most earnestly
> interested in his good opinion of you—

In polite society, word of a betrothal was passed informally among family and friends, with only the wedding announcement itself appearing in the public press. Once the news was out, women friends visited the bride-to-be, who was then expected to pay a return visit at each home, the last time she would leave her calling card with her family name. The wedding cake was a dark fruitcake with double layers of white icing. The bride carried a prayer book, not flowers.

Elizabeth wore a gold filigree brooch, a Seton family heirloom sent by Will's grandmother, when she and Will were married, Bishop Samuel Provoost presiding, in the parlor of her sister's house on Sunday evening, January 25, 1794.

Richard Bayley did not come to his daughter's wedding, although he was just across the river, in Newark, New Jersey. He did not mention it in a letter he wrote her the day before, saying he was "vexed and disappointed" that he had not had a letter from her, asking her to find a certain French translation for him, sending "a cordial how do you do" to Will, and ending with "Farewell my Daughter."

William Seton was delighted with his bright, lively daughter-in-law; she called him "Father," suitable for a man with thirteen children. While the five from his first marriage were grown and gone, those from his second marriage ranged from one to fifteen years old. Until the new house that Elizabeth and Will were having built on Wall Street was ready, they lived in the family house on Stone Street— formerly Brewer Street, where the draft horses kicked up so much dirt that the residents paid for cobblestones, making their renamed block the first paved street in the city.

When Elizabeth and Will married, Seton resigned as cashier at the Bank of New York, having steered the new nation through its early financial troubles. (In 1790, the national debt was already $80 million, according to Treasury Secretary Hamilton, whose fifty-page report on the economy spurred a flurry of insider trading.) He set up a large shipping firm—Seton, Maitland, and Company—with a fleet of merchant ships named for some of his children: the *William Magee,* the *Henrietta,* the *Cecilia,* the *Samuel Waddington.*

James Maitland was a businessman who managed the London branch of the firm. The Setons were William, Will, and James. The firm was so prominent that Will's grandmother's letters were addressed simply to William Seton, Esq., Merchant in New York, America. He had his portrait painted by his neighbor Gilbert Stuart, whose rendering of George Washington became the face on the one-dollar bill.

⚜

When the Dutch owned, or at least occupied, the island of Manhattan, they'd built a protective wall of logs thirteen feet high, vertically placed, with sharply carved points, stretching from river to river. With only one entrance, "the Watergate," locked every night at nine o'clock, the wall seemed an unbreachable defense. But when the British arrived by sea, with a fleet of warships in the harbor, the wall was merely a geographic accessory. Without a shot, within two days in 1664, New

Amsterdam was given as a birthday present from King Charles II to his brother James, the Duke of York. The wall came down and, little by little, the simple gabled houses of the Dutch were replaced by the bigger and bolder—some in classic Palladian style, then in the Federal style: two- and three-story houses painted red, gray, or cream.

Elizabeth was pregnant when she and Will moved into their new house at 27 Wall Street in late 1794.

My own home at twenty—the world—that and heaven too,
quite impossible! So every moment clouded with that fear
My God if I enjoy this I lose you—
Yet no true thought of who I would lose
Rather fear of hell and shut out from heaven.

As a child, Elizabeth had turned to God as a loving father, a source of comfort and assurance. She had instinctively—and joyfully—known God through God's creation in the world, with no thought that her physical world, the world she lived in, was opposed to her spiritual world. The two were equally real and whole. But as she grew, that sunny view was clouded by the theology, influenced by Calvinism, that she read and heard at Sunday services. Calvinistic preachers emphasized the total depravity of human nature, with the body and the soul as separate entities—the soul in a lofty position, the body lower and corrupt. Joy had no place in this worldview; God was a judgmental, punishing figure.

On an everyday level, the moral rigor of post-Calvinistic Puritanism led the Common Council in Elizabeth's New York to forbid Sunday sports and games, to prohibit children playing in the streets or making noise on that day, and to circulate petitions calling for "the annihilation of taverns, coffee-houses, billiard tables, ale-houses and theaters," not only on Sundays but every day. The message was unmistakable: Love of worldly pleasures was incompatible with love of God.

But it was a mixed message, according to the Bible she relied on. While she read in Genesis that "God saw everything that he had made, and indeed, it was very good," she was warned in John the Apostle's letter that she must "Love not the world, neither the things that are in the world." It would be a very, very long time before mainstream Christianity preached a balanced view, and although Elizabeth's thinking would slowly stretch toward that balance, she would never be entirely free from feeling that she could not love both God and the world God had made, not even at her happiest times.

Especially not at her happiest times.

By the time Elizabeth and Will moved to Wall Street, what had once been the wilderness edge of the city had become its lusty, pounding heart. Moneymen had gathered under a buttonwood tree on the block, then moved indoors to "a large convenient room for the accommodation of the dealers in stock," at number 22. Alexander Hamilton had rented, then bought, a pair of town houses at numbers 56 and 57, one for his residence, one for his law office, in a real estate deal brokered by Aaron Burr. The Bank of New York stood at the corner of Wall and William streets. Elizabeth's neighbors included Francis Childs, publisher of the *Daily Advertiser,* an influential newspaper in the city, and Daniel McCormick, an alderman who started a New York City tradition by sitting out on his front stoop.

Anna Maria Seton, named for Will's stepmother, was born on May 3, 1795. Naturally, the infant was "one of the loveliest beings my Eyes ever beheld," the new mother wrote to Eliza Sadler in Ireland. "Her grand Father B will tell you that he sees more sense expression Intelligence and enquiry in that little face than any other in the world, that he can converse more with her than any woman in New York."

Grandfather B was Dr. Richard Bayley, who stepped out of the shadows into the light of Elizabeth's life when his first grandchild was born, and never again moved out. Elizabeth welcomed him with all her heart. Any resentment she felt at his past neglect was entrusted to God. "Forgive us our trespasses, as we forgive those who trespass against us." If a faithful prayer life and a spiritual consciousness had no effect on daily life in the world, in one's attitude and relationships, if it did not transform anger into acceptance and understanding, then it was all pointless, a doomed charade.

Richard Bayley was not a religious man. Elizabeth heard him say the word "God" only once, on his deathbed. He was not influenced by the views of conscience found in all the world's religions, from Confucianism to Christianity, but only by the secular view in which conscience is simply "the sense of right conduct," inborn, imprinted—like language—into a person's very being.

In Richard Bayley, that elementary view of conscience was reinforced by his medical training, with emphasis on the humanitarian. And so he gave up his society practice to work in public health, helped promote the New York Dispensary to give medical aid to the poor, and in the newly organized Medical Society formed a committee to investigate the causes of epidemics that regularly beset the city.

From midsummer until fall 1795, more than seven hundred people died of yellow fever. Governor John Jay and others blamed immigrants for the plague, but Bayley was convinced that the problem stemmed from the city's filthy conditions. Sewers had to be drained, he insisted, swampland filled in. His views would be vindicated in a medical journal more than a century later: "He proved yellow fever to be infectious and understood thoroughly the conditions under which it throve . . . In the study of fevers and croup he was very far ahead of his time."

But in his time, Dr. Bayley was assailed by the soap makers, tallow chandlers, and glue manufacturers who used the streets and sewers for effortless waste removal. Jacob Roosevelt's leather industry, centered in Beekman's Swamp, was particularly offensive as it had made Roosevelt's fortune, some of which he had bequeathed to his granddaughter Charlotte, Dr. Bayley's wife. When Dr. Bayley was appointed health officer, Elizabeth wrote to him in Albany, where he was reporting his findings to Governor Jay, warning him that "the Soap Boilers and Tallow Chandlers talk of removal of the Health Officer." The governor listened to the doctor, though, and began working with him on plans for a quarantine station where yellow fever victims could be isolated and treated.

When he was not traveling, Richard Bayley visited the Setons nearly every day, often playing cribbage with Will as Elizabeth played the piano. He was godfather to Anna Maria, then to the second Seton baby, William III, born on November 25, 1796. That first son was, Elizabeth wrote, "all a mother's heart can wish in health, Life and Beauty and from his promise of goodness sweetness of temper I have reason to hope he will indeed be a *third* William." He would be the only one of her children to marry, raising a family that would continue Elizabeth's line of descendants into the twenty-first century.

Julia Scott came by at least once a week for tea and gossip, to play with the children. One afternoon she and Elizabeth rode horses along the East River, to a point called Hornbrooks, where they rode up the hill and stopped. Below them, the heady rush of moving water; across the river, an embrace of thick, lush green, so artfully streaked with sunshine and shadow that it seemed less a forest than a painted landscape. Elizabeth had reveled in the colors and sounds of nature since she was a little girl. Now she turned to Julia. "The world is so good," she said, "I could willingly consent to be here forever."

Calling cards on a silver tray; maids and a cook and a male servant to clean and sharpen the kitchen knives; book stalls and flower stalls and dollars to spend at them; a summer house on Long Island; two hours of the Bible, with prayer, every morning.

The world and heaven too.

On the night of February 22, 1797, at the first Commemoration Ball celebrating the birthday of George Washington, Will was one of four aristocrats chosen to be an official host. Invitations on stiff white pasteboard with crimson lettering and border had been hand-delivered to the Roosevelts, the Astors, the Alexander Hamiltons—all the powerful, the prominent, and the privileged. Elizabeth wore cream silk dancing slippers, monogrammed.

FOUR

~⚜~

S mells from the toilet in the lazaretto seeped through the room. "One of the guards brought a pot of incense also to purify our air," Elizabeth wrote. But the toilet was simply a pot in a partially closed corner—she called it "the closet"—and between its odor and the chimney smoke, the air in the sealed space was never pure. With only a basin of cold water for washing, she slept in her clothes and would not be able to change until they were released.

She picked up her journal after a week. "W. goes on *gently,* but keeps me busy."

Rev. Thomas Hall, the Protestant chaplain to the British consulate in Leghorn, had come at daylight, after the night Will was expected to die, and had promised to come again. Elizabeth's half brother, Guy Carleton Bayley, who was working for the Filicchis, had come. Elizabeth was thankful that she had not been shattered by the nearness of death, thankful "that my God could and would bear me through even the most severe trials." She could tell herself that since Will followed her reading of the Psalms and portions of scripture, their imprisonment was a spiritual benefit, giving her "days of retirement and abstraction from the world which have afforded leisure and opportunity for so blessed a work—except the day which we thought his last, he has never failed one day in this course—he very often says this is the period of his life which if he lives or dies he will always consider as Blessed—the only time which he has not lost."

But their confinement had also stirred Elizabeth's anger. When the *capitano* reminded her of "le Bon Dieu": "Oh well I know that God is above, Capitano, you need not always point your look and silent finger there." If it were not for her trust in God, she wrote, "you would find me a lioness willing to burn your Lazaretto about your ears . . . to keep a poor Soul who came to your country for his Life, thirty days shut up in damp walls, smoke, and wind from all corners blowing even the curtain round his bed, which is only a mattress on boards and his bones almost through—and now the Shadow of death, trembling if he only stands a few minutes—he is to go to Pisa for his health—this day his prospects are very far from Pisa."

Much of the time, Will was unable to carry on a conversation. When he lay silently on his bed, Elizabeth wrote to him.

"Dear W it is not from the impulse of terror you seek your God, you tried and wished to serve him long before this trial came, why then will you not consider him the Father who knows all the different means and dispositions of his children and will graciously receive those who come to him by that way which he has appointed—you say your only hope is in Christ what other hope do we need."

The skipper from the *Shepherdess,* Captain O'Brien, came to visit, along with Mrs. O'Brien. Elizabeth ran down the steps to greet them. "Must not touch, Signora," said the guard, dividing her from them with his stick. O'Brien had tears in his eyes; when his wife saw Anna peering through the grate, she began to cry. A sailor from the ship came with them. "He turned pale when he saw my head out of the iron bars and called out 'Why dear Mrs. Seton are you in a Prison?'" As the little group left, the sailor kept looking back.

Elizabeth finished reading through the Bible, which she'd started on the sixth of October, when their ship had just left New York. Usually she read to herself, but now she wanted Will to hear: "Today read him several passages in Isaiah which he enjoyed so much that he was carried for a while beyond his troubles—indeed our reading is an unfailing comfort Wm says he feels like a person brought to the Light after many years of darkness."

Whether it was through the Filicchis' intervention, Will's dangerously failing health, or some arbitrary decision, the Setons' term in the lazaretto was shortened from forty days to thirty. They would be released in time for Christmas. The Filicchis had arranged an apartment for them in Pisa, on the banks of the Arno. Elizabeth could not conceal her bitterness. "My heart used to be very full of poetical visions about this famous river, but it has no room for visions now."

As the raw December wore on, Will shivered; Elizabeth hopped on one foot, "five or six times the length of the room without stopping—laugh at me my Sister but it is very good exercise and warms sooner than a fire."

"My Sister" was Rebecca Seton, Will's sister, for whom Elizabeth was keeping this journal, not only as a record of what was happening when, but as a way of feeling close to the young woman whom she'd come to know and love since her marriage. In a letter to Julia Scott, Elizabeth called Rebecca "the most truly amiable estimable young woman I ever knew." When Elizabeth left for Italy, she had left three of her children—William, Richard, and Catherine—in Bec's care.

ᴥ✿ᴥ

William Seton was a portly man, almost roly-poly, with a head of thick hair, smiling eyes, and an open hand and heart. "Let all come to my strong box while I am alive, and when I am gone you will take care of each other," he told his children, a prediction that would prove overly optimistic.

He became so fond of his daughter-in-law that he showed her family letters he'd shown to no one else, not even Will. "You are the first of my children to whom I have submitted a perusal of them, and I request you will return them to me unsullied by the eye of impertinent curiosity. Let no one look at them." So Elizabeth read the letters from Will's grandmother, in all their brisk variety: "an infallible cure for rheumatism" involving "twenty ounces of good brandy"; an order that Seton stop sending money to his sister and her husband, who was otherwise bound for debtors' prison: "While she has you to depend on, she will never exert herself, and as to him, let him rot in jail." At the time of Will's marriage: "I hope the Young Lady is in every respect good and amiable, that she may be deserving of such a partner as my sweet William with whom I hope she will think herself uncommonly fortunate."

Elizabeth thought herself more than fortunate. She had entered a changed landscape, a lush and loving country where the stark "What would become of us?" was silenced. She was living her own creation story, in a new state of being, which made new history possible. Her creation was a process, rooted in love: When Will traveled to Philadelphia on business, she tucked her picture into his shaving case; he wrote every day to "my darling little wife, whose picture I have now before me and would not have been without it for the world." In one letter she wrote while he was on that trip, she called him, in succession, "my dearest treasure," "my dearest Husband," "my Darly," and "my love."

Elizabeth had admitted to having "no true thought" of God; in marriage she was stretching toward that thought, toward an authentic spirituality grounded in human relationships. Loving Will, with Will loving her, reflected God's love for them both, as it affirmed and deepened her faith. "These arms, heart and bed are all forlorn without you," she wrote. "I will not go to bed as I did last night for although it was twelve I did not close my Eyes 'till three therefore I will take my Bible and read till I am sleepy."

In that long letter, she told Will about a conversation she'd had at a dinner with his father, where she'd met a business associate, Mr. Fisher. "He really is the most charming company that can be and I think I never was in my life more pleased with a stranger—We talked of you, you may be sure and he said that I must learn one thing which few women could acquire the first year of their marriage which was to let their Husbands 'Act for the Best.'"

Elizabeth could learn that. She understood the role of an eighteenth-century wife, as Thomas Jefferson had explained to his newly married daughter: "The happiness of your life now depends on the continuing to please a single person. To this all other objects must be secondary." Elizabeth was not a headstrong rebel: She knew the language of her society; she could speak it, and she did. When she and Will didn't agree on where they would spend one summer, Elizabeth said simply, "Willy's please must be my please." She also knew what she called "the true language of female determination," and when she needed to speak *it,* she did.

By the time Elizabeth was married, a Frenchwoman, Olympe de Gouges, had published a ringing "Declaration of the Rights of Woman and the Female Citizen," a bold response to a key document of the French Revolution, "The Declaration of the Rights of Man and the Citizen" in 1789. The first article of the "Rights of Man" said that "men are born and remain free and equal in rights." The first article of Olympe de Gouges in 1791 declared that "woman is born free and remains equal to man in rights." She was guillotined as a reactionary.

But early feminism was taking hold. Mary Wollstonecraft, an English writer, published *A Vindication of the Rights of Woman,* claiming that women's subordinate position stemmed from their inferior education. Female education in the eighteenth century, she wrote, was intended to cultivate "that weak elegancy of mind, exquisite sensibility, and sweet docility of manners supposed to be the sexual characteristic of the weaker vessel." Many women were delighted with the book—John Adams teased Abigail for being "a Disciple of Wolstoncraft"—and so were some progressive men: Aaron Burr declared it "a work of genius," vowed to read it aloud to his wife, and had their nine-year-old daughter, Theodosia, tutored in Latin and Greek.

Wollstonecraft contended that because the faculty of reason existed in both males and females, they were therefore equals. In that age of Enlightenment, rational thought had become a primary value of a free, democratic society. In philosophy: "Have courage to use your own reason!" The minimal faith known as deism, common to the founding fathers of the republic, rejected dependence on biblical revelation in favor of unaided natural reason. Elizabeth thought of herself as eminently reasonable, as she explained to Eliza Sadler. "Every hour I can catch shows me the Instability of every expectation that is not founded on reason. I have learnt to commune with my own Heart, and I try to govern it by reflection."

Still, the heart had its reasons. She was also reading the Romantic philosopher Jean-Jacques Rousseau, whose *Emile; or, A Treatise on Education* stressed emotion, not reason, as the better guide to truth and emphasized maternal love and the importance of feeling. "Three volumes I have read with delight," Elizabeth wrote. Then she added, cryptically, "Were I to express half my thoughts about it . . . I should lose that circumspection I have so long limited myself to and be E.A.B[ayley] instead of E.A.S.—dear JJ I am yours." She marked pages with a honeysuckle branch.

Reason and emotion: a study in balance. When a family friend, Mr. Olive, called her a "Specimen of Philosophy, one who reasons and reflects on the Consequences of actions," she admitted to her father, "He little thinks how the frail Bark is tost by contending commotions, and how dearly earned is that spirit of accommodation he thinks so great an ornament."

Wollstonecraft wrote at length about marriage, saying that husbands "are often only overgrown children." Elizabeth read the book as soon as the publication reached America, and copied a section in her notebook: "In the choice of a Husband they should not be led astray by the qualities of a lover, for a lover the Husband, even supposing him to be wise and virtuous, cannot long remain. Friendship and Forbearance takes place of a more ardent affection."

Wollstonecraft was wrong about Elizabeth and Will not remaining ardent lovers. Elizabeth was no longer a rapturous bride but a burdened wife and mother when she wrote to Julia, when Will was in Philadelphia: "Send me a kiss by my Husband—*One,* mind you, no more, or you will be putting notions in the man's head . . . [I] will make your *one* many, by all the rules of multiplication."

But Wollstonecraft was right about friendship. A new phrase had crept into the late-eighteenth-century vocabulary, one that both co-incided with and contradicted the traditional view of marriage. In the new notion of "companionate marriage," the wife remained subordinate, yet the spouses could be equal as friends. Successful marriages validated the idea: Abigail Adams called John "Friend," and when Elizabeth referred to Will as "friend," both in an early courtship note and throughout their marriage, it was not a casual term.

When Elizabeth wrote to Eliza Sadler in Paris on a wintry February night, her letter reflected the comfort of friendship within marriage.

"Mrs. Sad, *il facto,* you go to Balls on Sunday night, you depraved creature, and what Balls or amusement can compensate for that quiet calm tranquility which Sunday and particularly Sunday evening affords with Husband shaking his Slipper by a good coal fire and a volume of Blair★ opened on the table . . .

"Peace and a potatoe for me I care not for rooms as big as a Church, great Buildings, busy servants or Perugues and as for your Boulvards I dare say they are very inferior to the pure air, fine prospect and gliding cement of our Battery . . . At this moment William is playing 'Rosy Dimpled Boy,' 'Pauvre Madelon Return,' 'Enraptured Hours' and 'Carmignol' all as fast as the violin can sound them in rotation . . .

"The clock strikes ten, and my fingers are cold I must say good by tho' suddenly for my friend William only gave me 'till tomorrow or the vessel will go without this."

Largely in response to Wollstonecraft's book, newspapers and magazines were running essays and letters speaking against the general subjugation of women in all areas: political, legal, social. In New

---

★ A book of sermons by Hugh Blair, minister of the High Church and a professor at the University of Edinburgh.

Jersey, women had been allowed to vote until the election laws were revised and the right to vote restricted to "free, white, male citizens." A wife had no legal identity separate from her husband; Will owned Elizabeth as a person, along with the dresses and shoes and hats she wore. Like children and slaves, women were considered to have "limited powers of reason"; under New York's law of "couverture," based on English common law, a woman could not hold property in her own name and was thus ineligible to vote. In 1777, New York had officially disenfranchised women in its constitution by specifically defining the electorate as male. But an influential group of New York intellectuals had formed the Friendly Club, where the rights of women were beginning to be discussed by the members—all male—including the role of women as mothers.

In colonial times, fathers were seen as the exclusive locus of authority, which often meant physical punishment, in the home. After the Revolution, as an aspect of Enlightenment thinking, being a parent was considered more than a biological fact; it was a cultural responsibility. In the new republic, mothers were seen as eminently suited to raise sons to be good Christians, active citizens, and successful competitors in the wider arena of life, and to raise daughters to be republican mothers. Discipline meant a temperate, rational approach that stressed affectionate guidance.

But how could women excel at republican motherhood without themselves being educated in history, philosophy, and literature? When schooling for girls became fashionable, even a priority, New York families who could afford it sent their daughters to boarding schools outside the city—Philadelphia, Boston, Connecticut—or, locally, to Mrs. Graham's academy on lower Broadway.

Isabella Graham was a fifty-five-year-old Scotswoman, so forceful and determined that when her husband died in Antigua and was promptly buried, according to custom, she refused to leave the country until she had his grave reopened, "to convince her that no symptoms of returning life had been exhibited there." In New York, she opened her school for girls in 1789, when it was still considered daring work. But the curriculum was so decorous—reading, writing, spelling, grammar, geography—that Mrs. Graham was acceptable in New York society, and society needed her. In Edinburgh, she had established a "penny society" to help the destitute sick; in New York, she was struck by the many women with children but without men, the poorest of the poor. Elizabeth Burgin, who had helped American prisoners of war escape during the British occupation of the city, had written directly to General Washington in 1779: "I am now Sir very Desolate without Money without Close or friends to go to, as helping our poor preseners Brought me to Want Whitch I don't Repent."

Elizabeth was twenty-three when she met Isabella Graham at a ladies' gathering. Mrs. Graham, an intensely religious Presbyterian, brought up the plight of poor women in the city, often forced to seek shelter in the almshouse, along with the blind and those called "the lunatic." By the end of the afternoon, this small group of women in a parlor had set up the first benevolent organization in the United States to be managed by women, the Society for the Relief of Poor Widows with Small Children.

Feminism as an organized movement was nearly a century away, but Wollstonecraft had laid the groundwork, along with her American contemporary, Judith Sargent Murray. In her essay "On the Equality of the Sexes," published in 1790, Murray declared that women were inferior to men in reason and judgment only because of their inadequate training. A little boy growing up "is taught to aspire," while his sister "is early confined and limited." Although Mrs. Graham's project did not directly address the question of women's rights, clearly it was a feminist initiative in its emerging into the male realm of public activity. Elizabeth was enthusiastic; thanks to her father's insistence on prolonged and serious education and her own independent spirit, she felt neither confined nor limited.

She rallied family and friends: Will's sister Rebecca; Eliza Sadler; her wealthy godmother, Sarah Startin; and "Dué"—Catherine Dupleix—who, along with Sad and Julia Scott, formed Elizabeth's closest trio. Membership in the society cost three dollars a year and meant visiting widows in their homes, assessing need, as a form of social work. By the end of the first year, "the success has been beyond our most sanguine expectations," Mrs. Graham wrote. "We now have a hundred and ninety subscribers . . . and nearly a thousand dollars in donations." Within two years, it was supplying food, firewood, clothing, and shoes to some 150 widows and 420 children.

While many citizens applauded the women's work, others were outraged. Shockingly, scandalously, these women were calling meetings, negotiating with government officials, incorporating their group so they could legally own property and engage in fund-raising, and going around the city without a male escort. One Episcopal clergyman publicly denounced them for laying aside "delicacy and decorum, which can never be violated without the most corrupting effects on themselves and public morals."

Certainly Elizabeth was not concerned with decorum when, as treasurer, she petitioned the state legislature for authority to run a $15,000 lottery, aiming to secure a permanent fund for women in need. "The poor increase fast," Mrs. Graham noted. "Emigrants from all quarters flock to us, and when they come they must not be allowed to die for want." Authority for the lottery was granted, the society flourished, and Elizabeth realized what women without male leadership could accomplish on their own.

"I am rocking the cradle with one hand, with a book on my knee to substitute my cabinet which is left in New York," Elizabeth wrote to Eliza Sadler in Paris. "Anna Maria is close by my side putting her Dolly to sleep and I will cut a lock of her beautiful hair for you which curls in a thousand ringlets over her head . . . *I* only have the least influence with her, because her disposition is exactly my own . . . she possesses from her Mother a most ungovernable temper and with all my endeavours is past all management. My William leaves her to me, My Father tells me, conquer her by gentleness. Post and my Sister recommends *Wipping,* which is to me an unnatural resource, and the last I shall have recourse to—Send me a word of advice on this subject, or rather make hast to set me right, and assist me in a case which demands more resolution, than any situation I have hitherto experienced."

Eliza Sadler had no children, and any advice would have been a long time coming from Paris, but she was older than Elizabeth—she'd served as chaperone when Elizabeth and Will were courting—and Elizabeth needed to talk. She and Will were sharing a house on Long Island, the summer of 1797, with Mary and Wright Post; Elizabeth was aware of "the inconveniences which a union of families always occasions." At breakfast one morning, Mary criticized Mrs. Sadler for being immersed in the pleasures of Paris, hinting that the fashion and glamour of that city would make her lose interest in Elizabeth. Elizabeth reported the exchange to Eliza. "I observed . . . that as you probably would never see Paris again you were right in enjoying all the good it affords . . . and I dread no alienation from a Heart that values candour and nature more than refinement and grace."

Seven-month-old William was sick that summer, so sick, Elizabeth wrote, "that my Father thought he could not recover . . . should I attempt to express what passed in my Heart in any moment of that time whilst his recovery was uncertain, you would lament that Heaven had allowed me the privilege of being a Mother, for what is there in the uncertainty of human happiness to repay the agonizing convulsions of those twenty-four hours in which I witnessed his sufferings."

The privilege of being a mother: Elizabeth both embraced and anguished over that role as long as she lived. Anna was only three when Elizabeth wrote to her, "In you I view the Friend, the Companion, and Consolation of my future years." Such an emotional connection at such an early age, Elizabeth later admitted, was "the great error." Near the end of her life, with her reputation for holiness spreading, when she was writing profound essays and reflections on Christ and the spiritual life, she was writing to her son William in Italy, sometimes three times a week, weeping as she wrote.

From the livery stable at the foot of Wall Street, below the Merchants Coffee House, the drive led up the Post Road on the east side of the island, past the Dove Tavern. There it turned along the Bloomingdale Road and headed south for the seven miles back, through the country village of Greenwich and down the west side, along the river, into the heart of the city. The drive, called the "Fourteen Miles Round," had been a favorite diversion of President Washington. Along the route, the Dutch had settled a small town called Bloemendael—"field of flowers"—which became an escape for affluent New Yorkers. William Seton leased a country house there, called Cragdon.

Elizabeth and Will celebrated their fourth wedding anniversary in the loving harmony they'd become accustomed to. Home was a miniature paradise, sunny and serene; Elizabeth kept songbirds in a pretty cage by the window. Will was quiet and mild-mannered, a perfect foil to his lively little wife, as they read together, played duets together, kept up on events together. They subscribed to newspapers from Baltimore and Philadelphia, as well as to local papers—usually four large pages, ten by fifteen inches, with extracts of news from European papers, advertisements, descriptions of French fashions (taffeta gowns, a muff of Siberian wolfskin), shipping news and weather, and a poet's corner. New York City news included wedding announcements, mostly formal and polite, with an occasional flight: "Captain Thompson Baxter was married to Miss Ann Whitman after a long and tedious courtship."

Late in January, Will's father fell on the ice while escorting a guest to his carriage. He could no longer ride his horse from Stone Street to Cragdon, but he was able to make the trip by carriage, and no one was particularly worried. No one had any reason to think that the new year would be anything but another year of prosperity and promise.

The city was buoyant. With Europe in turmoil following the French Revolution, New York's neutral position made it the nation's foremost port and marketplace. A weekly newspaper, the *New-York Price-Current,* was exclusively dedicated to financial affairs. The city expanded its shoreline around the southern tip of Manhattan, for more wharves and piers. Street signs had been put up, houses numbered, street names changed, befitting the new republic: Crown Street became Liberty

Street; King Street was now Pine. A "modern" hotel had opened on Broadway—the City Hotel, five stories, 134 rooms—for merchants and stockbrokers and their wealthy clients. Duncan Phyfe's shop— chairs, sofas, settees—around the corner from the Seton business at- tracted the rich and fashionable and made Phyfe's fortune. And in the spring, the new Park Theatre opened—a proud stone structure, which, including the pit and the gallery, had space for 2,400 people, fireplaces in the lobby, and a coffee room with, in deference to sensitive ladies, a no-cigar policy.

One stormy April night, Elizabeth and her sister went to the Park, husbands left at home. They had places in the red-cushioned box seats arranged in three semicircular rows around the stage, under a glass chandelier.

Elizabeth was six months pregnant, but this was 1798, before Vic- torian strictures would have kept her home by the fireside, and be- sides, her work with the widows' society proved that she need not let strictures stand in her way. And she'd loved going to plays since she'd been to the first permanent theater in the city, on John Street. That red-painted wooden building had opened when the Puritan ethic considered the theater a social menace, "a dangerous assault upon the Passions." In those austere days, Shakespeare had been the respectably correct staple. Even the Cherokee Indian chiefs who saw *Richard III* the night of the John Street opening had been serious and attentive, if uncertain about the plot.

But the American Revolution had brought freedoms beyond the political. In the one glorious year that New York City had been the capital of the new republic, President Washington had seen *The Clan- destine Marriage* on John Street and had laughed out loud, so unusual for that reserved gentleman that the moment had been reported in the press. On this night, Elizabeth and Mary saw *The Will,* with comic characters named Sir Solomon Cynic and Mrs. Rigid. A blond, blue- eyed soprano, Mrs. Hodgkinson, sang "Blue Bells of Scotland," "Sweet Passion of Love," and "One Kind Kiss Before We Part." Elizabeth called it "a frolick."

By the time the women came out onto the Park's broad portico, the storm had turned the street into a clamorous jumble. Horses were rearing, coachmen shouting at one another in their efforts to control the carriages. At a violent burst of thunder, the horses leapt again, with the wheel of first one carriage cracking, then another. It took Elizabeth and Mary's coachman half an hour to inch his way through the tangle.

Elizabeth was more embarrassed at her driver's quarreling than she was frightened. She considered it an adventure to be recounted to friends, just another entertaining diversion in the city she loved. Although as an authentic New Yorker she was dismayed by the "exorbitant" cost of a rental on Long Island, she was looking forward to a happy summer there.

In June, William Seton died from the effects of his fall on the ice.

In July, Elizabeth nearly died giving birth to her third child.

In August, yellow fever hung like a doomsday cloud over the city.

Seven years earlier, the fever had appeared in the city for the first time since the Revolution. Each succeeding year, the epidemic hit harder. A property called Bellevue, on the East River, was used as a hospital for the first time in 1795, but the drinking and the quarreling of the nurses was a scandal; two-thirds of the patients died.

Now, in the summer of 1798, Dr. Bayley called the disease more plague than fever. The sickness began with chills, headache, and a high temperature. After a few hours' respite, the fever shot up again; the skin and the eyeballs turned yellow as red blood cells were destroyed. The patient vomited black blood. In earlier years, the shabbier parts of town, where sanitation was secondary to survival, had been hardest hit. Now yellow fever crossed class lines, killing the rich as well as the poor. The Bank of New York moved from Wall Street to a country lane to the north, which became Bank Street. People sniffed sponges saturated with camphor, wore bags of the pungent medicinal herb asafetida around their necks, and carried bits of charred rope to use when touching doorknobs and railings. Within a few months, more than two thousand people died. A wealthy merchant helped families left without a provider by collecting money and goods: One man gave "one ox, two pigs, two lambs, eighty chickens and sixteen bushels potatoes. From a farmer in Staten Island he received "two sheep, ten bushels of Potatoes, six bushels turnips and twenty-five pumpkins." Others gave beef, cheese, cider, ducks and geese, eggs, flour, bread and butter, shoes, and cash.

Dr. Bayley lived and worked around the clock at Bellevue. The Common Council warned: "Persons carrying the dead are not permitted to walk on the sidewalks close to the houses." Two boys walked the streets selling coffins from a wagon.

Elizabeth was anxious about her father, and about Julia Scott. Julia's husband had died and she'd moved to Philadelphia, where the fever killed more than three thousand people that year. Through their frequent letters, the women were able to stay nearly as close as when they'd been neighbors in New York. Elizabeth's letters sometimes ran for pages, giving a detailed picture of what was going on in her life. She wrote to Julia about her brush with death in childbirth.

"I was so terribly ill in my hours of sorrow that my Father could scarcely perform his office, tho' every exertion was necessary to save me. The dear little son was for some hours thought past Hope and the Mother within one more pain of that rest she has so often longed for—but which Heaven I hope for good purposes has again denied—my Father may truly be said to have given the breath of Life to my child for when it neither Breathed or moved he went on his Knees and placing his Mouth to its lips breathed or I may say forceably blew it into its Lungs." In honor of the grandfather who had saved him, the boy was named Richard Bayley Seton, nicknamed Dick, Dicksy, Ricksy, and Doxie; by whatever name, he would grow up to be the black sheep of the family.

Even before his marriage, when he was working in Europe, Will had talked in his letters about "pain in the breast." Tuberculosis was a common cause of death in the eighteenth century; George Washington had it, along with members of his family. Quite unlike yellow fever, the "white plague" was often considered a romantic disease; as the victim was "consumed"—hence its other name, consumption—and quietly wasted away, the soul was cleansed. Various tonics were used as remedies: powdered licorice mixed with water, cinnamon milk, cedar berries made into a cough syrup. Elizabeth called tuberculosis "the family enemy" and was always anxious about her husband's health, "that health on which my every hope of happiness depends."

Will had been so close to his father that after William Seton was buried in Trinity's churchyard, with nearly five hundred people attending, Elizabeth became her husband's only consolation. "He has no friend or confidant now on Earth but his little wife; his attachment to his Father was so particularly affectionate and uniform that his loss is one of the most severe afflictions to him that could possibly have happened—most men have the resource in an event of this kind either of particular friends, or habits to dissipate sorrow but my Husband has neither, for he has been so long accustomed to leave my Society only for his Fathers, and his Fathers for mine, that all now centers in the survivor."

So it was the survivor who had to tell the family in England. Seton's sharp-tongued mother had died; Elizabeth wrote a long letter to his sister. "What can I say to prepare your mind for the sad and distressing intelligence that our beloved one, best of parents, is no more . . . he died on the 9th of June after several hours of severe pain but possessing his senses to the last."

As the oldest son, Will was responsible for his father's second family. Rebecca was eighteen, able to care for herself. But there were six others: Mary, fourteen; Charlotte, twelve; Harriet, eleven; Samuel, nine; Edward, eight, and Cecilia, seven. The Wall Street house was too small for them all; Elizabeth's new home was to be the larger Seton house on Stone Street. But because that was in the heart of the infected area, everyone crammed into Cragdon's five rooms until the city was livable again. One day, when the house was reasonably still, she wrote a prayer:

Almighty Giver of all mercies, Father of all, Who knows my heart and pities its weakness and errors, Thou knowest the desire of my soul is to do Thy Will.

Thy will. The will of God. The phrase resounds, again and again, in Elizabeth's letters and prayers. Such a simple phrase, such historical ramifications: the belief that the divine right of kings, their right to rule, came directly from the will of God. In Christian theology, God's will is not what God *wants*—a good God does not want wars—and not guidance for personal decisions, such as deciding whom to marry, but a relationship with God, acceptance of a God who does not pre-ordain events, not a God of explanations, but a God beyond human knowledge or even imagination. For Elizabeth, the will of God meant being aware of God's presence in her life, not only when she was praying or reading her Bible but every day, in every happening, every circumstance.

৩৪৩

In the fall, with the fever past, Elizabeth returned to the city to get the Stone Street house in order. "We have painted, Papered and White-washed, so I hope there is no danger, tho' the Man who took care of the House was ill there with Fever, and not one House in the neigh-bourhood escaped." But she wept as she closed up the house on Wall Street, the only home she could truly call her own. "Oh Julia, Julia," she wrote. "Those hours are past which tho' I enjoyed them, I never knew their value."

Before the move, Elizabeth did not have a high opinion of Rebecca Seton: "Until I was under the same roof with her I always thought her an uninformed Girl . . . but I prove the contrary every day." Within months of her father's death, Rebecca had so endeared herself to Elizabeth that Elizabeth began calling her "my Soul's Sister." Like Julia Scott, Rebecca became Elizabeth's intimate, with one signifi-cant difference: The Seton women shared an exceptionally religious devotion. Julia was Elizabeth's constant friend all her life, but she considered religion to be superstition; Rebecca and Elizabeth prayed together and attended Trinity Church together. They were committed to Eucharistic prayer. In their Protestant Episcopal Church, the service of Communion was viewed as merely symbolic of the Lord's Supper, not the bodily presence of Christ in the bread and wine, and was celebrated only about six times a year. On those "Sacrament Sundays," Elizabeth and Rebecca rushed from one church to another in order to receive Communion again.

But, like Will, Rebecca had tuberculosis, with frequent attacks of fever and weakness. In the spring of 1799 she went south, to her sister in Delaware, in an attempt to improve her health. During the time she was away—almost a year—Elizabeth wrote to her often. In a letter from Cragdon, she said, "I never sweep the hall, or dress the flower pots, or walk around the pear-tree walk, but you are as much my companion as if you were actually near me, and last evening finding myself accidentally by the garden fence at the head of the lane where we once stood at sunset . . . I was so struck with the recollection and the uncertainty of when I should see you again, that I had a hearty crying spell, which is not a very common thing for me." And Rebecca returned the love: "The idea of my spending the winter away from you makes me miserable."

By summertime, the Setons were settled in at Stone Street. For Elizabeth, it was an unexpected chapter in her creation story: at twenty-four, she was the mother of nine children, from four months to fourteen years. She was changing from a volatile, emotional, untested girl to a volatile, emotional woman beginning to meet tests of her strength and faith and love.

❧✣☙

In the lazaretto, Elizabeth woke in darkness, to the ringing of church bells.

At eleven o'clock on the morning of December 19, the gate of the lazaretto was unlocked. She took Will's hand and squeezed beside him as two men carried him down the twisting stone steps to the road. A crowd of the curious—she called them "the gazers"—watched the Americans climb into the Filicchis' coach.

As they drove the fifteen miles to Pisa, along the narrow road shaded by Mediterranean pines, Will was cheerful, revived by the fresh air. Elizabeth was grateful "that what I had so fondly hoped and confidently asserted really proved in the hour of trial . . . that my God could and would bear me through even the most severe trials."

In the beautiful apartment, Will seemed stronger than when they set out. He rested on a sofa, "delighted with his change of situation, taste and elegance of everything around him, every comfort within his reach."

Two days later, he and Elizabeth and the landlady of the house, Madame de Tot, went for a drive. Through the winding medieval streets, they saw the cathedral with its frescoed dome, the storied Leaning Tower, the thirteenth-century cemetery built on shiploads of earth from Golgotha, outside ancient Jerusalem, where Christ was crucified. Will was so renewed that Elizabeth thought that more riding would be good for him.

Back in their comfortable apartment, they read. They talked about the past.

FIVE

W ill was an affectionate father, engaged with his children. In a
    letter to Eliza Sadler, Elizabeth described how four-year-old
Anna "throws handkerchiefs, sticks needles in him and chases him
around the room fifty times a day, a kind of mirth he delights in."
When Will was away, their little son Richard "looks everywhere for
[him]," Elizabeth wrote, and when Will returned, the child "began
kissing him and would not quit him a moment."

As much as she, too, reveled in their children—"my treasures"—
Elizabeth sometimes prolonged breastfeeding beyond the customary
year in the hope of postponing another pregnancy. Women in Philadelphia had access to "certain small contrivances" to prevent pregnancy, but for most women, childbirth in the eighteenth century was a
recurring fact of female life. (When Aaron Burr was born, his mother
wrote that when she had only one child, "my hands were tied but now
I am tied hand and foot—how I shall get along when I have got ½ doz.
or 10 children I cannot devise.") Elizabeth called childbirth "running
the gauntlet"; she and Will had five children in seven years.

Since the Reformation, Protestants had dismissed Christmas as another
example of Catholic ignorance and deception: The date of Christ's

birth was not given in the New Testament, and December 25 marked the beginning of the winter solstice, a day traditionally linked to pagan bacchanals. New Year's Day was the important winter holiday, when families exchanged small gifts and gentlemen made calls, often with a snifter of brandy, from house to house. No shooting was allowed on New Year's Day; anyone who allowed his hogs or goats "to go at large in any of the streets" had to pay a fine.

From Albany, Dr. Bayley sent New Year cakes and honey, raisins and keg biscuits and almonds. Each winter he traveled to the state capital there, where he lodged at the lieutenant governor's house, brought health issues before the legislature, and mingled with Alexander Hamilton and other men with "great brilliancy of wit."

All along, he kept in close touch with Elizabeth with letters that reflected his singular personality: "Sunday after twelve: 14 minutes and a half, for the sake of precision . . . if I knew how, I would plague you with enigmatical allusions—but as this would require much time, and a greater exertion of genius than I can muster, please to look about, look at the habitable globe, look at the seasons, look at the lamppost, hear the howling of the elements, the crackling and rattling of the thunderstorms . . . you are determined never to deceive your Father in thought word or deed, let it be so, and if ever I do you, may I perish—now live on my Child, let reason guide you, if your opinion wavers, take always the prudential side." When Elizabeth did not promptly reply to one of his letters: "Can you Lady Bet prevail on yourself to write me by every post—that is, three times a week."

Elizabeth's New Year's letter to Julia was not all happy wishes. "If the news of our Misfortunes has reached you," she wrote, "you must do as I do, *hope the best*. My Seton is in a distress of mind scarcely to be imagined . . . I must be thankful for what remains from the ruins of Wall Street."

The family shipping business was collapsing. For all his integrity, Will was not the businessman his father had been. In addition to pirate raids and shipwrecks, the conflict between the English and the French affected the Atlantic shipping trade. Some Seton ships—one carrying coined money, one carrying valuable cargo from Amsterdam—were lost at sea. Will was forced to give up Cragdon, although his brother James, the junior partner, bought a fine three-story house on Greenwich Street. Elizabeth wrote tartly, "Thank heaven we are not *all* sinking." James Maitland, the other partner, had stopped payments of the Seton-Maitland obligations in England. Unpaid bills stacked up; a lawsuit loomed. Will would soon have a grim choice: to declare bankruptcy or go to debtors' prison.

Elizabeth stepped in. As a woman, she had no business training, no legal standing. But she had a husband sunk "in the stillness of despair." She stayed up late with him, sometimes until two o'clock in the morning, studying papers, sorting the accounts, writing to creditors, learning "all the whys and wherefores which makes me a better companion for him, and I am his only one."

Elizabeth's father gave money and emotional support. He had separated from his wife and shrugged off the gossip: "Shall we be compelled to assign or connect motives to every action of our lives?" he asked. "To every impulse of mind? To every expression of a heart that feels? I hope not." He'd succeeded in his goal of establishing a quarantine station on Staten Island, to receive immigrants who suffered from yellow fever, and had built an adjoining house, enclosed by a high fence, where Elizabeth and the children spent the summer of 1800.

"I could not wish a pleasanter situation or more delightful rooms," she wrote. "We have an upper balcony that commands a view fifty miles beyond the Hook."* On mild mornings, even before sunrise, she walked along the piazza facing the sea; in the afternoons she sat on a favorite rock beyond a cornfield, reading, while the children romped in the haystacks.

On July 1, Will wrote to Julia Scott: "I have the pleasure to inform you that on Saturday last at dawn of day your little friend presented us with another daughter, if possible more lovely than the first. But as you are acquainted with my sentiments with respect to what is mine I will

---

* A spit of land extending into New York Bay.

forbear all description at present and let you judge for yourself. I left her and her mother yesterday at the Health Establishment where they cannot but thrive and indeed Eliza was never better." The baby was named Catherine—Cate, Kate, Kit—in honor of the mother whom Elizabeth had scarcely known. The birth was so easy, in contrast to Richard's, that "eight days after her Birth I continued my arrangements down stairs as usual and have never had an hour's Indisposition since."

Even with financial troubles, the summer was happy. Will was able to come over from the city four days a week. He rowed on New York Bay; he enjoyed cribbage with Dr. Bayley as Elizabeth played the piano and the children danced. Friends came by ferryboat for supper parties. In August, a long-awaited Seton ship, the *Liberties,* came into port. Elizabeth wrote to Rebecca, who had stayed in the city with some of the children, "You may be sure we have had a scene of pleasure such as does not often come, and one that you would have enjoyed as much as I did." Elizabeth poured "50 bowls of tea a day three days running." Dr. Bayley was so happy to have his daughter and his grandchildren with him that they stayed on Staten Island until October 25. He wrote her a letter the very next day, saying he'd heard "last night at 8 o'clock all the little iotas of your passage to New York, that Miss Cate became torpid on her leaving Staten Island and continued in that state until she made her appearance at Stone Street. A smart sensible child exhibiting at so early an age such forebodings of future character. My friend Dick shall be received with open arms whenever he will pay grandpa a visit—all whining excepted."

While Elizabeth was on Staten Island and Rebecca was in New York, they tried to arrange the day so that they would be praying at the same time. "Come come Soul's Sister—let us bless the day together one Body, one Spirit, one hope, one God." That winter, their shared devotions were heightened by the arrival of a new curate at Trinity Episcopal Church.

John Henry Hobart, twenty-five years old, had been ordained just two years when he came to Trinity. He'd been a divinity student at the College of New Jersey—later Princeton—where he studied "supernatural rationalism," the philosophy that human beings were intelligent creatures who could apprehend much of reality on their own, but that to understand the mysteries concerning salvation, the revelation of scripture and the light of faith were also necessary.

He was not an imposing figure: He was short, with a head that seemed too big for his body, and he wore thick glasses. With a salary of just five hundred dollars a year, his first home in New York City was a very small house on Greenwich Street; his study was in the attic, with "zigzag mazes" through the clutter of books and papers. He smiled often; when someone asked him what he was smiling at, he replied, "At my own thoughts. I am so apt to do it, I am sometime afraid of being taken in the streets for a simpleton."

His voice—deep, strong, and flexible—matched his preaching. At a time when most sermons were read from pages of notes and delivered in a dry monotone, Hobart spoke from memory, with such passion that he seemed to be speaking to each person individually—exhorting, consoling, challenging. As one admirer said of him: "He appeared in the pulpit as a father anxious for the eternal happiness of his children—a man of God preparing them for Christian warfare—a herald from the other world, standing between the living and the dead, between heaven and earth entreating perishing sinners in the most tender accents, not to reject the message of reconciliation which the Son of the living God so graciously offered for their acceptance." His style was either embraced or criticized for "enthusiasm and extravagance," which some considered in poor taste.

Elizabeth embraced it. Hobart kindled her naturally vibrant temperament; they became close friends. "The soother and comforter of the troubled soul is a kind of friend not often met with," she told Julia. "The convincing, pious, and singular turn of mind and argument possessed by this most amiable being, has made him, without his even having the least consciousness that he is so, the friend most my friend in this world." Even Will, who was accustomed to taking Elizabeth to church, leaving her there, perhaps going to a coffeehouse, then coming back to pick her up, occasionally went to Trinity with her and was affected by Hobart's preaching on the scriptural theme "What shall it profit a man if he gain the whole world but suffer the loss of his immortal soul?" Until she met Hobart, Elizabeth's spirituality had been somewhat scattered, without guidance; under his spiritual direction, her "vague and unconnected thoughts" of God were becoming a more powerful realization of the presence of God in her life, and she wrote a reflection:

"The cup which Our Father has given us, shall we not drink it? Blessed Saviour! By the bitterness of Thy pains we may estimate the force of Thy love . . . thou hast declared unto us that all things shall work together for our Good if we are faithful to thee, and therefore if thou so ordainst it, welcome disappointment and Poverty, welcome even shame and contempt and calumny. If this be a rough and thorny path, it is one which thou hast gone before us. Where we see thy footsteps we cannot repine."

Her new spiritual awareness was a crucial step toward the encompassing spirituality she would someday be known for. But it could also make her something of a scold. She and Rebecca had made a pact to observe each "Sacrament Sunday" as a special day of retreat from the world; when Rebecca spent one of those Sundays away from the house, Elizabeth chided her: "You should never violate the strict rule, not to leave home on any persuasion on Sacrament Sunday, and to say openly to whoever would request it that it is your rule. It can never be a breach of civility or seem unkind." When Elizabeth sent Eliza Sadler a birthday greeting advising her to prepare for a happy death, Mrs. Sadler did not take it well.

In mid-November, Kit was baptized at Trinity, by Rev. Abraham Beach, the assistant minister. She had five godparents, including, once again, Dr. Bayley, and Elizabeth herself, standing as proxy for Julia Scott, to whom Elizabeth wrote an account of the event. "The sweet creature mistook Mr. Beach for my Father as he had spectacles on and when he threw the cold water in her face, looked up at him and laughed so drolly that I could hardly keep from laughing and crying both . . . the whole family doat on her and you might suppose her the *first* child rather than the fourth." When Julia did not reply, Elizabeth wrote two weeks later: "Are you well? Are you happy? . . . it sometimes lessens personal sorrow to compare our condition with the case of others—therefore when you sit musing and thoughtful about your crosses and accidents, turn you[r] mind to your friend and view the changes in my lot."

In December, Mr. Garret Kittlet, the commissioner of bankruptcy, sat in the Setons' library, taking inventory of all their possessions— furniture, dishes, books, even the children's clothing. The official entry of the bankruptcy men was supposed to protect them from sheriffs serving writs on behalf of impatient creditors, yet Elizabeth spent the days of Christmastime keeping constant watch on the door. When Will handed over the keys to the business, it was the formal end to Seton, Maitland, and Company. The Stone Street house was now too expensive; the Setons would have to move to a rental on the Battery.

In their days of plenty, Elizabeth had had the luxury of complaining about unreliable household help: "Oh Julia how happy must have been the former days of Simplicity and ease, when cooks and Waiters had their proper rank in existence and had not the power of over- turning whole Families and tormenting us poor little Ladies until Life is almost a burthen." Now she mostly relied on Mammy Huler, whom Elizabeth called "my attentive friend, the constant companion of all my changes and chances . . . the second Mother of my chil- dren," who was very likely a slave.

Slavery in New York had been a given, and sometimes a chorus of contradictions, since the days of the Dutch. Black people then were allowed to worship in churches and were given schooling, but when a merchant, John Van Zandt, whipped a slave to death, he was acquit- ted by the coroner's jury because "correction given by the master was not the cause of death, but that it was by the Visitation of God."

Under British rule, slaves built Trinity Church but could not wor- ship there or be buried in its churchyard. The State Assembly had declared baptism "ineffective for slaves." Peter Williams, a black man, was bought by the trustees of the John Street Methodist Church, where he served as sexton, though he could not be baptized or take Communion there. George Washington tried to discourage black men from serving in his army, but when he needed soldiers at Valley Forge, he enlisted slaves.

In Elizabeth's time, New York was second only to Charleston, South Carolina, among urban centers of slavery. A slave market had been established at the eastern end of Wall Street, where black people, Indians, and indentured white people—mostly Germans and Irish—could be sold. Slaves could not gather in groups larger than three, black funerals had to take place in daylight, and a slave found in the streets after dark would be whipped. The question of slavery was riddled with irony: After the Revolution, John Jay, who owned five slaves, was elected president of the Manumission Society, an abolitionist group. Elizabeth's father, a model of humanitarian feeling and action, had at least one slave, "Young Bayley," who had been with him for years. Her grandfather the Anglican priest taught "Negroes" in his catechism classes but owned six slaves; in his will, he left one of them—a boy named Brenners—to Elizabeth, who was three years old.

Following Dutch tradition, all New York City leases expired on May 1. As one observer said, New Yorkers "are seized, on the first of May, by a sort of madness, that will not let them rest till they have changed their dwelling." The Setons moved to their new lodgings at 8 State Street, at the tip of Manhattan, in May 1801. They were next to a boardinghouse, but they had a balcony with such a wide harbor view that Elizabeth could see her father's house on Staten Island. She set up a schedule of homeschooling, and because Rebecca was often away, helping her sisters' families, Cecilia Seton became Elizabeth's assistant.

After two hours of private Bible reading, then breakfast, Elizabeth began classes by ten o'clock. "Anna Maria follows Cecilia as nearly as her inferior age allows and discovers a capacity and amiability of mind that give me a peaceful satisfaction," Elizabeth wrote, "for a Mother always 'rejoices with trembling.' William and Richard say their lessons: little Pieces, names of the United States, Divisions of the Globe, *some* of the Commandments, etc." The only thing Elizabeth disliked teaching was sewing, which made her cross. Julia Scott was visiting when Elizabeth had been mending shirts three days in a row; when Julia called her outside to look at the new moon, Elizabeth snapped, "I do not wish to see it."

Along with grammar, reading, writing, and figures, the children learned "Spelling of large and small words." Noah Webster's *Spelling Book,* published in 1783, urged the elimination of silent letters in a word: "bread" should be "bred," "neighbor" was "nabor." In his later *American Dictionary of the English Language,* he changed English spellings to American—"honour" became "honor," "theatre" was "theater"— but all her life, Elizabeth held on to the English spellings.

Another summer, another stay on Staten Island. The early June weather was a perfect 77 to 78 degrees; the wife of the ferryboat captain sent "a great punch bowl of garden strawberries." Elizabeth served "elegant blackfish and chicken pie" when her brother-in-law Dr. Post and a colleague, Dr. Miller, came over for dinner. Elizabeth had leisure time to read a novel, *Lady of the Haystacks.* One day, a picnic at Sandy Hook; every day, the closeness and love of her father. "My Father cannot do more than he does to prove the regrets of the Past."

But yellow fever came early that year; by mid-June, ships were arriving with as many as a hundred sick passengers aboard. Dr. Bayley got up at three o'clock in the morning to attend them. The ten quarantine tents could not handle all the patients, and more had to be set up; from her side window Elizabeth could see lights from tents pitched all over the yard, with a large one adjoined to the Dead House. "I cannot sleep," she wrote to Rebecca. "The Dying, and the Dead, possess my mind. Babies perishing at the empty Breast of the expiring Mother—and this is not fancy, but the scene that surrounds me. Father says such was never known before, that there is actually twelve children that must die for mere want of sustenance, unable to take more than the breast and, from the wretchedness of their parents, deprived of it, as they have lain ill for many days in the ship without food, air or *changing*."

On Sunday, August 10, Dr. Bayley sat at the dining room window, admiring the sunset and a bright rainbow over the bay. He called Elizabeth to watch with him. "In my life I never saw anything so beautiful," he told her. At teatime, he played with the baby, Kit, fed her with a spoon from his glass, and sang along as Elizabeth played his favorite German hymns and "The Soldier's Adieu." He stayed up until ten o'clock, an hour later than usual.

Sometime in the late afternoon or evening, an Irish immigrant ship arrived. Although he had instructed his assistants that passengers were to be taken directly to the quarantine house, everyone had stayed on board. On Monday morning, the impetuous doctor strode into their midst—the sick, the dying, the dead, all in one unventilated room.

At breakfast, he drank his tea in silence, then headed back to the wharf, where he sat in the merciless August sun, his head in his hands. When Elizabeth saw him, she rushed out, crying. On the way back to the house, he collapsed, and was taken to his bed. "All the horrors are coming my child, I feel them all." Except for Kit, who was nursing, the children were sent back to the city with Rebecca. Elizabeth's sister, Mary, came, with her husband, Dr. Wright Post, who brought in a colleague, Dr. James Tillary, to stay with the dying man.

Elizabeth was terrified that because her father had not been faithful in his practice of religion, he would not be saved. In the middle of the night, Elizabeth carried six-week-old Kit onto the piazza and lifted her up. "O Jesus, my merciful Father and God! Take this little innocent offering; I give it to Thee with all my heart; take it, my Lord, but save my father's soul."

Elizabeth's desperate impulse to offer her baby as sacrifice came not from her spirituality but from her religion. Although Hobart considered Calvinism to be "repugnant to Scriptures," his preaching was streaked with that gloomy theology, stressing that "we are miserable sinners, born in corruption, inclined to evil." Sin and eternal punishment were familiar subjects in the religion of the time; Abigail Adams wrote to her son Johnny: "I had much rather you should have found your Grave in the ocean you have crossed or any untimely death crop you in your Infant years, rather than see you an immoral profligate or a Graceless child."

Apparently God did hear Elizabeth's prayer, and the answer was no. Catherine Seton lived to be ninety, an astonishing length of time for someone born in 1800, when the average life span was thirty-seven years.

Richard Bayley lived for one terrible week. He was sometimes delirious and kept reaching out of his bed for Elizabeth's hand. When she was not with him, he called for her: "Come sit by me, I have not rested a minute since you left me." Once in the night he said, "Cover me warm, I have covered many—poor little children, I would cover you more, but it can't always be as we would wish."

On August 17, at two-thirty in the afternoon, he called out, "My Christ Jesus have mercy on me." He reached for Elizabeth's hand, turned on his side, and died.

Because of his contagious disease, Dr. Bayley's body could not be carried through Staten Island to the church. A grave was dug in a corner of the yard near the house; then, "as if the Mercy of my Heavenly Father directed it, we thought of taking him in his barge . . . which could go within half a mile of the churchyard." At the landing, the coffin was placed on a lorry and taken over the twisting hill road to St. Andrew's Episcopal Church, where Elizabeth's grandfather had been rector, where she and her mother and sister had once been sheltered. Two wagons came, full of family members and friends paying their last respects as Dr. Bayley's servant and the boatmen lowered the coffin into the ground. A white marble tablet would mark his grave:

In Memory of
Doctor Richard Bayley of New York
Who after practicing the various branches of his Profession
With unwearied diligence and high Reputation
For thirty years in that city
Projected a Plan, and for five years
Conducted the operations of a Lazaretto on this Island
Intelligent in divising and indefatigable in pursuing
Plans subservient to the cause of Humanity
He continued to guard the Public Health with persevering Industry
And in the midst of dangers to perform with Invincible Fortitude
The hazardous duties of Health Officer
Until in the discharge of this important Trust
He was seized with a Malignant Fever
To which he fell a lamented Victim
And thus terminated a life of Great Usefulness
On the 17th August 1801
Aged 56 years.

Before she left Staten Island, Elizabeth wrote to Rev. Richard Channing Moore, rector of St. Andrew's, asking him to reserve two gravesites, one on either side of Dr. Bayley's, for herself and her sister. Both she and Mary had husbands and children, but, overwhelmed with grief, Elizabeth could convince herself that this request was rational, "not the impulse of unrestrained sorrow." Mary Post would indeed be buried there, but Elizabeth would be buried in a distant place she'd never heard of.

In just one decade, from 1790 to the turn of the century, the population of New York City had nearly doubled, from thirty-three thousand to sixty thousand. Battery Park was filled with both visitors and locals who came for the sea breezes, the ice cream, the punch, the wine, the cake, and sometimes a concert. Music and laughter drifted across the street to the Setons' house, where in the winter of 1802

Elizabeth resumed homeschooling, nursed Mammy Huler, and went door to door asking for donations for her poor widows' society—one day, a dozen calls before noon. She had backaches and headaches and such a severe toothache that she had to go to a dentist. In pulling the tooth, Dr. Woffendale broke it off short, "the three prongs remaining for life, I suppose." One or another of the children seemed to be always sick: colds, sore throats, upset stomachs, diarrhea, minor fevers, measles. "I rise up early and late take rest," Elizabeth wrote to Julia in her New Year's letter of 1802. "Never before after twelve, and oftener one. Such is the allotment, and as everybody has their *Pride* of some sort, I cannot deny that this is mine."

Will's grandfather in Baltimore wanted the family to move there, where he would get Will set up in business. When Will went to Baltimore to discuss the plan, he and Elizabeth exchanged letters at once, as they had in their early days of marriage.

"Is it possible that I am not to see you again for so long a time?" Elizabeth wrote on the afternoon of the day he left. "Heaven protect you and return you again in safety. Your darlings have enjoyed this cool day and are as merry as birds. They cannot understand that Papa is not to come, nor tomorrow, nor next day, nor the day after—that is for their mother to feel—Dear, dear William, farewell!"

From Baltimore, William replied: "It is needless to say how much I long to enjoy the view with you, and although we are in the midst of plenty and elegance, I long to come home to commence business in earnest, for this idle life will never do; and I fear the jaunt of little utility in point of business, unless I should determine to establish here, for which my grandfather is very anxious; but I shall enter on nothing decisive until I see you yourself, with my friends at N.Y."

The Setons did not move to Baltimore. Will's health was visibly failing; he was stubbornly trying to piece together fragments of the shipping business and talked gloomily about their dire financial situation, with debtors' prison "the black river." When Julia sent money without explanation, Elizabeth wrote: "A thousand thanks . . . is it to go to the Society funds, or is it for MY use?" James Maitland, the former partner, had already gone to debtors' prison; Will felt obliged to provide James's wife and children with milk and bread. One unhappy day, Elizabeth confided to Rebecca, "My soul is very, very, very sick. I call to my Physician every moment, from the bottom of my heart, but find no peace."

Her mood was always changing, though; she conceded that her temperament was "inconsistent," even "hair brained," and two days later, she could write that "all is well—the best thing I can tell you—sweet *Peace* today in anticipation of tomorrow." Tomorrow meant Sunday, when Hobart would preach, when Elizabeth could immerse herself in the palpable presence of God. "Going to Hobe's," the children sang; when five-year old Bill said sleepily, "Dear Henry Hubbard I wish you would preach for me," Elizabeth had a momentary hope that her firstborn son would become a priest.

Elizabeth had had no letters from Julia in months. On August 19, she began a letter of her own. "We have not heard one word of or about you . . . do say how you have managed thro' the Summer . . ." She broke off in midsentence; Will finished the letter. "Thus far, my very amiable little Friend, did our dear Eliza write last night at 11 o'clock & this morning at twelve I have the satisfaction to tell you she was safely delivered of [a] girl, *Great and Beautiful,* equaled, but not excelled by any of our others, which is all I should say of her at present and that the Mother is as well as she usually is on such occasions, *better* than would be expected for we had neither *Doctor* or *anything of the kind,* till a quarter of an hour after the Young Lady made her first appearance . . . the *Old Lady* hopes to write you again soon herself." The baby was named Rebecca, after Will's mother, who had died when Will was seven years old.

For the rest of the year, and into the next, Elizabeth's letter writing was limited, as she began keeping a journal of spiritual notes and themes: "The restless Soul longs to enjoy its liberty and rest beyond the bond when the Father calls his child how readily he will be obeyed." When she did write to Julia, a month after Rebecca's birth, the letter took an austere tone: "I will tell you the plain truth, that my habits of both Soul and Body are changed—that I feel all the habits of society and connections of *this* life have taken a new form and are only interesting or endearing as they point the view to the next . . . this is not to say my affection for you has lessened, for oh with what tender pity and love do we regard one who is dear to us when we see them walking in a path that leads to sorrow and pain, unconscious of their danger . . . bless you again and again my Julia I never loved you so well as at this moment while I speak my heart freely to you—your friend *forever* E.A.S."

Julia did not reply. Elizabeth did not send her a New Year's greeting for 1803; when she finally wrote again, it was a short note saying good-bye. She and Will were going to Leghorn, Italy, where Will had friends from his early days in business, where the sunnier climate might improve his health. They would take Anna with them. Thirteen-month-old Rebecca, newly weaned and sickly, would go to Elizabeth's sister, Mary; William, Richard, and Catherine, along with Will's young siblings, would stay with his sister Rebecca.

No one, family or friends, approved the trip, calling it "next to madness." But Elizabeth was determined. She wrote notes to her boys. "My dear William—you know how dearly your own Mother loves you and how much I wish to see you good . . . I am glad that you go to school and learn so fast—for that will please dear Papa."

"My own Richard—your dear Mother loves you more than she can tell and hopes you will be a good Boy—if you love me, do not plague your sweet Kate for that would make dear Maman very unhappy. Remember My Dick to pray for us every Night and Morning."

Elizabeth spent the month of September making arrangements for the children and breaking up housekeeping; she entrusted her beloved piano and her writing desk to the Hobarts. She did this briskly, in a matter-of-fact way. "My tears are dry—they are left with all the agonies that occasioned them on the garret floor at Staten Island."

On October 3, 1803, Will and Elizabeth and Anna boarded the *Shepherdess,* bound for Leghorn—and the lazaretto.

SIX
ꝏꙮ

Will died two days after Christmas.

He had known it was the end. When Captain O'Brien came to visit, Will gave him the charge to take Elizabeth and Anna home. He spoke so solemnly that "it made us cold."

On Christmas Eve he could not get out of bed. With a sedative, he slept until midnight, when he awoke to see that Elizabeth was not sleeping. "No, love," she told him. "Christmas Day is begun—the day of our dear Redeemer's birth . . . the day that opened to us the door of everlasting life." When Will asked for Holy Communion, Elizabeth put a little wine in a glass and they said portions of Psalms and prayers. "We took the cup of Thanksgiving setting aside the sorrow of time, in the view of the joys of Eternity."

Elizabeth stayed at Will's bedside around the clock. He wanted no one else in the room. When he imagined that he had won the lottery, and that his brother James had written to say that all their financial problems were solved, Elizabeth thought it best to let him think so. When he dreamed that he saw Rebecca, their infant daughter, Elizabeth worried about the sickly baby she'd left behind. "Is she too in heaven—thy will be done—how do I know how many are gone— thy will be done."

On the night after Christmas, a cold sweat washed over him. He wanted the candle taken out of the room. "Tell all my dear friends not to weep for me that I die happy, and satisfied with the Almighty will," he murmured. Elizabeth knelt by his bedside, in the dark, holding his hand, praying aloud. She heard Will following her prayers; when she stopped for a moment, he continued to pray: "My Christ Jesus have mercy." At four o'clock in the morning he stopped talking. At a quarter past seven, "his dear soul separated gently, without any groan or struggle."

Elizabeth sent for Anna, embraced her, and they knelt by Will's bed, to "thank our Heavenly Father . . . for the Joyful assurance that thro' our Blessed Redeemer he had entered into Life Eternal and implored his Protecting care and pity for us who have yet to finish our course."

By Italian custom, the body had to be washed, coated with scented oil, and wrapped in layers of white cloth. But when Elizabeth opened the door to tell the household, Madame de Tot and the servants would not come in to help, terrified that Will's disease was contagious. With the aid of an old washerwoman, Elizabeth prepared the body, then set out for Leghorn in the Filicchis' carriage, on the road shaded with Mediterranean pines that she'd traveled with a cheerful Will just nine days earlier. Guy Carlton Bayley, and Louis from the lazaretto, stayed behind to oversee the transport of Will's body to Leghorn. Elizabeth had not slept for three days and had eaten only one meal in that time; by the time she reached the Filicchis' house, she was drained.

"Oh Oh Oh what a day—close his eyes, lay him out, ride a journey, be obliged to see a dozen people in my room till night—and at night crowded with the whole sense of my situation—O MY FATHER, and MY GOD."

At eleven o'clock next morning, Will was buried in the graveyard at St. John's Anglican Church in Leghorn, the prayer service led by Reverend Hall, who had seen him in the lazaretto. The grave marker read: "Here lies the remains of William Magee Seton, Merchant of

New York, who departed this life at Pisa, the 27th day of December, 1803."

❧❧❧

Leghorn was a maze of old streets, crisscrossed by canals and surrounded by fortified walls. The teeming waterfront, bordered with palms and pines, was alive with the sound of ship's horns, bells, and whistles. Originally a small settlement, an outpost of Pisa, the town had been enlarged in the sixteenth century, when the Medicis expanded the population by offering amnesty for crimes, forgiveness of debts, and freedom from persecution. So many people came— Armenians, Dutch, English, Greeks, and especially Jews fleeing Catholic Spain—that Leghorn became known as "the city without a ghetto." By the time Elizabeth saw it, the city had become one of the most important ports in the Mediterranean, as energetic and prosperous as New York City.

Antonio Filicchi and his wife, Amabilia, with his older brother, Filippo, and Filippo's wife, Mary, an American from Boston, welcomed the widow and her daughter with open hearts. Until the *Shepherdess* set out for New York, Elizabeth and Anna would live in Antonio's cream-colored stone house on the Via del Corso, within sight of the sea.

But she could not yet rest. On New Year's night, Captain O'Brien came for her; his pregnant wife was ill. When a carriage could not be found, Elizabeth walked, mud over shoes, and was hoisted up the ship to remain on board, caring for the woman, till the next day. She was not fond of Mrs. O'Brien, who'd brought a child with whooping cough on the voyage to Italy, which had greatly disturbed Will, but helping when needed was a command of conscience. "These three months has been a hard lesson—pray for me that I may make good use of it."

The *Shepherdess* would sail on February 19. On an earlier ship bound for Boston, Elizabeth sent the news of Will's death—she called it departure—to her sister, Mary, and to Eliza Sadler, her uncle Dr. John Charlton, and John Wilkes. She wrote a long letter to Rebecca, asking her to tell the children "that they shall see their Father no more in this world." She thought of sending the journal she'd been keeping for her, then decided against it; if she never made it back to New York, she did not want her last message to be that saga of sorrow.

In her room at the Filicchis', and in their private chapel, Elizabeth tried to pray her way through currents of grief and worry. Will was gone. She had no money. She had no home. She had five children under eight.

What would become of us?

Even in a country where Catholicism was the state religion, the Filicchis were prodigiously Catholic—Amabilia rose for Mass at four o'clock every morning—and they promptly began trying to interest Elizabeth in their faith. In New York, Catholics were the despised immigrants, people who smelled bad; now Elizabeth found that Catholics could be her social equals, and then some. Antonio had studied philosophy and law; Filippo spoke five languages and had been named by President Washington to be American consul general at Leghorn. When they brought in a scholarly Jesuit priest, Peter Plunkett, to talk about Catholicism, Elizabeth was amused. "I am hard pushed by these charitable Romans . . . but they find me so willing to listen to their enlightened conversation, that consequently as learned people like to hear themselves, best, I have but little to say."

Filippo Filicchi gave her a copy of *Introduction to the Devout Life*, written by St. Francis de Sales, who had worked to convert Protestants to Catholicism. Filicchi told Elizabeth that there was only one true religion and without it we would not be acceptable to God. "Oh my Sir," Elizabeth exclaimed, "if there is but one Faith and nobody pleases God without it, where are all the good people who die out of it?"

"I don't know," he told her, "but I know where people will go who can know the right Faith if they pray for it and enquire for it, and do neither."

"You want me to pray and enquire and be of your Faith?" Elizabeth laughed, but Filicchi was very serious.

"Pray and enquire," he said. "That is all I ask you."

Elizabeth reported the exchange in her journal. "So dearest Bec I am laughing with God when I try to be serious and say daily as the good gentleman told me in old Mr. Pope's words, '*if I am right O teach my heart still in the right to stay, if I am wrong thy grace impart to find the better way.*' Not that I can think there is a better way than I know— but everyone must be respected in their own."

As a distraction, Amabilia took Elizabeth and Anna on a sightseeing tour. In Florence, the little group lodged in a villa on the Via Cavour, once a home to the Medicis, where Elizabeth could look out at the Arno and its bridges "thronged with people and carriages." At the Uffizi Gallery, she was attracted to a statue of the young Jesus, about twelve years old, and to a Madonna holding an hourglass in one hand and a skull in the other, "with a smiling look expressing I fear neither time nor death." The nudes were beautiful in bronze, she decided, but "being only an American, [I] could not look very straight at them." The Museum of Natural History interested her so much that she wished her brother-in-law Dr. Post were with her to lead her through everything again.

The wife of the Grand Duke of Tuscany was called "the queen." Elizabeth and Anna saw her twice; the disappointed child pointed out that "she would not be known from any other woman but by the number of her attendants." But they were dazzled by the "elegance and taste" of the queen's palace, with its gold ceilings, floors of patterned satinwood, tables inlaid with precious stones. At the gardens behind the palace, with their vine-covered walkways, its statues of cherubs and horsemen, Elizabeth ran up flights of steps to the top of the hill, where she was "sufficiently repaid" with a wide view of the warm terra-cotta rooftops of the city.

Among the sculptures in the gardens was one of a wistful woman, head slightly upturned, with a look of melancholy. Will had often talked about the glories of Europe; now she "felt the void of him who would have pointed out the beauties of every object, too much to enjoy any perfectly—*Alone but half enjoyed* O My God!" In the carriage she closed her eyes, pretending to be sleepy, and wept.

When she and Will were courting, he'd raved about the famous tenor Giacomo Davide, whom he'd heard when he was working in Italy; he'd told Elizabeth that one day she must hear him, too. One evening, Amabilia Filicchi asked Elizabeth to go with her to hear Davide. In loving remembrance of Will, Elizabeth put on a black hat and veil and went to the opera.

She hated it. "I could not find the least gratification in their quavers, felt the full conviction that those who could find pleasure in such a scene must be unacquainted with *real pleasure*—My William had so much desired that I should hear this *Davide* that I tried to be pleased, but not one note touched my heart. At ten I was released from the most unwilling exertion I had yet made, and returned with redoubled delight to my *pleasures,* which were as the joys of heaven in comparison."

On January 8, Elizabeth entered a Catholic church for the first time.

At the Church of La Santissima Annunziata—the Most Holy Annunciation—Sunday Mass was in progress. In the shadowed church, lighted only by one small, high window covered in green silk and by wax tapers on the altar, Elizabeth could just make out "hundreds of people," as an organ played distant music. She fell to her knees on the stone floor and wept, "a torrent of tears."

Before she left New York, Reverend Hobart had warned her not to be seduced by the "sumptuous and splendid worship" she would see in Italy, in contrast to "the simple but affecting worship at Trinity Church." But as she visited more churches, with their ceilings of carved gold, richly colored frescoes, marble altars inlaid with precious stones, and vividly stained glass, she saw not idolatry but exquisite offerings like the tributes of David and Solomon in the Old Testament. And she was intrigued by the faith they represented. In the Church of

Santa Maria Novella, a painting of Jesus taken down from the cross "engaged my whole soul. Mary at the foot of it expressed well that the iron had entered into her." Prayers and litanies to Mary were not a part of her Episcopal Church practice; here, Mary was an honored presence. From one of Amabilia Filicchi's books, Elizabeth read the prayer to Mary, the Memorare. "I felt really I had a Mother which you know my foolish heart so often lamented to have lost in early days." She began to say the Hail Mary.

On February 18, Elizabeth and Anna said fond good-byes and boarded the *Shepherdess,* "loaded with their blessings and presents," ready to sail the next day. During a nighttime storm, another ship rammed into theirs; the sailing was delayed, and the passengers returned to shore. As the *Shepherdess* was being repaired, Anna developed a rash and a high temperature, which the doctor pronounced scarlet fever. Captain O'Brien refused to take them on board, as his ship was scheduled to make a stop at Barcelona; without a Bill of Health, a quarantine there would be disastrous.

No other ship in port then was bound for America. Elizabeth would have more time in Italy now—time to weep again at Will's grave, time to revisit Florence, time to learn more about the Catholic faith, time to fall in love.

When King Henry VIII rejected the Catholic Church and established the Church of England, he held on to the theology of the "Real Presence" of Jesus Christ in the sacrament of the Eucharist: the belief that in some way surpassing human understanding, the elements of bread and wine truly become the body and blood of Christ. Even when Martin Luther rejected some Catholic doctrines, he maintained belief in the Real Presence, as the bread and wine "verily taken and received." Then Queen Elizabeth's Prayer Book of 1559 reflected a major shift in understanding. The new book spoke of remembrance, so that the bread and wine were "spiritually taken and received," only as a memorial and a symbol, and Communion distributed only a few times a year, on "Sacrament Sunday."

So the Catholic belief in the Real Presence, with people able to receive Communion daily, came as an astonishment to Elizabeth. "Mrs. F took me with her to Mass as she calls it, and we say to church—I don't know how to say the awful effect at being where they told me God was present in the blessed Sacrament." Elizabeth had always prayed in a personal relationship with God; now she was hearing how personal it could be. "My Sister dear," she wrote to Rebecca, "how happy would we be if we believed what these dear Souls believe, that they *possess* God in the Sacrament and that he remains in their churches and is carried to them when they are sick . . . my God how happy would I be even so far away from all so dear, if I could find you in the church as they do." When she saw a priest from Santa Caterina Church, on the corner of the Filicchis' street, passing by, carrying the Eucharist, "I fell on my knees without thinking when the Blessed Sacrament passed by and cried in an agony to God *to bless me* if he was *there.*" At the chapel of Montenero, on a cliff overlooking Leghorn, when she heard an English visitor mocking people's belief in the Real Presence, "my very heart trembled with shame and sorrow for his unfeeling interruption of their sacred adoration."

As the weeks went on, Elizabeth was more and more taken with Catholic beliefs and devotion. Montenero's chapel had a painting of Mary, dressed in red with a blue cloak, holding the Child Jesus, whose little hands held a thread delicately tying a tiny bird to Mary's arm. "I am a *Mother,* so the mother's thought came also how was my God a little babe in the first stage of his mortal existence in Mary." At the Church of St. James, with its insistent bells, next to the lazaretto—"at no loss to know the hours"—she was impressed to see men as well as women absorbed in prayer. "With us a man would be ashamed to be seen kneeling, especially of a weekday." It was the season of Lent, the penitential time leading to Easter Sunday; when Elizabeth saw that Mrs. Filicchi fasted until three o'clock in the afternoon, she remembered asking Hobart what was meant by saying to God, "I turn to you in fasting, weeping and mourning," after her bountiful breakfast of buckwheat cakes and coffee. He had dismissed fasting as an old custom; now Elizabeth saw that fasting could be a meaningful spiritual practice. "I like that very much," she wrote to Rebecca. "I don't know how any body can have any trouble in this world who believe all these dear Souls believe . . . they must be as happy as the angels almost."

By the end of her four-month stay with the Filicchis, Elizabeth felt sure she would become a Catholic. Filippo pointed out that her Protestant Episcopal Church was founded only "on the principles and passions of Luther, and consequently that it was separated from the Church founded by our Lord and his Apostles without a regular succession from them." Antonio Filicchi taught her to make the sign of the cross on her head and heart as he stood under a window, the moonlight shining directly on his face.

Antonio was thirty-nine years old, a handsome, dashing man. When Elizabeth and Anna finally sailed for New York, he said he would accompany them, out of friendship for Will. Elizabeth wrote to Rebecca, telling her that she felt "so ill at my ease that I scarcely know how to go on—my whole heart, head, all are sick." Two days before leaving, she wrote him a note.

"My most dear A. We often receive blessings from the hand of God and convert them into evils this has been my fault in respect to the very sincere and uncommon affection I have for you, and I am determined with God's help no more to abuse the very great favour he bestows on me in giving me your friendship . . . I intreat you will behave to me with Confidence and affection—the more you confide in me the more Careful I shall be."

At half past four on the morning of April 8, Antonio came to her room to wake her for Mass. After Mass, she entered the confessional, as she had seen the Filicchis do, but once inside, not knowing what to do, she simply knelt in silence. Finally the priest came out of the confessional into the aisle, to ask why Elizabeth did not speak.

At sunrise, Elizabeth stood on the balcony and embraced Amabilia as the ship sounded its warning bell. Amabilia gave her a lock of her baby son's hair, and one of his dresses, as a remembrance. At eight o'clock, Elizabeth and Anna were seated on the quarterdeck of the *Pyamingo,* the anchor weighed and the sails hoisted, heading home.

Seven months earlier, when she left New York, she did not know that her trip to Italy was the first step on a path that would take her to an unimagined place, where who she was and what she did would reshape the American world.

She still did not know.

The *Shepherdess* had taken forty-eight days for the Atlantic crossing; the *Pyamingo* took longer. The ship was becalmed off the coast of Valencia, Spain, and boarded for inspection by the crew of Lord Nelson's fleet. Elizabeth had fifty-six days to marvel at the dazzling whiteness of the snow-capped Pyrenees, to view the waves as a sheet of glass reflecting the sunshine, to think and cry and pray, and to write to Hobart about her decision to become a Catholic.

"As I approach to you, I tremble; and while the dashing of the waves and their incessant motion picture to me the allotment which God has given me, the tears fall fast thro' my fingers at the insupportable thought of being separated from you. And yet, my dear H., you will not be severe: you will respect my sincerity; and tho' you will think me in an error and even reprehensible in changing my religion, I know that heavenly Christian charity will plead for me in your affection."

She did not begin writing in her journal, though, until the ship had been under way for two weeks.

April 19: "So many days on board and could not find courage to begin my journal."

April 21: "Beset by the lowest passions of human nature, and from tears and prayers of earnest penitence can, by the apparently, most trivial incitements, pass to the most humiliating compliance to sin . . . Most dear Antonio, a thousand times endeared to me by the struggles of your soul, our Lord is with us."

April 24: "I have sinned against heaven and before thee, O my Father . . . I know I deserve death as the punishment of my sins."

April 25: "Lord of all mercy, I have sinned, I have offended thee . . . Lord Jesus Christ, still be merciful to a miserable sinner."

A priest who wrote about Elizabeth in 1853 answered the obvious question proposed by these entries by simply omitting that section of her journal.

A nun who wrote an article in 1993 concluded that there certainly was "sexual desire" between Elizabeth and Antonio, that Elizabeth considered herself to have sinned but remained trustful of God's mercy, and that with no other evidence, "one cannot say more than this about the events of the voyage."

Antonio was continuing on to Boston, on his firm's business. "My Sister do not write to me," he told her. When the ship docked in New York, Elizabeth lost him in the crowd.

Just out of curiosity, John Adams had once dropped in at a service at the "Romish Chappell"—St. Mary's Catholic Church in Philadelphia. He saw everything that his people had abhorred and rebelled against, yet he was so taken with the music, the chant, and the bells and candles that he wondered the Reformation had ever succeeded.

It had succeeded so completely that the penal laws against Catholics were not repealed in New York until 1784, when Elizabeth was ten. Catholics were still excluded from holding public office, but Catholics in the city—about two hundred out of a population of nearly thirty thousand—met in a carpenter's shop until they could raise funds for a church. In 1786, St. Peter's, the first Catholic parish in the city as well as in the state of New York, had opened on Barclay Street, with the first High Mass concelebrated by chaplains of the French and the Spanish legations.

Elizabeth's family, friends, and neighbors were aghast at her announcement that she would become a Catholic. "She is going to the church that persecuted our ancestors!" her sister Mary wailed to their cousin Anne in New Rochelle. Mary had heard scandalized gossip about the large painting of the Crucifixion at St. Peter's: "They say, my Sister, there is a great painting of Our Saviour, ALL NAKED!"

Some caring friends thought that Elizabeth simply needed a change of religious venue, to distract her from her grief at losing Will. Be an Anabaptist—a Methodist—the Church of Scotland—anything but a Catholic! A Quaker friend whom Elizabeth particularly admired pleaded, "Betsey, I tell thee, thee had better come with us."

Rebecca Seton, who would have understood, was gone. She never read the journal that Elizabeth had kept for her. When she did not appear at the dock to welcome Elizabeth home, Elizabeth went immediately to see her, and for a month rarely left her sister-in-law's bedside. She wanted desperately to tell Rebecca what she had learned about the Catholic faith, but all Rebecca could say was "Your people are my people, your God my God."*

On the morning of July 8, they prayed Psalm 51 together—"Have mercy upon me, O God, according to thy loving kindness"—and talked of their "tender and faithful love." When Rebecca seemed delighted with the sunny morning, Elizabeth raised Rebecca's head and drew her close. She died within minutes, in Elizabeth's arms. "With her is gone all my interest in the connections of this life," Elizabeth wrote despairingly to Julia Scott. "A cave or a desert would best satisfy my Natural desire, but God has given me a great deal to do." Julia invited Elizabeth and the children to come to live with her in Philadelphia, but Elizabeth wanted to stay in New York, where she had roots, where she had been so happy with Will, and where she was now caught up in a crisis of faith.

Not surprisingly, Hobart was *very* severe. He considered the Protestant Episcopal Church to be the most perfect branch of the Church of Christ, purified from the superstitions, the errors and corruptions, and "the oppressive influence of Papal power of the Roman Catholic Church."

"When I see a person whose sincere and ardent piety I have always thought worthy of imitation in danger of connecting herself with a communion which my sober judgment tells me is a corrupt and sinful

---

* Book of Ruth 1:16.

communion, I cannot be otherwise than deeply affected," he told her. "If it should appear that you have forsaken the religion of your forefathers, not from prejudices of education, not for want of better information, but in opposition to light and knowledge which few have enjoyed, my soul anxiously inquires, what answer will you make to your Almighty Judge?"

Elizabeth wavered. Hobart had been her mentor, spiritual director, and beloved friend for nearly five years. She was his daughter's godmother. She loved and trusted him so completely that she'd asked him to take her sons to raise if she never returned from the voyage. Both the Roman Catholic Church and the Protestant Episcopal Church claimed to be the one true church. Which did she see as the one true Christian religion? Which did God?

The choice was crucial. Doctrinal boundaries were so strict that a person's choice of church might indeed dictate the chances of salvation. If Elizabeth chose wrongly, what answer *would* she make to her Almighty Judge? Would she even have a chance to answer, or would she go directly from her deathbed to the abyss of hell? In Italy, she had been impressed by the penitential practice of fasting; now, thinking it would clear her mind, she began to fast. She lost so much weight that Eliza Sadler told her she had penance enough, as a penniless widow with five children, without seeking more penance among Catholics.

For Henry Hobart, following his conscience was a simple matter of right and wrong. For Elizabeth, it was not so simple. Did love and duty require her to stay with the religion she'd been born in and was expected to die in? What did she owe to her sister and brother-in-law and to the friends who were paying her rent? Should she follow the heartfelt yearnings that were calling her to Catholicism? What did conscience ask of her?

Specifically, Hobart challenged the Catholic doctrine of the Eucharist as the Real Presence of Christ. "How can you believe there are as many gods as there are millions of altars and tens of millions of blessed hosts all over the world?" Elizabeth herself worried about prayers to Mary, since the scriptures on which she relied made no mention of Marian devotion. Her godmother, Mrs. Startin, gave her a book about saints, with the chapter on Mary scissored out.

She wrote to both Antonio and Filippo Filicchi that she had decided to remain at Trinity. From Boston, Antonio replied that "your mind is over-influenced by an unaccountable awe towards the friends of your old communion." Filippo was harsher. "You have acted as though God was not to be obeyed without the consent and advice of your friends. You have met the predicament you deserve."

Elizabeth's most pressing predicament was finding shelter and support. When she moved into the second floor of a cottage on North Moore Street, with another tenant below, her rent was paid by John Wilkes, Wright Post, and Mrs. Startin, who always asked for a receipt. Elizabeth wrote to John Wilkes in Albany that his brother, Charles, had seen the house and approved it, but "he was really so affected at the tolling of the Bells for the death of poor Hamilton that he could scarcely command himself."

Elizabeth had just settled into her new house when, on July 12, muffled bells tolled all day, dawn to dusk, throughout the city; all inhabitants were ordered to suspend business. Alexander Hamilton, Elizabeth's former neighbor, a close friend of Will's father, was dead, and New York City was in mourning.

Hamilton had long been the enemy of Aaron Burr, caught up in the rancor of partisan politics: When Burr ran for the presidency against Thomas Jefferson, Hamilton campaigned against him, calling Burr an unprincipled rogue, "the most unfit and dangerous man." When Burr lost the election, he challenged Hamilton to a duel. On a barren field in New Jersey, just across the river from New York City, the men stood ten paces apart as Burr took Hamilton down with one shot. Dr. David Hosack, Richard Bayley's former student, who had accompanied Hamilton to the dueling field, attended the dying man (and sent his estate a bill for fifty dollars). Elizabeth called it "a melancholy event— the circumstances of which are really too bad to think of." On July 14, her brother-in-law, Dr. Wright Post, joined the long funeral procession, with its riderless horse. A band of uniformed soldiers, followed by artillery, infantry, and militia companies, led the way along Pearl and Beekman Streets to Broadway, toward Trinity Church. Hamilton's family and friends followed the coffin, as British and French frigates in the harbor fired their guns, the French sailors perhaps unaware of the irony in honoring this pro-British American on Bastille Day.

Will's siblings were now being cared for by other members of the Seton family. Elizabeth had only her own five children in her house, where she was now one of the poor widows for whom she had once begged food and firewood. When Amabilia Filicchi sent figs and raisins, Elizabeth sent her a letter of thanks: "I boil them in rice and it makes an excellent dinner." She learned a new routine that she described to Julia Scott: "Turn out at daylight in the coldest mornings, make fire, dress and comb, wash and scold the little ones, fill the kettle, prepare breakfast, sweep, make beds, and the etcetera work, nurse the old woman,★ keep the school, make ready dinner, supper and put to bed again . . . You will say where are all the friends, but must consider every one has their own occupations and pursuits and often for ten or twelve day[s] I see no one."

When she did see someone, it was family, or nearly so: Mary and Wright Post, Harriet and Cecilia Seton, Eliza Sadler. Guy Carleton Bayley was still working in Leghorn, but he sent his support: "I will say nothing to you about your change of faith, as you must know what you do. I can only assure you that it will not diminish in the least the sincere affection I have always had for you . . . if ever fickle fortune should place me in a situation to assist you, nothing would afford me more pleasure." John Wilkes never forgot that Will's father had housed him and his brother, Charles, and started them in business, when they first came from England, or that for ten days and nights, going home only to nurse her infant, Elizabeth had tended

---

★ Her household helper.

John's dying wife. "If John Wilkes did not continue a faithful friend to us I should see my dear ones in a state of absolute poverty," Elizabeth wrote to Julia.

That summer of 1804, Julia came up from Philadelphia and offered to adopt Anna, to give her the advantages of a fine education and a privileged upbringing. Elizabeth declined. In a later letter, she told Julia of her "delight in the opportunity of bringing up my children without those pretensions and indulgences that ruin so many." But when Julia sent a hundred dollars, Elizabeth used it to pay for dancing lessons for Anna.

Although she and Antonio had agreed not to correspond, after the voyage from Italy, Elizabeth wrote to him. "You know my heart you know my thoughts my pains and Sorrows hopes and fears." And he wrote to her. "I love, I esteem, I venerate you . . . and for you I shall always be ready to fight men and devils."

Filippo Filicchi was less emotional. He sent her a "Brief Exposition of the Catholic Faith," which ran fifty-six pages; Hobart's rejoinder was seventy-five pages long.

Filicchi's manuscript summarized essential Catholic doctrines, including a belief in purgatory, the role of saints as intercessors with God, private confession, and the doctrine that the Church, not the individual, must be the interpreter of scripture. On the subject of confession, Hobart's treatise argued that private confession and absolution only encouraged further sinning and was therefore an abuse of true piety; the Episcopal practice of public confession was simply a part of the worship service of the Church. Elizabeth had given him her Italian journal to read; he pointed out that it was her faithful reading of scripture that helped her survive her trials, yet if she had been a Roman Catholic, would she even have had a Bible? Since Catholics were not encouraged to use the scriptures as their ordinary basis of piety, would not her knowledge of God be always filtered through the priests? He defended the Protestant belief in individual interpretation of the scriptures; he said that God intended us to worship him with our *mind* as well as with our heart.

Elizabeth's soul was "more perplexed and unsettled from day to day . . . like a Bird struggling in a net."

The little house where she and the children settled was half a mile from the center of town, but it was not secluded. As early as 1648, in the days of Peter Stuyvesant, a municipal market had been held at the foot of Moore Street, with "meat, bacon, butter, cheese, turnips, roots, straw, and other products of the farm" offered for sale every Monday. Early in the nineteenth century, merchants who were priced out of the city's heart settled into the area, near Bowery Village, the community that had grown up around Stuyvesant's country house. Artisans arrived, along with a grog shop, a brothel, an oyster house where the post rider left the mail, and an array of taverns: the Gotham Inn, the Duck and Frying Pan, the Pig and Whistle. And a new Episcopal church had been built, St. Mark's in the Bowery. John Wilkes suggested that she consider moving to a larger house and take in as boarders a dozen boys, including his sons and his nephews, who attended St. Mark's School, a plan that would give Elizabeth a measure of independence. He expected to have made the arrangements by the first of the new year.

Meanwhile, Elizabeth was still besieged by doubt. In her letters to Antonio, she poured out her heart. "Through the name of Jesus my prayers shall finally be answered, yet there seems now a cloud before my path that keeps me always asking him which is the right path." When she stopped going to Trinity Church, on Antonio's advice, she was chided by her brother-in-law, but when, to keep peace in the family, she went to St. Paul's Chapel, she sat in a side pew, "which turned my face toward the Catholic church in the next street, and twenty times found myself speaking to the blessed sacrament *there* instead of looking at the naked altar before me, or minding the routine of prayers."

Still, she could not make the move. "My hard case is to have a head turned with instruction without the light in my Soul to direct it where to rest."

Hobart lost patience with her. When he called on her for the last time, it was "a short and painful visit on both sides." Elizabeth was so disturbed that she began wishing for a bad-weather Sunday, so she would have an excuse to stay away from church. When she crossed the street that led to St. Peter's, she wrote to Antonio, "my heart struggles and prays O teach teach me where to go . . . I pray always for forgiveness, if indeed I pass by where He dwells, and light and grace to know his will."

Light and grace. According to Christian theology, she had received *sanctifying* grace—the habitual grace that is always present in the soul—at her baptism. Now she needed *actual* grace: a direct aid from God, which enlightens the mind and strengthens the will. Whether or when she would receive such grace was a mystery, because God is a mystery and, as Kierkegaard would put it, "life is a reality to be experienced, not a problem to be solved."

SEVEN

꧁❦꧂

A crowd of Catholics showed up at the gates of heaven.

"Right this way," said St. Peter and showed them to a room.

Later that day, Buddhists came, Presbyterians came, the Sikhs arrived, and then the Muslims.

"Okay," Peter said. "Now everybody's checked in, and we can get you all settled. But please tiptoe past the third room on the right . . . That's where the Catholics are, and we don't want to disappoint them. They think they're the only ones here."

❦

When John Wilkes made the traditional New Year's Day call on Elizabeth, he brought disappointing news. His plan of having her take in boys from St. Mark's School as boarders would be delayed until the spring. She would still need to rely, at least in part, on his generosity. Julia Scott had sent money, which Elizabeth used to buy firewood and bread; when Julia offered another three hundred dollars, Elizabeth asked for half that, to buy clothing for Anna and to hire a woman "who will rid me of the dreaded burthen of patching and darning."

The winter was harsh, with snow banked against houses, the roads impassable. Elizabeth and the children were isolated in their little house, with plenty of time—too much time—for questioning. The back-and-forth led nowhere, as she had written to Antonio. "Should I again read those Books I first received from Mr. H[obart] my heart revolted, for I know there are all the black accusations and the Sum of them too sensibly torment my Soul—should I again go over those of the Catholick Doct[rine] though every page I read is familiar to me and my memory represents in rotation the different instructions and replies?"

Her religious dilemma was all she could think about. "My Soul is so intirely engrossed by one subject that it cannot speak with freedom on any other." She needed Antonio, but he was still in Boston. On January 2, Elizabeth wrote a pleading letter. "Will you not return? . . . I have been watching and still watch for the footsteps of the only one I can welcome with my heart within my doors—this must sound shocking to you, but think only of a part of the contradictions to that heart, and you who know its most secret thoughts will not wonder if it desires to dwell in a cave or desert. But no more of this, it must go back to its lesson of 'Thy will be done.'"

Antonio had become friendly with a priest in Boston, John Cheverus, and asked him to give Elizabeth "instruction, comfort, advice." Cheverus told her to meet attacks on her religion with short, clear answers, and if the discussion became too heated, "silence is the best answer to scoffers."

"I believe you are always a good Catholic," he wrote. "The doubts which arise in your mind do not destroy your faith, they only disturb your mind. Who in this life, my dear Madam, is perfectly free from such troubles? . . . [I]n spite of dark clouds and the noise of thunder, we perceive some rays of the glory of the Lord and we hear His divine voice. I would therefore advise your joining the Catholic Church as soon as possible, and when doubts arise, say only: I believe, O Lord, help Thou my unbelief."

It was the reassurance she needed. "Help thou my unbelief." In the pile of documents that Filippo Filicchi had given her to study was a summary of the works of Thomas Aquinas, defining conscience as "the application of knowledge to activity." She had read *The Following of Christ*—the edition with the Protestant preface—which said that "the glory of a good man is the witness of a good conscience."

Knowledge to activity: Elizabeth knew that as a historical fact, the Roman Catholic Church could be traced back to the lifetime of Christ and his apostles, but the Protestant Episcopal Church only to the reign of a sixteenth-century English king. Quoting the biblical passage in which Jesus tells Peter, "Upon this rock I will build my church," Elizabeth decided to take Jesus's word for it. And when she met him in heaven, "if he says you fools I did not mean that," she would respond, "It is your Word which misled us, therefore please to pardon your poor fools for your Word's sake."

Beyond that biblical base, she felt closer to Christ in the Catholic Church because of the doctrine of the Real Presence, the belief that in the Eucharist, Jesus came to her in a profoundly intimate way that she accepted as mystery. "Years ago I read in some old book when you say a thing is a miracle you say nothing against the Mystery itself, but only acknowledge your limited knowledge and comprehension which does not understand a thousand things you must yet own to be true."

She felt close to Jesus's mother, taking toward the Hail Mary a practical American view. "Why should we not say it? If anyone is in heaven, his Mother must be there."

And, given the theological criteria of the time, when the Catholic Church declared that it alone was "the one, true church of Christ," she felt safer there. "How often I argued to my fearful uncertain heart at all events Catholics must be as safe as any other religion, they say none are safe but themselves—*perhaps it is true*—if not, at all events I shall be safe with them as any other."

Still, belief did not quell emotions. "I am between laughing and crying all the while," she wrote to Amabilia Filicchi, "yet not frightened for on God himself I pin my Faith—and wait only the coming of your Antonio whom I look for next week from Boston to go Valiantly and boldly to the Standard of the Catholics and trust all to God—it is his Affair NOW."

Antonio returned from Boston and went with her to Barclay Street on March 14, 1805, when Elizabeth formally entered what she called "the Ark of St. Peter's."

Then came the flood.

"Sister Seton," Wright Post asked her, "they say you go to the Catholic church. What is the difference?"

Elizabeth loved and respected her learned brother-in-law; her voice trembled as she replied. "It is the first church, my brother—the old church the Apostles begun."

Mary Post interrupted. "Well, apostles or no apostles, let me be anything in the world but a Roman Catholic, a Methodist, a Quaker, anything—but Catholics, dirty, filthy, red-faced—the church a horrid place of spits and pushing."

Elizabeth had to agree about the externals at St. Peter's: "I am forced to keep my eyes always on my Book, even when not using it." She had left her Episcopal community of prosperous, literate people for the congregation of poor, smelly immigrants. Leaving Trinity meant leaving behind all social status, all hope of prosperity and comfort, the respect and honor of those whom she respected and honored. In the meditation she had written under Hobart's direction, she had said, "Welcome, disappointments and poverty; welcome, sickness and pain; welcome, even shame and contempt and calumny!" When both her husband and her father were alive, when life was filled with promise, those had been pious if ardent abstractions. But the shame and contempt, now that she had become a Catholic, were very real.

And it was her own doing. Earlier adversities had been beyond her control, but she had brought this humiliation upon herself and her children. By her deliberate choice she had disgraced the honorable Seton name.

Why?

Some people thought she had literally gone crazy. "So much trouble has turned her brain." When the Filicchis set up an account for her with their financial agent in New York, gossip went around that she'd been bribed, "that you have bought me," she told Antonio. The handful of people who stood by her were simply mystified. They couldn't understand it, which was the most valid reaction of all, since what Elizabeth had done had no comprehensible explanation.

She had not engaged in extensive theological investigation. "The controversies on it I am quite incapable of deciding." And although on the day of her entrance into the Catholic Church, she had professed to believe the doctrines set out in the Council of Trent,★ she admitted that she was "laughing with my heart to my Saviour, who saw that I knew not what the Council of Trent believed, only that it believed what the church of God declared to be its belief, and consequently is now my belief." She was following a conviction with no provable basis, a gut feeling that her soul was called to Catholicism as a way "to give itself to God alone."

There it was again, that echo of her youthful longing: God alone. Throughout her life, Elizabeth had been spiritual. As an eight-year-old, when she had sensed the presence of God in "every little leaf and flower," she had instinctively known that every created reality is charged with the presence of God. From that incarnational spirituality, she had progressed, under the guidance of Henry Hobart, to a practical spirituality—a personal relationship with God and belief in a visible church. Now she would live a fulfilled, authentic life in another religious context. All along, though, her spirituality had been visionary: She had always seen through things to their spiritual core.

Once she made her decision, she wrote to Amabilia Filicchi, "I came up light at heart and cool of head the first time these many months."

But there was nothing lighthearted in people's attitudes. When two former neighbors, Mrs. Livingston and Miss Ludlow, came to

★ The Council of Trent (1545–63) was a gathering of Catholic officials that set out strict doctrines of the Church, including those on the sacraments and belief in purgatory, and declared that anyone who did not follow them was condemned to hell. Among its declarations was that any Christian who relied on his or her own interpretation of the Bible was a heretic.

call on her, Mrs. Livingston remarked that "generally a connection with a Deist was not feared, while a Roman Catholic was thought of with horror." She asked Elizabeth whether as a Catholic she believed that she could buy her way into heaven: The shameful selling of indulgences★ on sixteenth-century streets ("As soon as the coin in the coffer rings, the soul from purgatory springs") had triggered the Reformation. Elizabeth pronounced it "nonsense" and wrote to Julia about her trials. "I could go almost mad at the conduct of every friend I have here . . . I drive every thought away and meet it all with the smile of content, which however often conceals the sharp thorn in the heart."

When St. Peter's was built in 1786, its first pastor, William O'Brien, had been commended by Elizabeth's father, Dr. Bayley, for being the only clergyman to remain in the city during the yellow fever epidemics. The priest had traveled to Cuba and Mexico collecting money and religious objects for his little church in New York; one of the objects was the large painting of the Crucifixion by the Mexican artist José Maria Vallejo that scandalized Elizabeth's sister. O'Brien had violent attacks of rheumatism, which Elizabeth's uncle Dr. Charlton warned might lead to his inability to lead the parish.

By the time Elizabeth went to St. Peter's, another Irish priest, Matthew O'Brien, was acting as pastor. Elizabeth made her first confession to him on March 20. "So delighted now to prepare for this GOOD CONFESSION which bad as I am I would be ready to make on the house top to insure the GOOD ABSOLUTION I hope for after it—and then to set out a new life—a new existence itself." Afterward, she said it had been "easy enough," with O'Brien speaking "with the compassion and yet firmness in this work of Mercy which I would have expected from our Lord himself . . . I felt as if my chains fell."

The night before her First Communion, Elizabeth couldn't sleep,

---

★ An indulgence was a piece of paper, issued with the authority of the Church, that promised reduction of the time spent in purgatory. The invention of printing meant that indulgences could be printed and sold in the thousands.

fearful she had not done all she needed to do in preparation. It was a long walk—about two miles—to St. Peter's, counting every step.

When she was in Italy, the first Catholic church she had visited was the Church of the Annunciation. Now, on March 25, 1805, Annunciation Day, commemorating the visit of the angel Gabriel to Mary, Elizabeth received Communion in the Catholic Church for the first time. She had expected to feel humble; instead she felt "a triumph of joy and gladness that the deliverer was come, and my defense and shield and strength and Salvation made mine for this World and the next."

Antonio had gone on from New York to Philadelphia. "You have led me," she wrote, "to a happiness which admits of no description, and daily even hourly increases my soul's peace—and really supplies strength and resolution superior to anything I could have conceived possible in so frail a being."

Elizabeth soon needed all the strength and resolution she could muster. Again the plan of John Wilkes fell through; in May, Elizabeth moved from the house costing eighty pounds a year to one costing fifty. The affluent Mrs. William Magee Seton who had "a long custom of spending" had become the Widow Seton, who knew that "thirty pounds will buy winter cloths." But the house was within one block of St. Peter's, "the greatest luxury this world can afford, as I shall be enabled every morning to sanctify the rest of the day." As an alternative to the plan of boarding boys, Elizabeth joined a couple, the Whites, who planned to open a school, with Elizabeth as teacher.

But word went out that the Whites were Catholics, and Hobart made sure to let people know of "the dangerous consequences of such an establishment." Even though the Whites were not Catholics, even though Elizabeth's friends Eliza Sadler and Catherine Dupleix explained that Elizabeth's intention was not to preach her new religion but to "obtain Bread for her children and to be at Peace with all the world," and even though Hobart tried to make amends, the school attracted only three students. In July, the Whites told Elizabeth that they could not pay their share of the rent. To prevent the landlord from seizing Elizabeth's belongings, Wright Post took her and the children to his family's country house in Greenwich. Mary's sisterly devotion had overcome her shock, and Dr. Post had parsed Hobart's point—("a corrupt and sinful communion")—about the most unholy activities of some early popes. "His cool and quiet judgment could not follow the flight of my Faith," Elizabeth wrote to Julia, "but was so candid as to admit that if before God I believed the Doctrine of the Church to be true, the errors or imperfections of its members could not Justify a separation from its communion." Still, the Posts had children; six more people formed a crowd. "Does your Sister and her husband really desire your remaining with them?" Eliza Sadler asked bluntly. Elizabeth wrote to Antonio: "Some proposals have been made me of keeping a tea store—or china shop—or small school for little children (too young I suppose to be taught the Hail Mary). In short, Tonio, they know not what to do with me, but God *does*—and when His blessed time is come we shall know."

Antonio had been to Canada; he suggested that Elizabeth and her children move to the Catholic city of Montreal, where her boys could attend a fine school, and Elizabeth, fluent in French, could get a teaching job. But the boys were rejected, on the grounds that they were ill prepared. And in November, John Wilkes's plan finally came about. The Setons left the Post home and moved to "a pleasant dwelling two miles from the city" where, Elizabeth wrote happily, she expected to have twelve or fourteen boys "to board, mend and wash for."

She also had two boys of her own for whom she wanted a Catholic education and a Catholic male influence. Antonio had promised to help pay for their schooling, and although he never completely gave up the idea of Montreal, he agreed to send them to the new school for boys near Washington, D.C. William was almost ten and Richard was eight when they were enrolled at the "Academy at George Town, Potomack River, Maryland." The beginning curriculum included Greek and Latin, poetry, and rhetoric; by the time the Seton boys arrived, Spanish had been added because it was considered "the most valuable in the country" and also, people suspected, because the president of the school was fluent in that language. The president, William Dubourg, did not think schoolboys should be somber: They wore uniforms of blue coat and trousers, and a dazzling red waistcoat with glittering gilt buttons.

Besides adjusting to her various new dwellings, to her financial plight, and to her changed social status, Elizabeth had to accept a change in her Bible.

Until the middle of the fifteenth century, Bibles were handwritten. The first book Gutenberg printed was a Latin Bible. The first English Catholic Bible, translated from the Latin, appeared in 1609. It differed in significant ways from the Protestant King James Bible: Among the disagreements, the Catholic edition said that both faith and good works were necessary for salvation, while Protestants relied on faith alone. The Catholic Book of Maccabees referred to purgatory, an article of faith that Protestants did not accept.

The first Catholic Bible in the United States was published by Mathew Carey in 1790, when Catholicism had only recently become legal. Carey was a well-educated, prosperous Irishman, a successful publisher who was determined to supply religious books for Catholics who "because of lack of books . . . are ignorant of their religion and some even embrace other religious persuasions whose books they read." In his pamphlets, he quoted the Bible, and he formed a society, the Vindicators of the Catholic Religion from Calumny and Abuse. Carey was committed to an American Catholicism shaped by Enlightenment thinking—doctrine and reason combined.

Elizabeth had two Bibles—one she used from 1805, when she became a Catholic, to 1813, then one from 1813 until her death. She marked many passages in both, underlined phrases and words, and made marginal notes (a practice that has delighted Seton scholars but dismayed her fastidious grandson Robert Seton, who called it "a bad habit which spoils books"). Again and again in her Bibles, Elizabeth marked the word "eternity." And on one fragment of paper, she wrote, "Eternity—in what light shall we view it? What shall we think of the trials and cares, pains and sorrows we once had upon earth? Oh! What a mere nothing! Let then they who weep be as though they wept not; they who obtain as though they possess not. This world passes away. ETERNITY! That voice to be everywhere understood. ETERNITY!"

Will's sister Cecilia was seven years old when her father, the elder William Seton, died, and Elizabeth took over as his children's mother. She had always been attached to Elizabeth; now, at sixteen, she was becoming as close to Elizabeth as Rebecca had been. She was not a substitute for Rebecca—no one could be—but she followed Rebecca as Elizabeth's intimate friend and spiritual protégée.

Cecilia was staying sometimes with her sister Charlotte and sometimes with her brother James and his wife, Mary, with whom Will had once been romantically linked. On a visit to Elizabeth, Cecilia told her that she, too, wished to become a Catholic. Elizabeth knew that most of the Setons disapproved of her conversion to Catholicism, but their general attitude was more of pity for the "poor fanatic" and her foreign friends. And Elizabeth was only a sister-in-law, while Cecilia was a born Seton, living under a Seton roof, in everyday contact with other Setons. Elizabeth thought it best that Cecilia not talk about this for a while.

Nevertheless, Mary and Charlotte were suspicious. When Cecilia confessed that yes, she wanted to become a Catholic, they locked her in her room. When Cecilia wouldn't budge, they told her that she would be responsible for Elizabeth and her children being turned out into the streets. They threatened to send her to the West Indies on a vessel that was ready to sail. Charlotte's husband, Gouverneur Ogden, was a powerful lawyer in the city; he might petition the state legislature to banish Elizabeth from New York. They warned Cecilia that "if she persevered that they could consider themselves individually bound never to speak" to her or to Elizabeth again, and she would never again be welcome in their homes. Early in the morning of the day that Cecilia was to be turned out of the house, she tied her clothes in a bundle and went to Elizabeth.

When Charlotte discovered that Cecilia was gone, she wrote a direct question to the girl: "Are you a Catholic?" Cecilia wrote back: "My dear Charlotte: In consequence of a firm resolution to adhere to the Catholic faith, I left your house this morning; and can only repeat that, if in the exercise of *that* faith my family will again receive me, my wish is to return." Mary Seton went through Cecilia's bureau drawers and found Catholic literature. She, too, wrote to Cecilia: "In respect to your sister [Elizabeth Seton] I will be very explicit. If she had never been a Roman, neither would you. I decidedly say, I firmly believe that she has acted toward me both cruel and unjustifiable, and I candidly own to you so far from keeping your change of religion a secret, I openly shall confess it, that others may not trust Mrs. Seton's liberality of principle as I have done."

On June 20, 1806, Cecilia made her profession of faith in the Catholic Church.

In the lazaretto at Leghorn, Elizabeth had known the strengthening power of faith; now she was seeing its power to disrupt and destroy. Her daughters were not welcome to visit their cousins; her wealthy godmother cut her out of her will. "Mrs. Startin has excused herself from contributing to our support," Elizabeth wrote dryly to Julia. As word of Elizabeth's dangerous influence went around the city, some boarders were withdrawn. Elizabeth knew that she and her children had become "the laughing stock of their dinner tables at home, and the talk of the neighborhood here." Anti-Catholic feelings were so feverish that on Christmas Eve, as parishioners were leaving St. Peter's after midnight Mass, they were harassed and heckled by a gang of some fifty men. On Christmas morning, the Irish Catholic immigrants came back, armed with stones and brickbats, to take on the native Protestants. In the bloody melee, Andrew Morris, a city councilman who had befriended Elizabeth, was killed. Elizabeth thought that the intention of the mob was "to pull down our church or set fire to it—but were dispersed only with the death of a constable and the wounds of several others. They say it is high time the Cross is pulled down, but the mayor has issued a proclamation to check the evil." That riot of 1806 was a taste of the nativist American movement later in the century, when one Protestant minister described Catholicism as being "the ally of tyranny, the opponent of material prosperity, the foe of thrift, and the enemy of the railroad."

St. Peter's was usually overflowing—Matthew O'Brien hoped to build a chapel to accommodate the crowds—but the Catholic Church in America was still a shadowy presence. Nearly all its priests had come from Ireland or France, either sent as missionaries to the new republic or fleeing the French Revolution. The only seminary in this country, St. Mary's in Baltimore, was established at One Mile Tavern in 1791 by French priests, the Sulpicians, named for the Church of Saint-Sulpice in Paris. The Sulpicians were known for their strictness; they complained that at Georgetown, Dubourg hired "too many masters full of the spirit of the world; dancing, drawing, soldiering," and later they became something of a problem for Elizabeth.

Because most of the priests were still in the Northeast, Elizabeth knew them, either in person or by letter, in that very new, very small Catholic world. Along with Cheverus, Francis Matignon in Boston knew of her through Antonio. Cheverus wrote to her about another French priest, John Tisserant, whom she would meet in New York; he recommended Tisserant as "both learned and pious and of pleasing conversation." In Elizabeth's first year as a Catholic, Tisserant became her close friend and spiritual adviser. He cautioned her about dwelling on past faults and about her tendency to excessive austerities; in his more reasoned approach, he told her that when she was living with her sister at the Posts' country place, she could be dispensed from the obligation to abstain from meat on Fridays and Saturdays,* as well as the rule of attending Sunday Mass.

When Tisserant returned to Europe, Elizabeth found another trusted friend in an Irish priest, Michael Hurley, just twenty-five,

---

* Both Fridays and Saturdays were days of abstinence then: Friday in honor of the suffering and death of Christ, Saturday in tribute to his mother, Mary.

newly ordained, who had been sent to New York from Philadelphia. During the storm caused by Cecilia's conversion, Hurley had "behaved like an Angel and our true friend," Elizabeth wrote to Antonio. In another letter, she called Hurley "my rigid, and severe friend in a calm, but whenever I have any trouble the most indulgent and compassionate." She often referred to him as "St. M."

The only American-born cleric was John Carroll of Maryland, the first Catholic bishop in the country. Elizabeth met him when he came to New York in May 1806 for a week of instruction and spiritual direction before her confirmation. The bishop was charmed by the lively little widow and kept up a correspondence with her after he returned to Baltimore. The two became so friendly, in fact, that the dignified bishop felt free to joke with her. In one letter, he told her that he was writing it "amidst continued interruptions, one of which arose from a drunken woman finding access to my study, and another from a drunken sailor, who was informed by inspiration or revelation . . . to write and publish a book highly important to the United States. When it comes from the press you will allow me to send you a copy."

Because her house was a distance from St. Peter's, Elizabeth began spending most of the day there on Sundays. After the first Mass of the day, she had breakfast with either John and Joanna Barry, who were among the very few members of New York society at St. Peter's, or Michael Hurley. Sometimes she attended three Masses in one morning. She often stayed for dinner at the parish house; once, Elizabeth wrote that she and a priest, John Byrne, had dined on "beefsteak and claret" when he returned from Georgetown with news of her sons.

She missed William and Richard and began to think again of moving to Canada. The boys' studies in Georgetown might have made them eligible for the Montreal school, and she would flourish spiritually, she felt, in a Catholic environment that was not limited to church. Cecilia no longer needed her as she had at the time of her conversion; when another Seton sister, Eliza, was dying, she'd asked for both Cecilia and Elizabeth. Except for Charlotte and her husband, who never forgave them, most of the Setons came around. In June, Mary Seton died in childbirth; when James asked Cecilia to come back, to care for his eight children, he and Elizabeth were reconciled. "James walked in my room the other morning and took me in his arms like one of the children . . . and seemed to have met me every day of the twelve [months] I have not seen him. I like that. So all the world should do."

She missed her friends. Julia was permanently settled in Philadelphia; Eliza Sadler and Catherine Dupleix had gone to Ireland. Michael Hurley would be recalled to Philadelphia. Antonio had sailed for home; she never saw him again.

Of the six boarders Elizabeth had left, four would be off to college in the fall; the fees for the remaining two would not be enough to pay the baker or the rent. John Wilkes told her frankly that he didn't know what she should do. With the backing of the Filicchis, Elizabeth was about to move to Canada when, at dinner one Sunday after church, she met a visiting priest from Baltimore. It was Louis William Valentine Dubourg, formerly the president of Georgetown, now president of St. Mary's College, connected with the seminary in Baltimore. He'd come to New York in the venerable Catholic fund-raising tradition—selling tickets for a lottery, to support his school for boys.

Dubourg was a Frenchman, educated in Bordeaux. Known as a man "of flashing intellect and wit, of overpowering persuasiveness and charm and almost ruinous generosity," he'd made an impulsive decision to come to the United States when he met an American sea captain who was sailing to Baltimore.

"When do you return there?" Dubourg asked. "Soon?"

"Tomorrow," the captain replied.

"Good!" Dubourg said. "I will go with you."

When he met Elizabeth, he was intrigued by her story and invited her to Baltimore, where she could open a school for girls. "Come to us, Mrs. Seton, we will assist you in forming a plan of life." He said he would receive her sons in the college at no expense; she and the girls would live in a small house that had just been finished, with as many girls in her care as she could manage. Elizabeth protested that she had no talents. "We want example more than talents," he told her.

Canada or Baltimore? The Filicchis, who were her main financial support, urged Canada. All the priests she knew voted for Baltimore. Matignon wrote: "I believe you are destined for some great good in the United States."

In fact, Dubourg had only two prospective students for the proposed school—his own nieces, Aglaé and Celanire. But he had escaped the French Revolution disguised as an itinerant fiddler, so he knew about taking risks. And the Seton family motto, emblazoned on its coat of arms, was *At Whatever Risk, Yet Go Forward.*

On Thursday, June 9, 1808, Elizabeth and her daughters boarded the packet boat the *Grand Sachem,* their fifty-dollar fare paid by Dr. Post. Her last view of New York was sunlight glinting on the windows of the house on State Street, where she had lived with Will.

Almost immediately, she wrote to Cecilia. "My own Cicil would scarcely believe that we are only now passing the light house, just 30 miles from the city . . . every one is so kind—a very mild modest man came down before we had been half an hour on board and said Madam my name is James Cork—call on me at all times—I will help you in everything . . . O sweet Mercy how kindly you are mixed in every cup."

But Anna, who had crossed the Atlantic without ill effect, was so seasick that she refused to come up on deck. Rebecca and Kit wanted to go back home; they sent paper ships overboard to New York. "Friday, Saturday and *Sunday* are past," Elizabeth wrote, "with many a prayer—many a sigh—rocking and rolling without getting on."

Monday night brought a ferocious storm. The younger girls slept with Elizabeth in her berth, as she reached down to the lower berth to hold Anna's hand, trying to quiet her own misgivings. "Do I go among strangers—No! has an anxious thought or fear passed my mind—No! can I be disappointed—No!"

She slept uneasily and awoke in darkness.

EIGHT

❦

Two centuries before Elizabeth arrived in Baltimore, an Englishman, George Calvert, had found a place in American history. As secretary of state for King James I, he was made a knight. By the time the king died and his son became King Charles I, Sir George had distinguished himself as a statesman and loyal subject. But when he became a Catholic, he had to resign his offices in the royal court. Because he was a favorite, he was not beheaded but was granted a charter for a chunk of land—nearly eight million acres—just north of the colony of Virginia. The new colony was named Maryland, not in honor of the mother of Jesus but as tribute to Charles's French wife, Queen Henrietta Maria.

By Elizabeth's time, Maryland was the third-largest state of the Union, and Baltimore had grown into a city of vigor and purpose. At Fells Point, named for Edward and William Fell, the early Quaker settlers, the deep-water port, rich with the tang of tar and saltwater, was a noisy tumble of factories, warehouses, sailors' boardinghouses, and merchant vessels bound for Europe with cargoes of tobacco, wheat, and flour, returning with wool and leather. Shipyards turned out the Baltimore clipper ships, so narrow and speedy that they clipped over the waves. Near the waterfront, workers lived in gabled redbrick houses built flush with the street and stretching from block to block. Outdoor market stalls sold fresh-dug potatoes, spring lamb, strawberries. In the center of the city, the first Catholic cathedral in the United States was being built, designed by Benjamin Latrobe, architect for the Capitol in Washington.

The *Grand Sachem* docked at Fells Point shortly before midnight on June 15, but the passengers were not allowed to disembark until the next morning, when their belongings could clear customs. When Elizabeth and her girls stepped off the boat, they were alone in a strange city. Dubourg had not come to meet them because the new chapel at the seminary was being dedicated that morning. In a thrashing rain, Elizabeth found a carriage to take them there.

That day, June 16, was the feast of Corpus Christi—the Body of Christ—an especially meaningful day for Elizabeth because of her devotion to the Eucharist. Bishop John Carroll celebrated the High Mass; the chapel was filled with priests, seminarians, and students. Elizabeth knew many of the priests, including her spiritual adviser from New York, Michael Hurley. He'd brought a friend, Samuel Cooper, a wealthy man, formerly a sea captain who had recently converted to Catholicism and who was to change Elizabeth's life.

St. Mary's Chapel was small and elegant. An English writer called it "a little *bijou* of a thing . . . more calculated, perhaps, to generate holy thoughts, than even the swelling anthem heard beneath the resounding dome of St. Peter's." Beautiful, not ornamental: students sat on backless benches and knelt on the stone floor, although there were benches with backs and places for knees for "the people who come in from outside."

Elizabeth was late. Just as she opened the door of the chapel, with candlelight shimmering on crimson curtains, the organ sounded a solemn peal, the Kyrie Eleison—the prayer for mercy—echoed from the altar, and the choir burst into song. Elizabeth was transfixed. The girls, wide-eyed, clutched their mother's skirt. "Human nature could scarcely bear it," she wrote to Cecilia. "Your imagination can never concieve the Splendor—the Glory of the Scene all I have told you of Florence is a Shadow."

After Mass, she was warmly greeted by the priests, then "I was in the arms of the loveliest being you ever beheld, Mr.★ D's sister— surrounded by so many caresses and Blessings—all my wonder is how I got thro' it." Françoise-Victoire Dubourg Fournier had come from France to be her brother's business manager for the college; now she welcomed Elizabeth as her charge. Dubourg advised Elizabeth to rent a house for the first year, rather than buying one. In New York, he had told her about some plots of ground in Baltimore that the priests owned; he hoped that her school would so expand as to require a larger house on one of those lots. "If one year's experience persuades us that the establishment is likely to succeed," he told her now, "and if it pleases Almighty God . . . we will then consult HIM about the means of perpetuating it by the association of some other pious ladies who may be animated with the same spirit."

Madame Fournier helped Elizabeth settle into a house off the Hookstown Road, adjoining the grounds of the seminary and college. The ivy-covered redbrick house was small, but to Elizabeth it was "a neat, delightful mansion . . . in the new French style of folding windows and recesses." One room on the first floor served as parlor, community room, and classroom; another was designated as dining room, separated from the kitchen by a low brick partition. A staircase led from the front hall to the second-floor room that Elizabeth would use as classroom, with a bedroom alcove; her girls and the boarders would sleep dormitory-style in the attic.

The house was between two orchards, abundant with cherries, peaches, pears, apples, grapes, and figs. In the vegetable garden: potatoes, onions, celery, eggplant. Only a fence divided the house from the chapel, open from daylight until Benediction at night. "Imagine twenty Priests all with the devotion of Saints clothed in white," Eliza-

---

★ Priests were called "Mr." until about the middle of the nineteenth century, when Irish immigrants brought the title "Father" with them.

beth wrote to Cecilia, "accompanied by the whole troop of the young Seminarians in surplusses also, all in order surrounding the blessed Sacrament exposed, singing the hymn of the Resurrection, when they come to the words 'Peace be to all here' it seems as if our Lord is again acting over the scene."

Just as she had in the lazaretto, Elizabeth heard church bells first thing in the morning. Chapel bells rang at five-thirty in the morning, fifteen minutes before two o'clock in the afternoon, and fifteen minutes before eight o'clock at night. The bells announced the Angelus—a prayer in honor of the mother of Jesus. Elizabeth's dedication to Mary was linked to her own motherhood. "Jesus on the breast of Mary, feeding on her milk! How long she must have delayed the weaning of such a child!!!!" She had taken the name Mary as her confirmation name, and she prayed the Angelus wherever she was, always on her knees. Behind the chapel was a narrow path, no wider than a sheep track, that led up to a little mount with shrubbery and olive trees and a large cross, with four graves at its foot. When Dubourg was showing Elizabeth around the property, he gestured toward the graves and said, "There is your rest."

He was wrong.

After the hostility and hatred she had known in New York, Elizabeth felt she was in paradise. "I find the difference of situation so great that I can scarcely believe it is the same existence . . . in every respect my condition is like a new being." She was sure she would spend the rest of her life here, in prayer and quiet service.

She was wrong, too.

Not since Leghorn had Elizabeth known, or even seen, so many Catholics. Maryland's Catholic population was 16,000, to New York's 1,500. And these Catholics were the landed gentry, along with an educated, prosperous middle class. Catholicism was never the official religion in Maryland; Catholics there had once been as burdened by the English penal laws as Catholics in New York. After the Revolution, though, Maryland, unlike New York, was a place where Catholics could live peacefully and enjoy full citizenship—so fully that Charles Carroll of Carrollton, a Catholic reputed to be the richest man in the United States, had signed the Declaration of Independence. His cousin the priest, John Carroll, had gone to Canada in 1776 with Benjamin Franklin and Samuel Chase to seek support for the Revolution in that Catholic country. The mission failed in its aim but succeeded notably in enhancing the Catholic reputation at home. After the war, Washington wrote: "To the Roman Catholics of the United States: I presume that your fellow-citizens will not forget the patriotic part which you took in the accomplishment of their Revolution, and the establishment of your Government." Washington banned the burning of the pope in effigy, an annual spectacle that observed the attempt by the crazed Catholic zealot Guy Fawkes to assassinate the British royal family. Washington called it "a ridiculous and childish custom," made a personal donation for the building of a Catholic church in Philadelphia, and invited John Carroll and his sister to dinner at Mount Vernon.

As a homegrown priest, born and raised in Maryland, Carroll was a rarity among the Irish and the French. He studied philosophy and theology in France and was ordained a priest, then in 1773 returned to his homeland as a missionary. After the Revolution, when the English penal laws were repealed, the new American Catholic Church had no bishop. Carroll urged the pope to adopt some method of appointing Church authorities that would not make it look as though they were receiving their appointments from a foreign power. The Protestant belief that Catholics owed allegiance to the pope first and to their country second was widespread; the Sons of Liberty had carried signs that said NO POPERY.

Carroll's appeal to the pope worked. In 1789, his fellow priests elected him bishop of Baltimore, the first bishop of the United States.

John Carroll was a short man with a frail voice, but he was a figure of stature and strength. Open-minded and articulate, with an ecumenical sensibility, he had joined a Mason and an Episcopalian priest in founding the Maryland Society for Promoting Useful Knowledge. He replied to a critic of the Catholic Church with "An Address to the Roman Catholics of the United States of North America" in which he said, "General and equal toleration, by giving a free circulation to fair argument, is a most effectual method to bring all denominations of Christians to a unity of faith." He spoke of "an enlightened faith"; like Mathew Carey and other well-educated, thoughtful Catholics, Carroll saw no contradiction between Catholicism and the rationalism of the Enlightenment. He blended religion with the democratic American culture in a way that was typical of the republican era. He preached tolerance, and he was respected throughout the city; when he died, newspapers were bordered in black. Carroll referred to his people not as Catholics but as Catholic Christians, and was so progressive that one change he urged in the Church—the use of the vernacular in place of Latin—was not adopted for nearly two centuries. "Can there be anything more preposterous than an unknown tongue[?]" he wrote. "The greater part of our congregations must be utterly ignorant of the meaning and sense of the public office of the Church."

As a bishop, he had authority over churches and priests in New York, Philadelphia, Boston, and Bardstown, Kentucky, as well as in Baltimore. Four of the five were running peacefully, but New York was a mess. William O'Brien, the pastor of St. Peter's Church— Elizabeth's "Ark"—could not get along with the priests who were needed to minister to that swarming congregation. When the trustees of the parish suggested one candidate, O'Brien said he hated that man "above all men." Most priests whom O'Brien asked for were unfit, Carroll said. "New York is a city of too much consequence not to demand superior abilities." Even Matthew O'Brien, who had received Elizabeth into the Catholic Church in 1805, caused such public scandal with his drinking that he had to leave the parish. Michael Hurley, to whom Elizabeth was so attached that she had his picture sent from New York to Baltimore, was accused of being too proud, too forbidding, and too much of a meddler in local politics. At least a dozen priests flitted in and out of Elizabeth's hometown church in the three years she was there.

Elizabeth was so anxious to see her boys that, four days after her arrival, she went to Georgetown to fetch them. They would be enrolled as boarders at St. Mary's. Michael Hurley went to Georgetown with her, along with Samuel Cooper, who intended to enter the seminary in the fall. Cooper was thirty-nine, Elizabeth was thirty-four; the two were drawn to one another, and both were free to marry. As Elizabeth candidly acknowledged in a letter to Cecilia, "If we had not devoted ourselves to the heavenly spouse before we met I do not know how the attraction would have terminated." Cooper was so interested in Elizabeth that when he went to New York, after the Georgetown trip, he wanted to meet people who knew her. He had coffee with Cecilia. Elizabeth reminded her that Cooper planned to enter the seminary, adding, "I should not wish you to know him as I do."

With William and Richard settled in at St. Mary's, just across the orchard, Elizabeth set up housekeeping. She had saved—"at interest," she pointed out—the $600 that Julia had sent, and the $400 a year provided by Antonio Filicchi. Her little house cost $200 a year instead of New York's $350. Madame Fournier had hired a woman, Ann Nabbs, to do the washing, cleaning, and cooking, for $4.50 a month. Elizabeth was able to buy firewood at $3 a load instead of New York's $5.50; because the seminary bought everything by the gross, they could get it for her wholesale.

Spiritually, Elizabeth was thriving under the direction of her new adviser and confessor. Pierre Babade was an emotional, warmhearted man with a romantic imagination: Along with his religious ministry, he composed music and wrote poetry. At the First Communion of children, he wept. Elizabeth called him "our Patriarch," and told him that Cecilia wanted to come to Baltimore but had to stay in New York and take care of her brother James's children. She wrote often to Cecilia, sometimes enclosing a letter to Harriet "under cover to you."

And Cecilia wrote back. She couldn't risk being seen writing to Elizabeth in the parlor, so she wrote from her cold bedroom: "My fingers
are almost frozen, I can scarcely hold the pen." Harriet was staying
with her older sister Charlotte, who was still incensed at Cecilia's
change of religion. When Charlotte demanded that Harriet promise
to never become a Catholic, Harriet refused, although she expected
to marry a man who was not Catholic—Andrew Barclay Bayley,
Elizabeth's half brother, who was working in the West Indies.

Three weeks after her move, Elizabeth wrote to Antonio. In the
long letter, she told him all about Baltimore, thanked him for his
generous allowance, and sent "tenderest love" to Amabilia and the
children. She asked to be remembered to all in Leghorn who remembered her, particularly Dr. Tutilli, who had tended Will, and Peter
Plunkett, the Jesuit whom the Filicchis had brought in to talk with her
about Catholicism ("I am hard pushed by these charitable Romans . . .").

Near the end of the letter, she got to the point. "The gentlemen of
the Seminary have offered to give me a lot of ground to build on, it is
proposed . . . to begin on a small plan admitting of enlargement if
necessary in the hope and expectation that there will not be wanting
ladies to join in forming a permanent institution—but what can a
creature so poor in resources do? . . . [W]ith that frankness I owe to
you from whom no thought of my mind should be concealed I dare
to ask my Brother how far and to what sum I may look up to yourself
and your honoured Brother in this position of things—what you have
done is so unmeritted by the reciever, what you are continually doing
for us is so much more than could in any way be expected that I *force
myself* to ask this question."

A month later, she wrote to him again, reminding him that Dubourg and his fellow priests, especially Cheverus and Matignon, were
waiting for his word. "So much of my or rather *the scheme* of these
reverend gentlemen depends on your concurrence and support that I
dare not form a wish . . . if we succeed in forming the purposed establishment I shall look upon it as a mark that Almighty God intends
an extended benefit." Elizabeth may not have formed a wish, but she

wrote, more in prophecy than she knew, "It is expected I shall be the Mother of many daughters." On March 25, she made a private one-year vow in the presence of John Carroll.

Except for two hot weeks in late June—the temperature on the thirtieth was 94 degrees Fahrenheit—the summer days were pleasant. The pears and apricots were beginning to ripen, along with the early apples and figs. Most of the priests, and Dubourg's sister, went on vacation, "which lasts six weeks," Elizabeth wrote to Cecilia, "and Sister will again be ALONE WITH GOD."

The chapel had a lower level, darkened and still, dedicated to Mary. Elizabeth delighted in this lower chapel—she prepared children for their First Communion there, and she prayed there often. She did not need to be in a chapel or a church to pray, but the chapel was a sacred space, where God seemed nearest in the quiet. Now, with everyone away, with school not yet started, and with Anna taking care of her younger sisters, Elizabeth was free to kneel and to sit in the chapel for hours in prayer and contemplation.

Was she a mystic? If being a mystic means having an emotional experience of God, completely shutting out the world, having visions and miraculous happenings, she was not. If being a mystic means being constantly—*constantly*—aware of the presence of God in her life, going beyond spiritual reading and vocal prayer to a deep basking in the grace and love of God, then she was. "Oh, be with me and I shall be whole."

Early in July, Elizabeth interrupted her retreat to write an encouraging letter to Cecilia, who Harriet had said was very ill and who was disconsolate over not being able to come to Baltimore. "*My* Cecilia . . . you *will triumph,* for it is Jesus who fights, not you my dear one . . . He will not leave you one moment, nor suffer the least harm to approach you, not one tear shall fall to the ground nor one sigh of love be lost—happy, happy child—and if you are not removed to the sheltering fold that awaits you, he will make you one in his own bosom until your task is done."

Elizabeth herself was showing signs of "the family enemy," tuberculosis, which had killed her husband and her sister-in-law, her beloved Rebecca. Even the children worried about her: "Not one of them but anticipates the sorrow of being dispersed." The "pain in the breast" left her weakened, and the stiffness she often felt led her to send an urgent letter to Cecilia. "Do not fail to send me five yards of the Salisbury flannel of which we made *our coats*—the Shop is on the corner of Mott St and Bowery I believe—do not omit it my love as it is necessary for my Rheumatism to wear it all winter—*you must find time to get it.*"

By October she had four students; with her three girls, that was as many as she felt she could manage, at least in the beginning. The boarders paid two hundred dollars a year for the basic lessons in reading, writing, arithmetic, English, and French. A girl who wanted "extra accomplishments" such as music, dancing, and drawing paid a separate fee. When classes ended at five o'clock, Elizabeth herself sat down to study. "What would amuse you," she wrote to Julia, "would be to see Your old Lady seated gravely with a slate and pencil with a Master of Arithmetic stuffing her brain with dollars cents and fractions, and actually going over the studies both in grammar and figures which are suited to the scholar better than the mistress."

She had written only two letters to Julia in the five months since she had left New York. "My Boys appear to be the most innocent and well disposed children that can be imagined for their age," she told Julia. "Neither of them appear to me to show any distinct marks of genius, but their progress in their classes is superior to that of most Boys of 10 and 12. William will be 12 in November Anna was 13 the third of last May—but your little Kate has more talents than either of the three elder, and Rebecca more than all of them together."

Toward the end of the letter: "Now pray tell me Julia if it is possible that with your intelligent mind, long experience of human vicissitudes and very critical moment of life, tell me if you do not sometimes reflect on the long long long life to come? . . . [A]nswer me this question in some moment that you are alone with God. I will never preach to you, but I wish I could pour your heart in my bosom and tell you how sweet it is to have him our best friend . . . do do promise that you will pray to him for this Knowledge, you are sure of being heard with peculiar pleasure . . . oh do do think of it."

Julia did not answer the question; she was used to Elizabeth's declaring that she would not do something, then doing it. When Elizabeth was still in New York, she had written to Julia: "Not to moralize or repine, but in the common language of every day and hour, what is life except we consider it a passage . . . in the dear, the strong and anxious hope of soon reaching our happy heavenly home, where peace and all we prize most awaits our arrival." Julia scorned Catholicism as "folly, madness, bigotry and superstition," yet she was always Elizabeth's best friend. She sent gifts—beaver hats, dresses for Kit and Rebecca, a gown for Anna. "They are much more useful to us than you would perhaps imagine," Elizabeth wrote, "as I am *obliged* to be more attentive to appearance here than in N[ew] York—not myself, but the family, poor little self is always dressed for the grave."

Many of Baltimore's distinguished families were calling on Elizabeth. She met Major General Robert Goodloe Harper and his wife, Catherine, who was a cousin of John Carroll; the Harpers were to become like family to Elizabeth. She met Dr. Pierre Chatard, who had studied medicine in France, and his wife, Marie Françoise; when he became physician to Elizabeth, he prescribed for her a bottle of ale every day. She met Polly Carroll Caton, a cousin of John Carroll, and Polly's husband, Richard; their daughters—Louisa, Mary, and Elizabeth—were so beautiful that they were known as "the Three American Graces" and were presented at the court of George IV. She met Robert Patterson, whose sister Betsy married Jerome Bonaparte, Napoleon's brother; Elizabeth later met their son, Jerome Napoleon, called "Bo," a student at St. Mary's. She met Colonel John Howard, a former governor of Maryland, who offered Elizabeth a home in his own mansion, promising to educate her daughters as his own.

By December 6, three more students had arrived at the little house off the Hookstown Road. "From half past five in the morning until 9 at night every moment is full, no space even to be troubled—ten girls three of them almost women, keep the wheel going continually— many very advantageous offers of assistants have presented themselves, but in the present state of my family we are so happy and live so much as a Mother surrounded by her children that I cannot resolve to admit a stranger, yet it must be eventually."

"Eventually" came quickly. The next day, Cecilia O'Conway arrived from Philadelphia with her father, who offered her to Elizabeth as a child consecrated to God. Cecilia was twenty years old, the sister of Isabella O'Conway, one of Elizabeth's boarders. She wanted to live in a religious setting, and Elizabeth's school fit that description perfectly. Religion was the framework of the school day, beginning and ending with chapel. The girls also said the rosary, with examination of conscience, every day. On Fridays they read the story of Christ's passion and death. Babade was constantly in and out of the house, giving religious instruction.

An early snow had fallen in October, and the winter continued icy. On Christmas Eve, snow and sleet fell all morning. The new year began with temperatures below zero, and another letter to "My dearest Antonio":

"The subject of my letter to you last July so nearly concerns all my hopes and expectations for this world . . . that I am sure you would give me some encouragement if you had any opportunity, or your reasons for not encouraging our plan . . . I cannot help begging always in Communion while my heart is turning toward Leghorn . . . Mr. Wilkes writes me from New York 'the Filicchis have made a *mint* of money and he hopes they will not forsake me tho' the old proverb says out of sight out of mind' . . . My dear Antonio neither you nor Filippo must be displeased with me for so freely addressing all my affairs to you—I repeat it is not to make any formal request, but only by showing you the situation in which our Lord has placed us."

In fact, Antonio *had* written to Elizabeth on November 30, telling her that she could draw one thousand dollars from his account, and "if something more should be wanted, you are *commanded* to quote it to me plainly & positively." But the Embargo Act, signed by President Jefferson in 1807, closed ports to shipping trade; letters from Leghorn could take a very, very long time. (When Antonio wrote to Cheverus in 1806, the letter reached Boston in 1809.)

Elizabeth interpreted Antonio's silence as disagreement with her plan, and, a week after she'd written to him, she wrote to Filippo:

"This morning at communion . . . the thought crossed my mind ask Filicchi to build for you—the property can always be his—to be sure thinking of it at such a moment shows how much it is the earnest desire—indeed it is as much wished as I can wish any thing . . . and if really the thought is practicable on your part the lot of ground stands always ready and if a building is placed upon it you could regularly attach it to yourself and secure your property while you would promote so good an action . . . so do do, dear Filicchi, hold me up . . . but hush, Our Lord will direct all, whatever you say or do I shall consider as his voice and Will."

His will. The will of God. To Elizabeth, the phrase meant that she was to adapt herself to whatever circumstances she was in, living day to day in the trust she had in her God. Cecilia Seton felt that the will of God was for her to come to Baltimore, which she could now do; her brother James had released her from her promise to care for his children. But Anthony Kohlmann, the priest in New York who was her spiritual adviser, wanted her to stay and open a school for Catholic children. He told her it was the will of God that she not go to Baltimore, where she could do no good. Five other priests in New York agreed with him. The phrase was tossed back and forth between New York and Baltimore like an ecclesiastical football until Bishop Carroll intercepted. Elizabeth showed him Cecilia's letter. Carroll wrote to Kohlmann. Cecilia wrote that she was coming, and Elizabeth wrote back: "Bring only a black gown and flannels."

Along with praying and teaching and studying, Elizabeth kept up with her fund-raising. At Mass one morning, "Mr. Cooper being directly in front of me at his thanksgiving, I thought, 'He has money.

If he would but give it for the bringing up of poor little children to know and love You.'"

That spring, three more young women—Maria Murphy and Mary Ann Butler from Philadelphia, and Susan Clossy of New York—came to join Elizabeth and Cecilia O'Conway in a life of prayer, service, and community. In one letter to Julia, Elizabeth referred to herself as "your poor little Nun."

The word "nun"—from the late Latin *nonna,* a tutor—traditionally refers to a woman who takes solemn lifetime vows and lives in cloister, separated from the world by an iron grille, in an ascetic life of prayer and contemplation. In the late fifteenth century, a papal edict had decreed only cloistered life for nuns, often as a punitive measure. "Get thee to a nunnery" could be a death sentence: One girl was so miserable at being unwillingly sent to a convent that when her family was visiting, she strangled herself on the bars of the grille.

A woman who takes simple vows, usually for one year at a time, lives an active life through teaching and nursing and serving the poor. Although an active woman in religious life is not, technically, a nun but a "sister," the terms slowly became synonymous: Cloistered nuns are addressed as "Sister," and active women are usually referred to as nuns. Another one-name-fits-all is "woman religious"—not "religious woman," which could be any woman, but a woman who has taken religious vows in the service of God and the people of God. By whatever term, they rarely have children. But Elizabeth made clear that her children were her priority. "The dear ones have their first claim which must ever remain inviolate . . . I have solemnly engaged with our good Bishop Carroll as well as my own conscience to give the darlings their right and to prefer their advantage to everything."

The little house off the Hookstown Road was crammed when Mr. Cooper stepped forward—but not to build the house that Elizabeth wanted in Baltimore. He offered instead a large farm—269 acres—that he had bought at Emmitsburg, in the Maryland wilderness.

All Elizabeth wanted was a bigger house. She was living the perfect life in Baltimore. "Your friend is breathing the air of Peace and tranquility," she had written to Eliza Sadler. Her health was beginning to improve. "I am now so well, so free from weakness of the breast etc that I can hardly believe it. Winter has always been my cheerful season, and here I am sheltered from all cold and changes of weather wet walks etc." Besides, the move from city to country would take her further away from her New York roots. She was born and raised and married in New York; her children were native New Yorkers. She hadn't written to Mrs. Sadler until six months after she left New York because sometimes she was homesick. "I am a coward in thought," she wrote, "and try to drive away the past as much as possible in whatever occasions regret . . . as my heart is more drawn toward the summit, it looks backward with added tenderness to anyone I have ever loved."

But Dubourg had had a long talk with Cooper. Recalling his conversation, Dubourg wrote to a friend that "Mr. Cooper, even while protesting that he did not wish to exert any influence on the choice of location, or the direction the work should take, repeated in an assured tone that it would be at Emmitsburg."

And so it was Emmitsburg. The will of God. As Elizabeth's beloved Psalms said, "I know the plans I have for you, says the Lord."

Julia objected to the move. "You are giving up a certainty for an uncertainty . . . you will be overwhelmed with the responsibilities . . . no peaceful hours, no peaceful moments will you know." Moreover, Julia thought it would be a mistake to move the girls away from the city to an isolated, rural environment. "Will your girls have the same advantages of education of Society they certainly will not." Baltimore had a theater, coffeehouses, and a circulating library, along with an engaged, active population. Four months after Elizabeth arrived, citizens had held the "Baltimore Gin Party." Seven hundred and twenty gallons of gin from Holland were taken off the brig *Sophia* at Fells Point, having been taxed by the British en route. More than a thousand horsemen, with trumpeters, marched through the city to Hampstead Hill, where they circled a gallows with the gin stacked on it. When the torch was applied, some fifteen thousand Baltimoreans watched the burning of the gin that had paid tribute to England, as they sang "Yankee Doodle."

Elizabeth thought it could actually be good to remove Anna from the distractions of city life. Anna, who had her fourteenth birthday that spring, was blossoming into a beauty, "so marked in her appearance and manner," Elizabeth told Julia, "that indeed you would scarcely know her—her chest is very prominent and the shoulders quite in their right place." Already Anna was secretly receiving tokens and letters from an older student, Charles DuPavillon, a young man from Guadeloupe who'd been interested in her since he'd seen her in the chapel. William and Richard acted as go-betweens. When Elizabeth found out what was going on, she had Charles come to the house for "an interview." From Babade, who knew the young man, Elizabeth learned that he had a good character as well as an immense fortune; in fact, he had urged Anna to tell her mother about them. But Elizabeth still believed that the separation would be "an effectual means of extricating Anna from the effects of her imprudence, for if *young D* is hereafter true to his attachment he may easily claim her, if not her happiness depends on seeing him no more."

Once the decision was made, Elizabeth moved fast. On June 1, the feast of Corpus Christi—the same day she'd arrived in Baltimore the year before—she and her four companions went to Mass together in the clothing they would wear as nuns. The dress was very like the widow's garb that Elizabeth had worn since Will died: black dress with short shoulder cape, white muslin cap tied under the chin, plus a black rosary draped from a leather belt.

Twelve days later, Cecilia Seton arrived from New York. In her trunk she had yards of black fabric: plain material to make a shroud, silk for a dress if she lived. Harriet had come with her as helper and supporter, although she had not become a Catholic, nor did she intend to stay. Her intended husband, Andrew Barclay Bayley, had written that he would return to New York sometime in the summer, to marry her and take her back with him to Jamaica.

On June 21, 1809, Elizabeth left Baltimore, taking Anna, Cecilia, Harriet, and Sister Maria Murphy with her. The others would follow, under the charge of Rose White, a widow who had just joined the community.

Emmitsburg was fifty-two miles from Baltimore, but Elizabeth was traveling an incalculable distance. This little woman, a Protestant for thirty-one years and a Catholic for just four, was on her way to establishing the first order of active nuns in the United States—the first religious community founded by and for Americans.

This was the path she had started on when she stepped off the *Shepherdess* at the port of Leghorn. She didn't know it then. She didn't know it when she became a Catholic—the only nun to be seen in New York was made of wax, an object of curiosity in a museum on Greenwich Street. But she had the risk-taking energy of a child of revolution, so she did what Americans would always be able to do: She reinvented herself.

NINE

❧

Winchester Friday Afternoon

We are so far safe tho' our progress is so much slower than
you expected—your turnpike road is to be sure a very rough
one and we were obliged to walk the Horses all the way—
and have walked ourselves all except Cecilia nearly half the
time—this morning four miles and a half before Breakfast . . .
all the natives astonished as we went before the carriage—the
dogs and pigs came out to meet us and the geese stretched
their necks in mute demand to know if we were any of their
sort to which we gave assent.

Elizabeth wrote this report to Dubourg when she was in a village
thirty miles northwest of Baltimore. She wanted to keep him informed, every step of the way. He had supported her when she was
persecuted in New York. He had rescued her by bringing her to Baltimore. He had kept his promise to educate her sons at no charge.
And he would cause trouble for her almost as soon as they reached
Emmitsburg.

———

Before the Revolutionary War, English settlers had ventured into the poplar woods in the dense Maryland countryside. Near Toms Creek, the long tributary of the Monocacy River that flowed into the Atlantic, the colony of small farms was called Poplar Fields until a wheat farmer, Samuel Emmit, took out patents for land and began to sell lots to newcomers for two pounds ten shillings. By the time Elizabeth arrived, Emmitsburg had a three-page newspaper, a general store, and more than one tavern—twelve and a half cents for a meal, three cents for a drink. One Catholic priest, John Dubois, served the one Catholic church, St. Joseph's, as well as Mount St. Mary's College.

Halfway up the mountainside between Mount St. Mary's and its chapel, Dubois lived in a two-room log cabin. At the height of the French Revolution, he'd escaped from Paris, in disguise, helped by a classmate, Maximilien Robespierre. With a letter of introduction from the Marquis de Lafayette, Dubois met Patrick Henry, who gave him English lessons. The priest worked as a circuit-riding missionary in central Maryland until 1808, when he founded Mount St. Mary's, where students called him "Little Napoleon."

To Elizabeth, Dubois was "an excellent, superexcellent priest." When the women arrived, their farmhouse in the valley was being made ready, so Dubois loaned them his cabin as their first home. William and Richard had already been accepted at the college, where a classmate was Jerome Bonaparte, nephew of the man whom Elizabeth called "Old Bony." She met John Hughes, a gardener and groundskeeper there, a man who would one day radically alter the course of her religious community.

Elizabeth loved the cabin on sight, being "half in the sky." But Harriet was unhappy. Torn between her wish to become a Catholic and the harsh truth that most family doors would then be closed to her, she wore Bayley's miniature around her neck and told Elizabeth, "If it were not for this engagement, I would remain with you." In the short time she had been in Baltimore, she had become attached to Pierre Babade. He had become the beloved confessor and spiritual director to Elizabeth as soon as she came to Baltimore; the other women had found in him a warm and caring mentor. His enthusiastic love for God was like a magnet drawing Harriet to Catholicism. Her middle name was Magdalene, and Babade called her "Magdalena, child of my heart." One evening, when Elizabeth and the other women went to the chapel on the mountain, Harriet sat on a rock outside in the moonlight and wept.

When the second group, under the direction of Rose White, left Baltimore a month later, it was the final good-bye to Elizabeth's time in Baltimore. Madame Fournier, Dubourg's sister, waved from her casement window. The travelers were women and girls except for William and Richard, Elizabeth's sons, all closely packed in the carriage as it lurched and heaved. "When we have gone a few miles the baggage will settle down and you will be more at your ease," the waggoner shouted. They drove all day without stopping until nightfall, when they came to a tavern where they would spend the night. The boys slept in the wagon, to guard the baggage. As it was a meatless Friday, they had eggs, bread and butter, and tea for their supper.

By the time they arrived in Emmitsburg, Elizabeth and the others had moved into the little farmhouse in the valley—another temporary home while a larger house for them was being built. Cecilia Seton's health had noticeably improved; she was one of the first to run down the path and welcome the travelers. The two priests, Dubourg and Dubois, rode into the village to buy cups and saucers, knives, forks, and pewter spoons, and half a dozen chairs.

Elizabeth had told Julia that she was going to "a beautiful country place in the mountains." Certainly the land was beautiful, nestled beneath the Catoctin spur of the Blue Ridge Mountains, near today's Camp David: acres of woods and meadows, hills and deep ravines, with cherry trees, cedars and magnolias, and butterflies "as large as one's hand . . . pearl blue and violet, delicate green, orange yellow, pale rose and vermillion." Elizabeth had looked for God in nature since she was eight years old; now she was dazzled by the splendor of God's creation. Even the place the women chose as the cemetery site was lovely, dappled in sunlight on the old trees. As they were walking around the property not far from the house, Harriet playfully threw her apple core toward a tall oak: "There is my place."

But the house was stark. The stone building had four small rooms, two down and two up in the garret, for sixteen people, most of them adults. The two cots were reserved for sick Sisters; the others slept on the floor. Snow drifted in through holes in the roof. There was no water pump; drinking water had to be carried from a spring in a hollow. Washtubs were carried several hundred yards to Toms Creek; on a rainy day, the clothes had to be brought back soaking and heavy. The frugal budget meant a lot of turnips, potatoes, and bread; "coffee" was made from shaved carrots roasted and dried, then steeped in boiling water. When the women went to Mass at the chapel on St. Mary's Mountain, they had to cross a creek where the water was sometimes so high that Dubois would send a horse to carry them across, one at a time. When the water was low, they crossed on stones and, with no bridge or road, sometimes got lost in the steep hills and thick woods. "We would carry our dinner in a sack and often fry our meat at the mountain," Rose White recalled in her journal, "and take it from the frying pan and place it on a piece of bread without knife or fork, eat standing, and take a good drink of water, and go up to church and wait for Vespers. Often we would be caught in the rain coming home, at this time we never wore a shawl, much less an umbrella."

When the little community came close to folding, however, it was not because of the hardships: So many women applied that there was a waiting list. It was because of Elizabeth herself.

Poverty, chastity, and obedience are the uncompromising vows of religious life. For Elizabeth, poverty was effortless. Chastity had been tested on the long Atlantic crossing with Antonio. But obedience . . .

Elizabeth had always followed the dictates and decisions of her faithful feminist heart. As a young wife, just twenty-two, she had asserted her independence by helping to set up the first charitable organization in this country to be managed by women. When the Seton family business went bankrupt, and Will was sick, she had pitched in, doing a man's work in dealing with creditors and banking officials. Then, on her own, without Will, she had taken charge. She had managed. She had coped. Now, in her rigidly patriarchal church, she was expected to submit to male clerical control, no matter how arbitrary.

Elizabeth had expected that Dubourg would be their Superior. She had written to Julia, "I shall be at the head of a community which will live under the strictest rules of order and regularity, but I shall not give those laws, nor have any care of compelling others to fulfil them if any person embraces them and afterwards chooses to infringe them they will only find in me a friend to admonish and it will be in the hands of Mr. Dubourg either to rectify or dismiss them."

She had *not* expected that he would forbid them to have any more communication with their beloved mentor, Pierre Babade.

The women were distraught. They had become close to their white-haired mystic, the priest-poet, as soon as he first met them in Baltimore. They had expected him to visit Emmitsburg often, to pray with them, to celebrate Mass, to hear their confessions, to celebrate their friendship that was based on Christ's unconditional love. Harriet was inconsolable. She had decided to become a Catholic after all, and was eagerly awaiting Babade's arrival, when he would receive her into the Church.

Elizabeth wrote the letter as soon as she received Dubourg's order. She went over his head and appealed to Carroll, telling him of her disappointment and distress, and accusing Dubourg of "acting like a tyrant."

"Both myself and Sisters have been greatly chagrined by a letter received from our Superior soon after I came here which required of me not only myself to give up a correspondance with the person in whom I have the most confidence, and to whom I am indebted for my greatest spiritual advantage, but also to eradicate as far as possible from the minds of the Sisters that confidence and attachment they all have for him."

Except Rose White. She had joined the community just before Elizabeth left for Baltimore, on the advice of her own spiritual director,

John David, another Sulpician at the Baltimore seminary. Rose re-garded David as "the father and friend of her soul," and Elizabeth knew that Rose had no attachment to Babade.

"There has been some very busy persons making exaggerations to our Superior about my writing large packages to Father Babade," Eliz-abeth continued in her letter to the bishop, "which package sent only twice I truly explained to him contained letters from Cecilia, Har-riet, my Anna, Maria Burk (and my little girls who are fondly at-tached to him and used to write him constantly when in Baltimore) and the packages he twice sent us contained the life of Clotilda of France, and the manner of regular meditation and mental prayer which I had never followed in a manner necessary for a community."

Dubourg resigned.

Elizabeth was so regretful that she wrote again to the bishop, urg-ing him to have Dubourg return as Superior. And in fact, Dubourg wanted to return. But Carroll turned the matter over to Charles Na-got, who was the head of the entire seminary, with overall authority over the women who had come together in Baltimore under Sulpi-cian auspices.

Nagot refused to reinstate Dubourg. He wrote Elizabeth a stern letter, saying it was God's will that a Sulpician priest, John David, take over as Superior. He ordered her to "obey in silence."

And so with the first community of active American nuns the pattern was established: Nuns would come under the heavy hand of clerical control. Women were already considered to be inferior to men; when that cultural stance was reinforced by clericalism, nuns were expected only to work, pray, and obey. The priest had far-reaching jurisdic-tion, including the authority to either grant or deny permission for a person to receive Communion. Dubourg had restricted the women to three Communions a week, sometimes fewer.

Sometimes that heavy hand became a fist. When a new commu-nity of American women—the Sisters of Loretto—was founded in rural Kentucky, not long after Elizabeth settled in Emmitsburg, their

Superior mandated a rigorous penitential routine. The Sisters were made to go barefoot year-round, when water froze in the pitchers, when beds were covered with frost and snow, all the while teaching, doing manual labor, managing a farm, and in general doing whatever the priest told them to do. All the women were young—under thirty— but in the first dozen years after their founding, half of them died. At the entrance to the chapel, they kept an open grave.

As more religious communities sprang up to meet the needs of the growing American church, the women often had to choose between submission and confrontation, with submission the norm. The typical seventeen-hour day included Mass, meditation, private prayer, common prayer, the rosary, stations of the cross, spiritual reading, examination of conscience, adoration of the Blessed Sacrament, and manual work in the convent; silence was kept even at meals, with the hour of recreation usually devoted to mending, sewing, and parish tasks. Within that same day, Sisters carried a full professional schedule in schools, hospitals, and other Catholic institutions, while subject to a rigid schedule that a Sister today wryly sums up: Home by five, dead or alive.

Elizabeth chose confrontation.

Her new Superior, John David, was French, schooled in the severe Sulpician spirituality, based on sin and fear, with a pessimistic view of human nature. Because of the evils of the flesh, the lower faculties had to be disciplined by the higher—that is, the intellect. Elizabeth saw the spiritual at the heart of everything around her; she and David clashed at the outset. He wrote out rules for her school, though it would not be opened until the new building was ready, without consulting the women who would be teaching there. He made it clear that he would run the community by himself, limiting the role of Elizabeth and her council to simply carrying out his orders. In a letter to Dubourg, Elizabeth called David a stepfather, not a father. "Our Lord did not give him that place with us—the charge was pointedly given to you." She wrote a weary letter to George Weis, a friend in Baltimore. "When and how it will end God only knows."

And she wrote again to Bishop Carroll. She told him of her "confusion and want of confidence in my Superiors . . . if my own happiness was only in question I should say how good is the cross for me this is my opportunity to ground myself in patience and perseverance . . . really *I have endeavored to do everything in my power* to bend myself to meet the last appointed Superior in every way but after continual reflection on the *necessity of absolute conformity with him,* and *constant prayer* to our Lord to help me, yet the *heart is closed.*" In his reply, Carroll told her she must sacrifice herself for the good of the community, "not withstanding all the uneasiness and disgust you may experience." As for "obey in silence," Dubourg asked her to be "fairly obedient."

The larger question, beyond Elizabeth's own happiness, was the fate and future of the first American Catholic sisterhood. And it was not just one woman versus one particular man, but the sheer newness of it all. This new American church was challenging the established European model: David's Catholicism emphasized penance and absolute authority, in clear contrast to Carroll's American view stressing democratic ideals.

In the Protestant culture of the early nineteenth century, an American Catholic Church was suspect, let alone an American convent. A Lutheran minister in Frederick, Maryland, near Emmitsburg, told his people that these women in black dresses were "female wolves . . . ferocious creatures." His warning was a forerunner of anti-Catholic sentiment that would deepen as the Catholic Church grew, through wholesale immigration. The nativist movement saw the Church of "foreigners" as a threat; the founder of the Know-Nothing movement based his political career solely on anti-Catholicism. In the summer of 1834, about fifty men disguised as monks, with painted faces, broke into an Ursuline convent in Charlestown, Massachusetts— where the Sisters taught more Protestant students than Catholics— and burned it in a rampaging fire that lasted all night. Three orphanages in Philadelphia were torched, with one run by Elizabeth's community saved only because Mayor John Scott, Julia's son, sent in police protection. Catholics in New York were advised to arm themselves.

Two years after the Ursuline convent was destroyed, Maria Monk's *Awful Disclosures,* a lurid account of the goings-on between priests and nuns in convents, was published. Harper Brothers, concerned about their reputation, set up a dummy corporation, Howe and Bates, to bring the book out. The stories turned out to be flaming fiction, but truth came only after three hundred thousand copies had been sold. By then, paranoia was reaching a peak. In midcentury, when the pope sent a two-thousand-year-old inscribed stone to be used in the building of the Washington Monument, the tribute was seen as a Roman takeover of America; the stone was either smashed or thrown into the Potomac River, and the finishing of the monument delayed for nearly thirty years. (A noticeable change in color, like a stripe, marks the place on the monument where the building was interrupted.)

Anti-Catholic sentiment simmered down, at least temporarily, after the Civil War. Throughout the war, Sisters became known for their work as nurses to soldiers on battlefields and in hospitals, perhaps less known for their hospitality to both blue and gray. At Emmitsburg, Sisters were sleeping one Saturday night when they heard the pounding of horses; they watched as "a vast army" camped on their grounds. On Sunday morning, Union soldiers approached the house. "One squad succeeded another," Sister Marie Louise wrote, "and each squad seemed hungrier than the last . . . Sisters were engaged all day slicing meat, buttering bread, filling canteens with coffee and milk." Encampments sprang up all over the property until one day, very early in the morning, the men struck the tents and marched the eleven miles to Gettysburg.

In a religious house, regulations are called the Rule—the guidelines for daily living. Since Elizabeth's community was the first of its kind in this country, there was no model to follow. But there was an order of active nuns in France—the Daughters of Charity of St. Vincent de

Paul, founded in 1633 by a French priest, Vincent de Paul, and a widow, Louise de Marillac. To evade the papal edict that all nuns be cloistered, they had the women take simple vows, binding for just one year, instead of solemn lifetime vows; "no other monastery than the houses of the sick or the school rooms, no other cell than a hired room, no other chapel than the parish churches, no cloister but public streets or hospital rooms, no enclosure but obedience, no other grate than the fear of God, no veil but that of holy modesty . . . in all their intercourse with the world they shall conduct themselves with as much recollection, purity of heart and body, and detachment from creatures, as nuns in the retirement of their monastery." Abigail Adams had visited one of their orphanages in Paris when her husband was in diplomatic service there and had been impressed by the Sisters' kind attention to the children.

John David wanted the Rule for these women to be applied to Elizabeth's community. But this French order worked mostly in hospitals, not schools, and certainly did not allow women with children. Elizabeth had five. Her sister, Mary, wrote, sounding bewildered and upset. "To my too worldly mind it seems almost incredible, surrounded as you are by dear little children, that you can familiarize yourself to the contemplation of any change that must incur the necessity of separation from them." To Elizabeth, though, separation from her children was not only unnecessary, it was not even to be considered. "The thought of living out of our valley would seem impossible if I belonged to myself," she wrote to Julia, "but the dear ones have their first claim, which must ever remain inviolate. Consequently if at any period the duties I am engaged in should interfere with those I owe to them I have solemnly engaged with our good Bishop Carroll as well as my own conscience to give the darlings their right and to prefer their advantage to everything."

John Dubois was opposed to a union with France, and so was Cheverus in Boston. But David intended to import some Daughters of Charity to Emmitsburg; three Sisters—Marie Bizeray, Marie Woirin, and Augustine Chauvin—were to make the journey. The nuns were eager to come. "I hope I shall have the pleasure of seeing you in a few months," Marie Bizeray wrote, "as the Almighty, who calls you to our holy state and has inspired me, as well as many of my companions, with the desire of being useful to you, will not fail to prepare the way for our departure."

Elizabeth vigorously opposed their coming. For all her French heritage, Elizabeth wanted her community to be uniquely American, staffed by Americans in service to the American people. Then, too, there was the question of leadership.

"What authority would the Mother they bring have over our Sisters while I am present?" she wrote to the bishop. "How could it be known that they would consent to the different modifications of their rules which are indispensable if adopted by us? What support can we procure from this house but from our Boarders, and how can the reception of Boarders sufficient to maintain it accord with their statutes? How can they allow me the uncontrolled privileges of a Mother to my five darlings? . . . [M]y duty to my Anina* alone would prevent my throwing her in her unprotected state in the hands of a French mother."

As the controversy continued, the women plowed ahead, working and praying under Elizabeth's direction. Although she had been a Catholic for a shorter time than most of the others, her spirituality had never been defined by doctrine but was a grace she naturally shared. "God is like a looking glass in which souls see each other."

She often wove her prayers around people:

Around Harriet, who'd been received into the Catholic Church by Pierre Babade in late September, and had had scathing letters from family in New York. Her brother-in-law Gouverneur Ogden told her that the establishments at Baltimore and Emmitsburg "are novel things in the United States, and would not have been permitted by the populace in any other place than in the democratic, Frenchified State of Maryland . . . I predict from many causes the demolition of every

---

* Anna, who'd been called Anina when she was in Italy.

building in that state in any wise resembling a convent or Catholic hospital." Harriet had also heard from her fiancé that he would not return from Jamaica for eight to ten years. He told her about a young man who'd been long away from the woman he was to marry, but when he returned, he'd found her old and ugly. Bayley asked Harriet whether her beauty had faded.

Around Cecilia, whose improvement in health had been temporary, who was again spitting blood, so weakened that she often fainted upon rising from a chair.

Around Anna, who was often moody and discontent. Julia, who sent money specifically for Anna, asked again to adopt her. "I will love her, nurse her, and amuse her . . . in all things she shall be at Home," Julia wrote. She underlined the word "Home" twice. "Indeed my Julia," Elizabeth replied, "if you had her she would be a source of perpetual uneasiness to you for as she grows up and looses herself from that blind obedience expected from a child under thirteen, she takes many varieties of temper which makes her disposition so unequal that until she is more matured and experience teaches her some necessary lessons it is very difficult to make her happy."

Without a permanent Rule, the Sisters lived under provisional regulations that were, as David had told Elizabeth they must be, "very strict."

The women rose at five, dressed, then immediately knelt in private prayer.

At five-thirty, vocal prayer and meditation.

At six-fifteen, walking two by two to church, saying part of the Rosary on the way and part on the way home. "One of the Sisters by turn shall keep the house, whilst the others go to church, and employ herself in sweeping and fixing everything for breakfast." After breakfast, a half hour of talking was permitted. Silence was kept the rest of the morning, as the Sisters did manual labor.

Just before noon, reading of twenty-five verses of the New Testament on their knees, then examination of conscience.

Dinner at twelve, with two Sisters in succession reading from the

Old Testament, chiefly of the books of Solomon, except his song, with its sensual theme—"How beautiful are thy breasts . . . more beautiful than wine."

After dinner, recreation until two o'clock. "Two will be appointed by turns to removing the things from the table, washing the dishes, sweeping the hall, etc. and the rest of the time they will spend together in friendly conversation, avoiding, however, anything that might degenerate into excessive familiarity."

At two, reading of a chapter of *The Imitation of Christ,* then manual labor for the rest of the afternoon, interrupted only by prayer at four.

At five, recreation for half an hour. At five-thirty, back to church for a half hour of prayer. "If on their arrival at home they do not find everything ready for tea, they will wait in silence. During tea, one will read out of *Spiritual Combat.*"

At eight-thirty, evening prayers, asking for the blessing of the Mother, then retiring to bed "in profound silence."

Three women were elected to form a council that would make community decisions: Catherine Mullen, Cecilia O'Conway, and Cecilia Seton. Rose White, as second in command, automatically belonged on the council. The community had grown quickly: Elizabeth wrote to Antonio that she had been placed at the head of "ten of the most pious Souls you could wish," and she expected that when he heard this news, "you will laugh."

She'd had no word from Leghorn since her move from New York to Baltimore. When she finally had a letter from Antonio, written a year earlier, she wrote to thank him for the thousand dollars he sent—"May you be blessed forever"—and she told him of their financial troubles. "We might be a very large family if I recieved half who desire to come, but your Reverend Mother is obliged to be very cautious for fear we should not have the means of earning our living during the winter. Yet as Sisters of Charity we should fear nothing."

This was the first time that Elizabeth referred to her community as Sisters of Charity.

———

No one expected Cecilia to live much longer, and no one expected Harriet to die.

Until late November she was strong and healthy, always following the daily schedule faithfully, attending Cecilia with loving concern. She had decided to stay in Emmitsburg, although her brother Sam had written to her, urging her to come back to New York. He would take a cottage near town, he said, and Harriet could live with him. Just about that time, she began having sick headaches, but Elizabeth was not alarmed: Sickness had become a constant in the household.

By mid-December, Harriet was critically ill, with what the doctor called an inflammation of the brain. In the last few days of her life, she was delirious, singing hymns, trying to touch items of Babade's— his handkerchief, his towel. She stealthily drank the water he had blessed. She stretched out her arms, calling to him, calling to Jesus. When Elizabeth asked her what Jesus was saying to her, Harriet replied, in her last rational words, "All love and Peace."

She had not formally joined the sisterhood, but her death, just five months into the settlement at Emmitsburg, was treated as the first community death. Elizabeth was so shaken that she immediately wrote to George Weis. "Our Harriet is gone without my even knowing she was in danger—she died at two this morning we have had Mass and the communions of all the community it is now five o'clock." Harriet was buried at the foot of the oak where she had gaily thrown her apple core.

The bishop wrote to Elizabeth. "It seems to be the order of divine providence to lead you to perfection thro' the road of sufferings, interior and exterior; and may you always correspond with the graces bestowed on you." David's reaction emphasized his stringent spirituality. He saw Harriet's death as "a happy event . . . perhaps God foresaw that, if she had lived, the persecutions and allurements of a wicked world would have shaken her constancy and caused her to forsake her good resolutions."

Anna became quieter than ever—she and Harriet had always walked together, read and worked together, and shared a bed. To Elizabeth,

Harriet was more like a daughter than a sister-in-law—Harriet had been just thirteen when her father died, when Elizabeth had become an instant mother to his children. "I can only offer a Mothers heart, a Mothers sighs and a Mothers tears," Elizabeth wrote in her letter to George Wels. And she reacted like an indignant mother in a letter to Andrew Bayley in Jamaica, reminding him of his letter in which he'd asked if Harriet had lost her bloom. She told him that Harriet had burned the letter.

The new year of 1810 came in with crushing cold. Sisters Rose and Sally shoveled two cartloads of snow from the garret rooms. Anna had chills and fever, with sweating. One by one, Sisters fell sick, to the point where Elizabeth wrote to Carroll, "I began to think we were all going." The stone house was so overcrowded that Sisters Rose, Sally, and Kitty moved to the unfinished log house with its multitude of inconveniences. With no way of telling time, they would often get up at one or two o'clock in the morning and trudge through the snow to the stone house, thinking it was time for morning prayer. In the log house, they kept at their spinning wheels, both to have something to do and to try to keep warm. On stormy days, the strongest of the three would cross the muddy ground to bring back something to eat.

As the winter continued freezing, the stone house was so cold and damp that Elizabeth felt they all had to move to the new log house, finished or not. On February 20, 1810, after a lifetime of moves— what would become of us?—Elizabeth settled into her last home.

She described it to a Catholic friend in New York: "We have an elegant little Chapel thirty cells holding a bed, chair and table each, a large infirmary, a very spacious refectory, besides parlour, school room, my room working rooms etc." This was more prediction than reality. The women had to carry mattresses from room to room, to be out of the way of the workmen; some slept in the hall. The hair kept in the building for the plaster was thick with fleas; women were so bitten that their faces turned purple.

And it wasn't paid for. The Sisters' attempts to make money by sewing quilts, along with coats and vests for the boys and men at the college, was pathetically slow work by hand and barely made a dent. When Elizabeth suggested that she go on a begging tour, called "questing," Dubourg vetoed the idea. He suggested instead that she send letters to "various ladies," including "Mrs. Bonaparte, who being now an imperial princess might perhaps think it suitable to her new dignity to pay for the honor of protecting the Sisters of Charity." Later religious orders sometimes depended on begging most of the time for most of their funds; one nun spent seven years begging on behalf of their hospital, from her Kansas convent as far as Albany, New York. "Oh, the humiliation of it," another nun lamented. Poverty in religious orders has always been not simply a vow but a way of life. In Elizabeth's community, there were not even enough little crucifixes to go around. "We have so few in the house that we cannot allow a poor Sister in her coffin that last possession." She had planned a school for "our Saviour's poor country children," but inevitably, the boarding students whose families could pay $125 a year would become the mainstay, while children from St. Joseph's Parish in the village would be enrolled at no cost as day students, a forerunner of the Catholic parochial school system.

"I remember when Anna was six months old and everything smiled around me," Elizabeth wrote to Julia in the spring. As she neared the one-year anniversary of her move to Emmitsburg, she thought more and more often of glad days past. She thought of Will, her father, her friends, and the enchanted time in her own house on Wall Street. "And I would say to myself . . . all these and heaven too? . . . [T]he dearest pleasure in the world I would now ask would be to see you quietly, and alone for a few hours."

In that letter, she talked of Harriet's death, and of Cecilia, who Elizabeth felt "will very soon follow her I think in a very few months more probably weeks." When the women moved from the stone house to the log house, Cecilia was so sick with tuberculosis that she had to

Above: The signature of Elizabeth Seton, who wrote in a firm, confident, graceful hand. *Photograph used with permission of the Daughters of Charity Provincial Archives*

Below: Richard Bayley (1744–1801), Elizabeth's father, was so dedicated to medicine that he left his wife and young daughters in New York just before the American Revolution, to go to England to study anatomy. He was absent from Elizabeth's life as she was growing up; later he became an intimate, irreplaceable part of her family. As the first health officer of New York, he was far ahead of his time in investigating the cause of epidemics and is cited in twentieth-century literature. He gave up his society medical practice to work with victims of yellow fever, and died among them. *Collection of the New-York Historical Society*

William Seton, Elizabeth's father-in-law, was a distinguished figure in New York both before and after the Revolution. He was a founder of the New York Chamber of Commerce and, as a friend of Alexander Hamilton, was appointed cashier of the Bank of New York, the first bank in the city. He was known for his open heart and hand, his abundant generosity. "Let all come to my strong box while I am alive, and when I am gone you will take care of each other," he said, a prediction that would prove overly optimistic. *National Gallery of Art*

Left: Elizabeth at nineteen in 1794. As a bride, she presented this miniature portrait to her husband, which was the custom. He carried it with him on his first business trip away from her, and wrote that he "would not have been without it for the world." The portrait was done by Francis Rabineau, a noted miniaturist, who charged eight dollars, with a money-back guarantee: "No likeness, no pay." *Sisters of Charity of New York*

Right: Born at sea on April 20, 1768, as his parents were sailing from England to New York, William Magee Seton, called Will, was Elizabeth's husband. He was educated in England, then worked in Italy, studying business methods. Like Elizabeth, he loved music; in Italy he went to the opera three times a week. He once considered a career as a concert violinist. In 1789 he bought a violin in Cremona, the first-known Stradivarius in this country, a family treasure until one of his grandsons, on his way to boarding school, left it on a train. *Photograph used with permission of the Daughters of Charity Provincial Archives*

This earliest known view of Fraunces Tavern is believed to represent the building as it was altered following a fire in 1832.
From Valentine's Manual for 1854

TRINITY CHURCH, NEW-YO

Top left: The Fraunces Tavern, at the corner of Pearl and Broad streets in New York City, was built as a house in 1719 and converted to a tavern called the Queen's Head in 1762. Before the Revolution, the Sons of Liberty met here. After the war, the name was changed to that of its owner, Samuel Fraunces, and it became one of the city's premier meeting places, with private dining rooms for ladies. General George Washington gave his farewell talk to his officers of the Continental Army in the tavern's Long Room. Said to be New York City's oldest surviving building, the tavern and its museum remain open today, a popular tourist site. *Courtesy of Fraunces Tavern Museum, New York City*

Bottom left: The Park Theatre was the most prestigious playhouse in New York City. A three-story stone structure, it opened on January 29, 1798, and became one of Elizabeth's favorite places. Opening night brought in a gross of $1,232, and hundreds of potential patrons had to be turned away. The lavish interior was modeled after London theaters, with a large pit, three tiers of red-cushioned box seats, a top gallery, and a dazzling glass chandelier. The Park had space for 2,400 people, with fireplaces in the lobby and a coffee room. It was located on Chatham Street at the north end of the city, today's Park Row.

Right: The second Trinity Church on Wall Street in 1789, after the first Trinity Church was destroyed by fire during the American Revolution. Elizabeth attended Trinity from childhood until she became a Catholic at age thirty-one. On April 30, 1789, George Washington stood on the sunny balcony of Federal Hall and took the oath of office as first President of the United States.

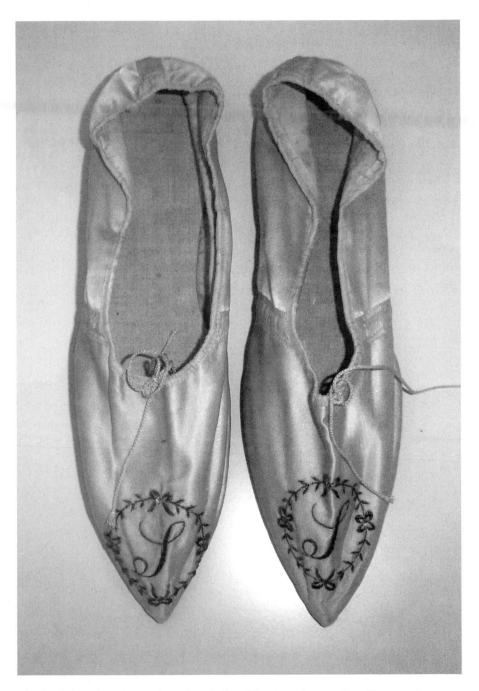

Elizabeth loved to dance. At a time in her life when she was literally counting pennies, she used a friend's gift of a hundred dollars to pay for dancing lessons for her daughter Anna. Elizabeth wore these cream silk dancing slippers, monogrammed with a swirling dark green S, to George Washington's sixty-fifth birthday ball in New York City on February 22, 1797. *Courtesy of Fraunces Tavern Museum, New York City*

Left: Elizabeth Ann Bayley Seton (1774–1821), the only American woman of her time who left a lasting imprint on this country's history solely because of her own life and work, not because she was married to a prominent man. In a society where women were subordinate, she knew what she called "the true language of female determination," and crossed gender and cultural boundaries when she thought it necessary. The Seton family motto, from its twelfth-century coat of arms, was "At Whatever Risk, Yet Go Forward." And she did. *Photograph used with permission of the Daughters of Charity Provincial Archives*

Right: This portrait of Will Seton was done in 1797, when he was twenty-nine years old and a partner in his father's successful shipping firm, with a large fleet of merchant ships. It was a very good year: Will was named an official host of George Washington's birthday ball. In this image, made by Charles Balthazar Julien Févret de Saint-Mémin, Will is wearing a wig, a mark of distinction at the time. But a year later, when the elder William Seton died, Will had to take charge not only of the business but also of his father's six children, from seven to fourteen years old. Will's health deteriorated, and within a few years, the family business went bankrupt. Will died on a trip to Italy, in a doomed attempt to regain his health, at age thirty-five. *Photograph used with permission of the Daughters of Charity Provincial Archives*

Left: Antonio Filicchi, the wealthy businessman who took in Elizabeth and her daughter after Will Seton died in Italy. He taught Elizabeth the sign of the cross and encouraged her interest in Catholicism. He was romantic and charming, she was a beautiful, vulnerable woman, and they were attracted to each other. He paid for her sons' college tuition and established a bank account that Elizabeth could always draw on. They kept up a warm, loving correspondence all their lives. She called him Tonio. *Photograph used with permission of the Daughters of Charity Provincial Archives*

Right: Filippo Filicchi, Antonio Filicchi's brother, was married to an American woman and appointed by George Washington to be the American consul at Leghorn, Italy, in 1794. Stern in his insistence that Elizabeth become a Catholic, he sent her a "Brief Exposition of the Catholic Faith," which ran fifty-six pages. *Photograph used with permission of the Daughters of Charity Provincial Archives*

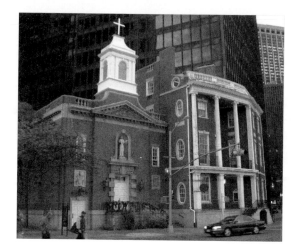

Above: 8 State Street at the southern tip of Manhattan, overlooking New York's wide harbor and its colorful Battery Park. Elizabeth and her family lived here for two years, from the spring of 1801 until the voyage to Italy in the fall of 1803. When she left New York for Baltimore, her last view of New York City was sunlight glinting on the windows of what had been her house. Now a shrine to St. Elizabeth Ann Seton, the house includes Our Lady of the Rosary Church, with a chapel open to visitors. *Courtesy of Father Peter Meehan*

Below: The sign in front of 8 State Street in New York City, where Elizabeth once lived. *Elena Miranda, Sisters of Charity of NY*

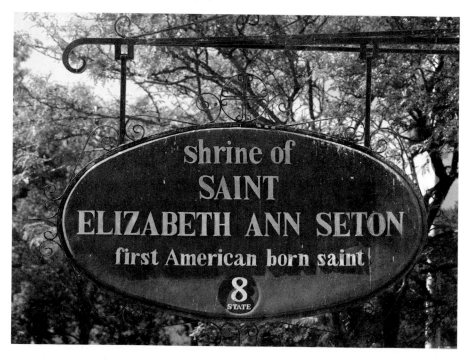

Above: St. Peter's Church on Barclay Street in New York City, the oldest Roman Catholic parish in New York State. The original St. Peter's, a simple log structure, was opened in 1786, after the English penal laws against Catholics were repealed. Because most Catholics then were the immigrant poor, the church was financed largely with a gift of a thousand silver pieces from King Charles III of Spain. Elizabeth was received into the Catholic Church here; she called it her "Ark" and was a faithful parishioner until she moved to Baltimore. This second St. Peter's, designed in the Greek Revival style, was built on the original site in the heart of the financial district in 1840 and is listed on the National Register of Historic Places. During the attacks of September 11, 2001, the church became a staging ground for rescue and recovery operations. When debris from the towers killed Father Mychal Judge, the Franciscan chaplain for the New York City Fire Department, who was the first publicly identified casualty of the attacks, his body was brought to St. Peter's and laid before the altar.

Left: This is the Baltimore house that Elizabeth lived and taught in for a year after leaving New York City. One room on the first floor served as parlor, community room, and classroom; another was the dining room, separated from the kitchen by a low brick partition. A staircase led from the front hall to the second-floor classroom and her bedroom alcove, with dormitories on the third floor. More than two hundred years after Elizabeth lived there, the house is still open to visitors today. *Archives of St. Mary's Seminary and University, Associated Archives at St. Mary's Seminary and University*

Top: St. Mary's Seminary Chapel in Baltimore. The seminary, founded in 1791, was the first institution in this country to educate men for the Catholic priesthood. Its new chapel was dedicated on June 16, 1808, the day Elizabeth arrived in Baltimore. An English visitor called the chapel "a little bijou of a thing," more inspirational than even St. Peter's in Rome. Designed by Maximilian Godefroy, the chapel was made of brick, bought for three thousand dollars by Charles Carroll of Carrollton, the only Catholic signer of the Declaration of Independence. Elizabeth's house in Baltimore was just across an orchard from this chapel, which was open from daylight until Benediction at night. And so Elizabeth heard church bells first thing in the morning, just as she had in the lazaretto in Italy. *Archives of the Associated Sulpicians of the U.S., Associated Archives at St. Mary's Seminary and University*

Bottom: When Elizabeth and her little band arrived in Emmitsburg in the summer of 1809, their permanent log house was not ready. For six months they lived in this stone farmhouse with four small rooms—two downstairs, two up—for sixteen people, most of them adults. The upstairs was really a garret, where snow sifted through holes in the roof onto women sleeping on the floor. There was no pump in the house; drinking water had to be brought from a spring in a hollow west of the house, and the washing—an all-day job—carried to a creek several hundred yards away. *Photograph used with permission of the Daughters of Charity Provincial Archives*

Left: Anna Maria, called Anina or Nina, born in 1795, was Elizabeth's first child, to whom she was always close. Too close. Anna was just three when Elizabeth wrote her a letter: "In you I view the Friend, the Companion, and Consolation of my future years." Elizabeth took Anna on the trip to Italy, when Will was dying, though an eight-year-old might have been better left at home with her brothers and sisters. When Anna died of tuberculosis at sixteen, Elizabeth was so bereft that for a time she doubted the existence of God. *Photograph used with permission of the Daughters of Charity Provincial Archives*

Right: Richard Bayley Seton, born in 1798, Elizabeth and Will's second son, named for her father, who saved both mother and child in a difficult birth. "As different as sun and moon," Elizabeth said of her boys. Dark-haired and dark-eyed, Richard was a boisterous, playful child who in a sense never grew up. His mother admitted that as a young man, he was thoughtless and irresponsible. Unable to keep the job Elizabeth found for him when he finished school, he became a navy clerk and died at sea at the age of twenty-five. *Photograph used with permission of the Daughters of Charity Provincial Archives*

Left: Rebecca Mary Seton was Elizabeth and Will's youngest child, born in 1802, as Elizabeth was writing a letter to a friend. Bec was always frail, and exceptionally sweet-tempered. At ten, she fell on the ice and never recovered. At fourteen, she died in Elizabeth's arms. *Photograph used with permission of the Daughters of Charity Provincial Archives*

Right: Elizabeth's daughter Catherine Charlton Seton, named for the mother Elizabeth had never known. Catherine was a talented musician and taught piano at Elizabeth's school. Called Kit or Kate, she became her mother's constant companion and was the only one of Elizabeth's children to be with her when she died. Later she became a Sister of Mercy, working in prison ministry in New York City. *Photograph used with permission of the Daughters of Charity Provincial Archives*

Above: Known as St. Joseph's House, this was the first motherhouse of the community and Elizabeth's last home. In the chapel here, on July 19, 1813, she and sixteen other women pronounced vows of poverty, chastity, and obedience as Sisters of Charity, the first active order of women religious in the United States. The house had thirty little rooms, called "cells," for the Sisters, each with a bed, chair, and table; a small parlor; a large infirmary; a refectory; and classrooms. Only a partition separated Elizabeth's room from the chapel; from her bed she could see the tabernacle and "keep the heart to it, as the needle to the pole." *Photograph used with permission of the Daughters of Charity Provincial Archives*

Left: Simon Gabriel Bruté, whom Elizabeth called "G," was a French priest, newly ordained when he was sent to work in Emmitsburg. He brought with him five thousand books, all in French, which Elizabeth could translate for the Sisters and in the process help him with his English. His religious exuberance matched hers, and they became close friends. He guided her through the blackness after her daughter Anna's death. As Elizabeth's spiritual adviser, he was aware of her profound holiness, and when she died, he told the nuns, "Save everything." *Photograph used with permission of the Daughters of Charity Provincial Archives*

Elizabeth, Mother Seton, in a portrait painted for her friends and benefactors, the Filicchi family. She is wearing the habit of the order she founded, the Sisters of Charity, very much like the widow's garb she'd worn since Will died: black dress with short shoulder cape, black rosary draped from a leather belt, and a muslin cap tied under the chin. The cap had been white until for practical reasons it was changed to black, leading to the nuns being called "blackcaps." *Photograph used with permission of the Daughters of Charity Provincial Archives*

Top: The original community cemetery at Emmitsburg, where Elizabeth was buried next to her daughters Anna and Rebecca when she died in 1821. Later her coffin was placed under an altar in the chapel. The names of the Seton girls, along with Harriet and Cecilia Seton, are still legible on the tombstones. *Photograph used with permission of the Daughters of Charity Provincial Archives*

Bottom: The Basilica of the National Shrine of St. Elizabeth Ann Seton in Emmitsburg, Maryland, ten miles from Gettysburg. After Elizabeth was beatified in 1963, her remains were placed under an altar here, which was dedicated as a basilica in 1965. In the museum connected with the shrine are mementos of the saint's life here, including the christening dress she made for her daughter Catherine in 1800. *Photograph used with permission of the Daughters of Charity Provincial Archives*

Top left: The interior of Chiesa di Santa Elisabetta Anna Seton in Livorno, Italy, the first church in the world to be named after St. Elizabeth Seton. Its pastor, Don Gino Franchi, insisted that the church be built in modern American style, to suit an American saint, so it has no cherubs, no marble statues, but vivid murals recalling Elizabeth's Italian journey. *Lara Bellagotti*

Top right: This statue of Elizabeth Seton stands in the garden of the Chiesa di Santa Elisabetta Anna in Livorno, Italy. It is flanked by bronze busts of the two most important men in her life: Antonio Filicchi, stern and high-collared, on her right, and her husband, Will Seton, curly-haired and casual, on her left. *Lara Bellagotti*

Bottom: This mural symbolizing Elizabeth's leadership of children is in the Chiesa di Santa Elisabetta Anna Seton, in Livorno, Italy. The artist is Paolo Maiani. *Lara Bellagotti*

be wrapped in a blanket and carried across the field to the new place. News of her condition reached Baltimore, where Samuel Cooper, who'd donated the property, was studying to become a priest. When he came to Emmitsburg, he brought Cecilia a barrel of honey, a barrel of molasses, and boxes of figs and raisins and prunes.

Cecilia was not the only one down. "Sisters became sick several at a time," Rose White wrote. Even Ellen Thompson, just twenty-two years old, was so sick that the women thought she might die. The doctor ordered a bath, with blisters to be applied, and her head shaved. But the community had no tub large enough for the bath, so they used an ash barrel, which leaked. Sister Sally took the barrel to the creek and placed it in the water to tighten; in the meantime, Dubois sent a large meat tub. But the staircase was too small for the tub to be carried up to Ellen's room. They then brought the barrel from the creek. But when they placed Ellen in the barrel of warm water, the barrel gave way; the women had to open the seam of the floor and sweep the water out of the room. Sister Rose noted that everyone, including Ellen, "was smiling at the drollery of the scene."

Sister Ellen did not die, and Cecilia did not improve. Elizabeth decided, on the advice of the bishop and the doctor in Baltimore, Pierre Chatard, to take Cecilia back to Baltimore for medical treatment. She wrote to John Dubois about it. "If you will accompany us on any part of our way we will esteem it as a particular favour . . . if she should ever die in the attempt I can only feel the conviction I have acted for the best, and done all in my power to serve her." And she wrote to Eliza Sadler, "My heart faints when I think of this separation. No one can conceive what she is to me."

Anna and Sister Susan went with Elizabeth on the journey to Baltimore, where Cecilia died on April 17. "A more consoling departure than she made you cannot imagine," Elizabeth wrote to Mrs. Sadler. "She was innocence and Peace itself." Elizabeth and Sister Susan took Cecilia back to be buried in the little wood, next to Harriet. Because there was no room in the wagon for Anna, Elizabeth left her with the Barry family.

Elizabeth knew that Charles DuPavillon, the young man whom Anna loved, or thought she loved, was still in Baltimore, about to sail home to Guadeloupe. She knew that the plan was for him to return with his mother and marry Anna. She knew that Anna would see him before he left, so she laid down the rules: Mrs. Barry was to see all notes that Anna wanted to send to Charles, and the two young people must never be alone together.

Charles was to sail for home on Saturday, May 5. Five days earlier, toward dusk, he came to the Barrys' door, asking to see Anna. He stayed until nine o'clock. "Oh my mother," Anna wrote, "how hard to be good in Baltimore!"

In June, Anna wrote again. "The Bishop told me the other day, tho' as in secrecy and you will keep it such, that you would probably be down in the fall again and, still more probable, not go back."

In July, Rose White went to Baltimore "on business."

David wrote to Elizabeth. "We must always rest contented when we have followed the advice of those who are to direct us." When a friend of Elizabeth's in Baltimore sat next to David at a dinner, she heard him openly discussing his plans for the women. He intended to replace Elizabeth with his favorite, Rose White, as head of the community.

TEN

❧

The *Common Rules of the Daughters of Charity* arrived from France, but the nuns never came.

At first they were held up by the government of Napoleon, which caused problems with passports. Then, too, although Vincent de Paul had included teaching as one of his nuns' possible ministries, by Elizabeth's time the Daughters were committed to serving the sick poor, not to teaching in schools where tuition was charged. There was a great difference between the needs of the fledgling Church on the American Protestant frontier and the situation of the Church in the stable, Catholic society of Europe. And there was disagreement over who had final authority over the Emmitsburg Sisters: Bishop Carroll or the Sulpicians. Even a priest who had favored the importation of the Daughters changed his mind. "I dread the arrival of the religious women who are to come from Bordeaux . . . Their hopes will be frustrated, they will be unhappy, be it at Baltimore or Emmitsburg."

So the French rules were adjusted to fit Elizabeth's situation as the mother of five children. The Sisters would teach children from the village at no cost, while relying on the boarders for income. These modifications meant rules that Elizabeth could live with.

If she stayed.

———

The vows that she had taken in Baltimore were binding for only a year. The year was up. "Certainly I have made no renewal of them," she wrote to Bishop Carroll, "and I intreat you . . . to relieve me from them if you think any obligation remains." In a letter to Catherine Dupleix, Elizabeth was more direct. "I am free."

She did not want to be free from her beloved community, but Elizabeth thought that she and her children would leave Emmitsburg if Rose became its leader. "Everything here is again suspended," she told George Weis, "and I am casting about to prepare for beginning the world again . . . as we have many reasons to expect from many things past, lately, that our situation *is more unsettled than ever.*"

Rose had returned from Baltimore, but David summoned her back. She was not well, but he insisted that she come "at any risk." She might come in a wagon, he said, as long as the wagon man was a Christian.

Elizabeth herself was ill much of the time. She admitted to Julia that her health was "a good deal altered, tho' always wrapped in a coating coat, with a lambs wool shawl and worsted stockings, some cold has penetrated to the breast and without cough or expectoration, or acute pain, it keeps an almost continual slow fever on me—Your first thought will be that comfort and good nourishment are wanting, but you will believe the sacred assurance that I have both, not only as I wish, but even as your tender heart would wish for me—have had fire in my chamber night and day all the winter, chicken broth, new eggs warm from the nest, little nick nacks of many kinds . . . be not alarmed, dearest, only after closing so many dear eyes and knowing so well the symptoms of our family enemy, perhaps I notice them more than one less acquainted with them would do it is not the first time I have had them, and recovered from them." Anna, too, was showing symptoms of tuberculosis. She had coughing fits; sometimes her cheeks were burning red, with a sweating fever.

Elizabeth was so concerned with the question of leadership that she wrote to Carroll. "Rose's virtues are truly valued by me and by us all, but from the time she knew she was proposed as Mother of this house in my place and that every one in it should prepare themselves for the change . . . her conduct has undergone an intire change and has been very unfavourable to her happiness and ours." She asked him not to tell Rose and David of this letter. "If you should ever be permitted to resign your maternal charge over your community," Carroll replied, "I would rejoice on your own individual account, but my hope for the continuance of the establishment would be very much weakened."

This intramural issue was essentially a human issue. Women who come to a religious community bring their attitudes and feelings and personalities with them. The closeness of community living can lead to disagreements, usually minor, sometimes so major that they disrupt lives. Twenty-five years after Elizabeth's death, the male Superior of the Sisters of Charity decided that the Sisters must return to the original Rules of the Daughters of Charity of St. Vincent de Paul. With Elizabeth out of the way, no adjustment need be made anymore for a woman with children, a woman who, with her community, had worn a simple black dress and cap rather than the habit of that venerable French order: the voluminous blue gowns modeled after seventeenth-century peasant clothing, and cornettes—the starched white-winged headdresses that won them the affectionate label "God's geese."

In New York, sixty-one Sisters were caring for orphans, both boys and girls; the Daughters' Rules allowed only for the care and education of girls. John Hughes, whom Elizabeth had known as a ground-skeeper at the seminary in Emmitsburg, was the bishop of New York, known as "Dagger John" because he signed his name with a cross that looked like a dagger, and because of his aggressive personality. He wanted the Sisters to stay, caring for both boys and girls, as a separate community under diocesan management. The women had to decide: New York or Emmitsburg? The choice was painful and harshly handled; when some Sisters wept, their Sulpician Superior, Louis Deluol, spoke sharply. "Now, behave yourself, don't cry—and be silent." He told them it was "the will of God" that all return to Emmitsburg, and if Sisters did not return, "let their names be heard no more in the

Valley." In the end, thirty-one Sisters stayed in New York, and thirty
returned to Emmitsburg, where the names of the women who stayed
were inscribed on the RIP plaque: women who were dead.

Amid the uncertainty over the leadership, Elizabeth kept to her usual
routine. "My days ever the same are spent in eating, keeping, walking, teaching, loving, and praying all the time." And worrying about
Anna, who'd had a letter from her Charles in Guadeloupe.

"Anna you always refused me, and I respected your delicacy, but at
the last moment when I left you perhaps for a watery grave could you
continue to refuse one single kiss—one only proof that I was dear to
you the remembrance that you persisted in doing so is a continuing
cloud of sorrow."

Elizabeth read the letter and told Julia about it. She called it "expressive of the romance of his age . . . this language is triffling—but
to me the music of heaven—that my darling should have had the
virtue and purity of an angel in the first dawn of youthful and ardent
affection (for she certainly is not without passion) is a joy to her
Mother which a Mother only can know."

While she waited to hear from the young man again, Anna was
"as quiet as a puss in the corner gathers nuts, dries fruits, and shares in
all the amusements of the Boarders of the house, and seems to have
resigned all *to him who knows best*—yet her D. may return when she
least expects it."

He never did. "The young DuPavillon to whom she gave her
foolish little heart found on his return to his family and possessions
someone who nabbed him on the spot . . . so much the better. I am
very thankful that she is left quietly with me."

The new American Catholic Church had its first archbishop when
John Carroll was invested with the pallium★ sent from Rome in the

---

★ A vestment worn by the pope and conferred by him on archbishops and sometimes
bishops.

summer of 1811. When three priests—Michael Egan, Benedict Flaget, and John Cheverus—were named bishops, none of them wanted the job. "Let me enjoy forever unmolested the humble post I occupy," Flaget wrote to Carroll. "I will prove more useful to your diocese in remaining in the college than in going to Kentucky as bishop." Cheverus told Elizabeth that "if there must be a bishop in Boston, I ought not to be the man. This affair has given me more anxiety and grief than I can tell."

The good news for Elizabeth was that Flaget wanted to take John David with him to Kentucky. With David gone, there would be no more talk of Sister Rose replacing Elizabeth. Before David left, though, he made one last attempt to conform the women to his wishes: He said he would conduct a retreat for them.

Again, Elizabeth protested. Now that David was leaving, with another priest succeeding him, with the Rules still being discussed, what was the point? She wrote to him at once. "What object can a retreat have at this time except it be followed by an immediate acceptance of those rules? . . . [O]f what use can it be to discuss those rules with any other than the one who is to take your place of Superior as he may on many points think differently from yourself and of course his opinions will subject us to new changes and uncertainty." She wrote to John Carroll as well, asking him to refuse permission for a retreat.

The retreat was not held. David left for Bardstown. John Dubois was named Superior of the Sisters of Charity. Elizabeth and Rose were reconciled, and Elizabeth remained head of the community for the rest of her life.

By that summer, the second anniversary of her arrival in Emmitsburg, the house had settled down. There were no more holes in the roof. Fifty boarders were enrolled at the school, most of them Catholic, although Elizabeth had insisted, contrary to the Superior's advice, that Protestant girls be admitted, including the daughter of the British consul. The education of females was not yet commonplace, but

Elizabeth's school was a decided step away from the derision that had prevailed, as in a late-eighteenth-century verse:

> *Why should girls be learn'd and wise?*
> *Books only serve to spoil their eyes.*
> *The studious eye but faintly twinkles*
> *And reading paves the way to wrinkles.*

Happily, Elizabeth's father had insisted that her learning continue, after the few years at Mama Pompelion's. He had given her one of his copybooks with scientific, political, and literary excerpts; in it she had written a French translation. In her second large copybook, eight by sixteen inches, she wrote a hundred pages from Rollin's *Ancient History,* along with Greek history and the history of England, and from then on, she never stopped.

Along with the school, the religious community was thriving. Fifteen women had joined the Sisters of Charity. They had not yet taken vows; the Rules had to be approved by Archbishop Carroll.

Anna did not want to wait to be a Sister of Charity. Already she was calling herself "Sister Anina of St. Josephs." She helped the younger children prepare for their First Communions; she instructed a group of ten girls that she called her "decury." She insisted on following the routine of the house: rising before daybreak, when no fires had yet been lighted; walking to Mass on the mountain without cloak or shawl; washing at the outdoor pump in the bitterest cold. When Elizabeth reproached her, Anna said she wanted to set a good example.

But she was slipping, and she knew it. "Pray for your Anina," she wrote to a friend in Baltimore. At the same time, she could say wistfully, "I can never believe that after all our dear Lord has done for me in this house, and attaching so much to it, that he would ever let me leave it. He knows I always will be his and his alone." Elizabeth, too, alternated between dread and hope, in a letter to Julia. "Anna my sweet and precious comfort and friend is undergoing all the symptoms which were so fatal to our Celia and so many of the family . . .

Yet she may not be as ill as I imagine." She took Anna on leisurely horseback rides, to rebuild her daughter's strength; she asked George Weis in Baltimore to send a stove and a carpet, so that Anna could be moved from the children's dormitory to Elizabeth's room downstairs, next to the chapel. When Anna said she would like some oysters, Weis, who owned a grocery store, sent them at once.

Elizabeth's sister, Mary Post, wanted her niece to come to New York, where Dr. Post could treat her. But Elizabeth wanted to hold Anna close—so close that Dubois was concerned. He felt that Elizabeth idolized her daughter, but he was never able to tell her so. He considered Elizabeth's character to be "like gold brocade, rich and heavy, how hard to handle."

That summer, a new man entered Elizabeth's life.

Simon Gabriel Bruté de Rémur from France had been ordained to the priesthood just three years earlier. He yearned to go to China as a missionary; instead, he was sent to Baltimore, then Emmitsburg. As assistant to John Dubois, he plunged into his ministry so vigorously that Dubois complained to Carroll: "He will go ten times to visit the sick . . . he even goes to visit those who are not sick . . . interrupting my simple but regular routine, mixing things up."

Bruté brought with him a religious exuberance and a spiritual awareness so like Elizabeth's that the two become fast friends. She called him "G" and confided in him as she had not in anyone else. When Bruté was in Baltimore, she wrote him a long, startling letter. "I tell you a secret hidden almost from my own SOUL, it is so delicate—that my hatred of opposition, troublesome inquiries, etc brought me to the church more often than Conviction—how often I argued to my fearful uncertain heart at all events Catholics must be as safe as any other religion, they say none are safe but themselves—*perhaps it is true,* if not at all events I shall be safe with them as any other . . . I was in the church many times before I dared look at the Sacred Host at the elevation, so daunted by [the Protestant] cry of idolatry—my thousand *ifs* to our God."

Bruté also brought with him some five thousand books, all in French, which Elizabeth could translate for the Sisters and in the process help him with his English.

They began with book 3, chapter 21 in *The Following of Christ,* the book that the Protestant Elizabeth had taken with her on the voyage to Italy. "Give me, O most sweet and loving Jesus, to repose in Thee above all things created; above all health and beauty; above all glory and honor; above all power and dignity; above all knowledge and subtlety; above all riches and arts; above all joy and gladness; above all fame and praise; above all sweetness and consolation; above all hope and promise; above all merit and desire; above all gifts and presents that Thou canst give and infuse; above all joy and jubilation that the mind can contain or feel; in fine, above all Angels and Archangels, and all the host of Heaven; above all things visible and invisible; and above all that is not Thee, my God; for Thou, O Lord my God, art supremely good above all things."

The prayer reflected perfectly the longing for God that Elizabeth had felt all her life, and that was now coming to full flower in her life as a religious. Always spiritual, she was becoming holy—not the holiness of a hermit or a contemplative nun, but as someone living a God-based life in the midst of her worldly work. Elizabeth knew that Christian holiness meant to live as Jesus lived. To love as Jesus loved. To follow the example of Jesus. In whatever situation or circumstance, what would Jesus do?

As contented as she was, Elizabeth longed to see old friends.

To Catherine Dupleix:

The very thought of your visiting gives a delight to us you can never imagine—the solitude of our mountains, the silence of Cecils and H[arriet]'s graves, your skipping children over the woods which in the spring are covered with wild flowers they would gather for you at every step—the regularity of our house which is very spacious and in an end wing contains our dear dear chapel so neat

and quiet, where dwells (as we *believe*) night and day *you know who,*
this is no dream of fancy and only a small part of the reality of our
blessing—You must be a witness to believe, that from Monday to
Saturday all is quiet, no violation of each other's tranquility, each
helping the other with a look of good will which must indeed be
seen to be believed—all the world would not have persuaded me if
I had not proved it so you may be incredulous till you come and see.

Julia Scott had written longingly that Elizabeth come to her for "a
change of air which your Physician will surely prescribe as the best
Medicine in the disease you apprehend, will give me the happiness of
receiving you in my House my arms and Heart—this visit would be a
mutual comfort to us . . . better than my coming to you, which my
fears of traveling alone, and over mountainous roads would render
almost impossible."

"I cannot give up the hope that you will one day come here,"
Elizabeth replied. "My going to you would be to me almost as difficult
as a voyage to the Moon."

To Eliza Sadler:

Since the weather is more mild and settled I am stronger. The
children are all health and spirits of course. I have more enjoyment
of a Mother's consolations every time I have the five together, which
is always once sometimes twice a week . . . my Anna, my William,
my Richard, my Kate my Rebecca especially if you could see her on
her knees milking her little white cow and afterwards loaded with a
little tin pail in each hand running over and her eyes glistening with
delight of the wonders she can do. Kits greatest pleasure is feeding
the lambs with salt from her hand Annas in decking the graves of
dear C[ecilia] and H[arriet] and the Boys in asking Mother
increasing questions about all their friends and connections and their
hopes and prospects in life . . . my dear Eliza will you write me
soon, give me at least the *hope* that you will sometime or other come

to the Mountain . . . Aunt Sadler and Uncle Craig is one of the unfailing sources of the Childrens remembrances. William will tell everything his Uncle Craig ever said to him every kind of indulgence—they can tell every article of your room up stairs, where the sofa stood on which you sat—the little Bird, wooden cow, the white dog etc. . . . I tell you *come* dear Eliza.

Elizabeth and her sister kept in touch. Mary wrote about her children—she had four boys and three girls. Their uncle William Bayley, with whom they'd spent so many of their young years, had been working in his garden when he complained of pain in his stomach; he went into the house, lay down on the bed, and died. Mary had gone into a Catholic church for the first time when she went to St. Peter's on Barclay Street for a concert of sacred music. She saw the famous painting—"Our Saviour, ALL NAKED!"—and remembered that Elizabeth had once spent a whole day kneeling in front of the painting, in prayer and contemplation. "The music did not answer my expectations," Mary wrote, "but I would have gone much farther to see the Picture over the Altar, although I must say I found it painful to see such a sight for the first time under the observation of such an assemblage of people."

On Christmas Eve, everyone went to Midnight Mass, slept briefly, then went back to the chapel for a 4:00 A.M. Mass. The chapel shimmered with light from the candles the Sisters had made. "Let all be hushed as the darling Babe when he first laid his dear mouth to the sweet breast of his Mother . . . I stop, adore, and listen."

Even in this joyful season, though, financial worries crept in. When Elizabeth asked Julia for two or three thousand dollars, Julia regretfully replied that she had spent her money on investment property. The women's flour merchant, grocer, and butcher couldn't—or wouldn't—extend any more credit. No money was coming from the Filicchis because of political disturbances; the Embargo Act, which had passed the U.S. House of Representatives in 1807, meant that she did not hear from her Italian friends for three years. The War of 1812, which was to severely affect Elizabeth's friends in Baltimore, was impending: British vessels had begun to impress American seamen, and in the Battle of Tippecanoe, an American force defeated Shawnee Indians, who were reportedly backed by the British.

Three days after Christmas, as a last resort, Elizabeth wrote to Robert Harper. He'd been elected to the House of Representatives and had become Elizabeth's financial and legal adviser. Three Harper girls—Mary Diana, Elizabeth, and Emily—were enrolled at St. Joseph's Academy. "If we sell our house to pay our debts," Elizabeth wrote, "we must severally return to our separate homes—must it be so—or will a friendly hand assist us." She appealed to him to ask his wife. "Mrs. Harper has a Heart of Pity She has proved it unsolicited—if we were relieved but from a momentary embarrassment her Name would be blessed by future generations." Harper advised Elizabeth to raise the tuition.

Elizabeth regularly gave instructions to the Sisters, which, considering her warm heart, could sound surprisingly stern.

"You must be in right earnest, or you will do little or nothing . . . What sort of interior life would you lead, if every time the door opens, or if any one passes you, you must look up; if you must hear what is said, though it does not concern you? Or, if you remain silent and in modest attention to your duty, what would be your interior life, if you let your thoughts wander from God? I once heard a silent person say that she was listening to everything around her, and making her Judas reflections on everything that was said and done; and another, that she delighted in silence because she could be thinking of her dear people. But you know better than that."

Along with teaching history and religion, Elizabeth gave formal instructions to the older girls twice a week, to prepare them for their lives after school. She was able to draw on her own experience as a woman in the world. "Your little Mother, my darlings, does not come to teach you how to be good nuns or Sisters of Charity, but rather I would wish to fit you for that world in which you are destined to live: to teach you how to be good . . . mothers of families."

When she was not fund-raising, or teaching, or preaching, Elizabeth was immersed in the running of the school.

The girls rose at 5:45 A.M., then Mass and study until breakfast at seven-thirty. Classes began at eight o'clock and ended at five, with breaks for dinner and some recreation. Supper was at seven-fifteen, followed by spiritual reading for the older girls, early to bed for the younger. When the girls went out walking, one Sister walked in front of them, one behind, keeping especially close watch when they went to Mass at St. Mary's chapel—the campus was full of boys.

Elizabeth visited each class at least once a month to judge the efforts of the teachers, to make suggestions, and to keep up with each pupil's progress, both in her studies and in her behavior. When Mary Harper bragged about her family to a classmate—"Do you know who I am? I am the daughter of General Robert Goodloe Harper!"—she was made to kneel beneath a picture of Christ until she was told she could get up. Names of careless or lazy students were read aloud in the refectory. Elizabeth thought that a girl's distractions might be caused by the devil, whom Elizabeth called Sam.

Sometimes she had to write to a girl's parents, warning them that if their daughter did not change her behavior, she would be expelled. And sometimes the warning did no good, as she said wryly to Bruté: "I will tell you what I know American parents to be most difficult— *In hearing the faults of their children*—in twenty instances, when you see the faults are not to be immediately corrected by the parents but rather by good advice and education it is best not to speak of them to Papa and Mamma who feel as if you reflected on their very self . . . they think it is not much and they will soften and excuse the child . . . and our efforts afterwards avail very little."

Early in the new year, ten-year-old Rebecca slipped on the ice. She had pain in her hip and leg and began to walk with a limp. Elizabeth noticed, but her daughter made light of it; the house was greatly distressed about Anna, and Rebecca did not want to divert attention from her sister.

In January, after nearly three years of discernment and discussion, Archbishop Carroll finally approved the Rules, which were read to the assembled Sisters. "We were at liberty to adopt these or not," Rose White wrote in her journal, "free to retire if we wished from the Community. All were invited to remain, notwithstanding bad health and other infirmities. Each was invited to raise her hand, if she was willing to adopt the rules. All were united but one voice." In February, Dubois told the women they would begin their novitiate—the probation period—after which those who wished could take vows as Sisters of Charity.

Even before the Rules were adopted, John David had asked Bruté to send a copy of them to Kentucky. "We are determined to form a society of virtuous women for the education of young people of their sex," he wrote. He wanted Sisters of Charity—specifically, Rose White, his protégée—to come to lead the new community. Elizabeth and Dubois agreed to help with the project, but they could not afford to lose Rose, Elizabeth's right hand. David complained to Bruté: "I am very annoyed that they could not give me Rose; she is perfectly suited to this important work. If Sister Kitty had enough health she would do very well for my purpose. Fanny is the one I need for instruction. But I see that after having given me a choice, they refuse the one I ask for." Elizabeth and David clashed again when he wrote, "I demand that we form all novices for Kentucky here." Elizabeth's council wrote an unusually large NO in the minutes of the meeting: prospective candidates for the Kentucky group, they decided, had to be interviewed in Emmitsburg, to judge the women's qualifications, then would need to spend their novitiate there, in the motherhouse. Finally, David gave up. The Kentucky community based its Rules on those of the Daughters of Charity in France but was never connected to the Sisters of Charity in Emmitsburg.

Anna died on March 12.

For weeks the pain had been relentless. She was wasting away.

Bones were pushing through skin; the raw spots were bleeding. One hip was festering; she could not stay in one position for more than five minutes.

On the morning of February 20, after Elizabeth had read the day's meditation to the Sisters, Anna had begged her to stay, for more prayers and reading. In the afternoon, when the pains had lessened a little, they sang hymns, with Anna reminding her mother of the tunes. At 8:00 P.M. she tried to get out of bed but began to strangle and fell back, bursting into a heavy sweat, the muscles of her throat constricting.

"Jesus Mary Joseph assist me in my agony," she said through the choking. "Jesus Mary Joseph may my soul depart peacefully in your holy company."

Elizabeth began to cry.

"Oh my Mother . . . rejoice for me," Anna said. She began to repeat prayers of faith, hope, and desire and the Litany of Mary. John Dubois came and anointed her with prayers for the dying. She took vows as a Sister of Charity, the first person at Emmitsburg to do so.

Elizabeth never left her bedside. She held Anna's hands, rubbed her cold feet. Other Sisters came, in turn, to stay with them. Anna was sometimes able to talk—of Jesus, of Eternity, of the love of God—but sometimes she could not get the words out. When her French teacher came, Anna said *"Je vais . . ."* then could say no more. Sister Rose came and repeated the name of Jesus over and over, with Anna echoing the name. At one point, her mind seemed to wander, and she laughed foolishly.

Bruté told her he would say Mass for her. As he went off to the altar, Anna called after him, saying she was praying for all. As she began to struggle, three women could hardly hold her down. She shrieked with pain. Elizabeth climbed up on the bed and on her knees, facing Anna, held the crucifix up high so her daughter could see it. Anna kept saying, "My Mother, my Saviour."

Elizabeth was kneeling at the bedside when Anna died, just weeks short of her seventeenth birthday. Her hands were clasped in prayer. Elizabeth told the Sisters who were with her to leave the hands in that position, then went to the chapel. The Sisters cut the seams of Anna's nightdress, then cut around her hands, leaving them clasped. In the little woods behind the house, next to the two other Setons, she was buried in that position.

Elizabeth stood woodenly. She did not weep. When her boys sobbed loudly, she turned to them. "You are *men,* and Mother looks for support from you." As she walked away from her daughter's grave, she said in a low, tight voice, almost fiercely, "Thy Will be done."

When Harriet Seton died, then Cecilia, Elizabeth had accepted their deaths with resignation. "We part, nature groans," she had written to Julia, "the soul is aghast, petrified. After ten minutes it returns to its usual motion and all goes on as if nothing had happened . . . Faith lifts the staggering soul on one side, Hope supports it on the other— Experience says it must be and Love says let it be."

This time, she could not let it be.

She had always been closest to her firstborn, who was most like her mother in her volatile personality. When Anna was only three, Elizabeth had called her "the Friend, the Companion, and Consolation of my future years." Anna had gone with her to Italy, where the child was indeed her friend, her companion, and, after Will's death, her consolation. A widow in the community who had lost a child said that "the grief of a mother is of no ordinary kind and admits no ordinary remedy."

Elizabeth lived that grief. "For three months after Nina was taken I was so often expecting to lose my senses and my head was so disordered that unless for the daily duties always before me I did not know much of what I did or what I left undone." She poured out her heart to her dear friends: Julia, and Eliza Sadler, and Dué. She sent her sister some of Anna's pious exercises, along with a flower from Anna's grave. Mary Post and her husband came to Emmitsburg at once.

The sisters had not seen one another in four years, since Elizabeth left New York. And Mary had never seen a nun. She had been strongly opposed to Elizabeth becoming a Catholic; now, she was so affected by what she saw in Emmitsburg that when she returned home, she wrote to Elizabeth:

"I left you, dear Sister, with sensations I cannot describe. It seemed to me as if I must have crossed the threshold of existence . . . It seemed to me I had actually seen an order of beings who had nothing to do with the ordinary cares of this life and were so far admitted to the company of the blessed as to take pleasure in the same employments, while they were at the same time exempt from the solicitude . . . for what usually [occupies] the attention of mortals."

Even with the love and sympathy of those who loved her, Elizabeth kept reliving Anna's deathbed scene, over and over.

When she was just three years old, Elizabeth had talked of joining her mother and her baby sister in heaven. She had spent her life loving God, following what she believed to be God's will, praying constantly. Now, when she knelt in the chapel, "it seems that he is not there for me." She was not simply finding that the "rough and thorny path" she had written about had become rougher and thornier: it had vanished. She was stranded in a void where, as the sixteenth-century mystic John of the Cross put it, "there is no path." Like other holy people—Thérèse of Lisieux in the nineteenth century, Mother Teresa in the twentieth, and countless people not as famously holy throughout all centuries—she was lost in a fog of anguished doubt. She was caught in what a modern writer calls "the dark, tangled visceral aspect of Christianity, the *going through* quality of it, the passage *into* death and suffering that redeems and inverts these things."

Elizabeth was trapped in the death and suffering stage. "Eternity" had long been her beloved word, her hope and belief. Now she was "uncertain of reunion." She was kneeling at Anna's grave when she saw a large, ugly snake stretching itself on the dried grass. Elizabeth was desolate, seeing Anna as "the companion of worms and reptiles! And the beautiful soul, *where*?"

———

In spite of her husband's opposition, Catherine Dupleix had become a Catholic, and she made plans to visit Emmitsburg. When Elizabeth heard of this, she was so excited that she wrote to Eliza Sadler: "Tell her the front door, the back, the side door which will lead her to the chapel and all the windows up and down will open at her approach." On the night that Dué arrived, Elizabeth wrote to Mrs. Sadler "to say Dué dear is behind my curtain with the children . . . she is safe and surrounded by love and tenderness."

It was Simon Bruté, though, who did the most to guide Elizabeth through her grief. He had her dwell on Anna's virtues and faith, to reawaken Elizabeth's belief in eternity and reunion with those she loved, while emphasizing her duty to her living children. He helped her through her anxiety over the snake by calling up a mental picture of Anna watching her mother at the grave. He drew sketches of Anna hovering near the altar when Elizabeth was in chapel. He taught her to savor the grace of each moment, and to finally see the graveyard as a "lovely little wood, happy little corner of earth."

The grace of the moment was tangible when the Sisters finished their long novitiate. On July 19, 1813, Elizabeth and sixteen other women took part in a powerful ceremony:

I, the undersigned, in the presence of God and all the company of Heaven, renew the promises of my Baptism and make my Vows of POVERTY, CHASTITY and OBEDIENCE to God and our Rev. Superior General until the 25th of March next, and engage myself to the corporal and spiritual service of the poor sick, our true Masters, the instruction of those committed to our charge, and to all the duties pointed out by our Rule in the Society of the Sisters of Charity in the United States of America.

Poverty meant that everything was held in common. If a Sister genuinely needed something, she was to submit her request to the Sister in charge, "and let them remain easy whether it is granted or not." If some article was given to them, then transferred to someone else, they should "be pleased with the opportunity of practicing holy poverty and mortification." Even when sick, they were to content themselves "with the common fare of the poor." Because Elizabeth had to provide for her children, she was partially exempt from the vow of poverty.

Following the rule of chastity meant shunning "any desire of pleasing, vanity, and affectation either in their dress, carriage, gait or conversations," and not running to the windows to look at strangers coming or going. They were to keep their eyes down, particularly in the streets, in church, in strange houses, and "above all, when speaking to persons of the other sex." Sisters could not go out alone. When they were sick and a priest came to see them, another Sister had to be present; if the room was too small, the door had to be left open.

"Rules, prudence, subjections, opinions etc dreadful walls to a burning SOUL wild as mine," Elizabeth wrote to Bruté. But now that she was Mother of the house, obedience was no longer as difficult as it had been in the beginning. Obedience for her meant primarily obeying the instructions and rules set down by the male Superior. (Dubois had once heard talking in the infirmary and had written in large letters: "Silence here at all times . . . also no one to go to the infirmary without permission!") Other Sisters could not open letters or notes addressed to them without permission of the Mother, who could read them first; when letters were written, the Mother was to read them before they were mailed. Sisters living outside the house were to write to the Mother two or three times a year, with a full account of their doings. The few Sisters who did not know how to write might ask another Sister to do them that favor.

Later, when the community was incorporated, with by-laws calling for the election of officers, Elizabeth was elected head of the community by acclamation. She had been in charge all along, but this was a formal arrangement, an Act of Incorporation in the State of Maryland, and she was suddenly unsure of her abilities. Sister Cecilia O'Conway wrote a letter of assurance. "My beloved Mother, how

[you] surprise me by your alarm . . . be a mild, patient but firm MAMMA, and you need not tremble under the burden of superiority. Jesus can never give you a task above your courage, strength or ability." Cecilia had been the first young woman to join Elizabeth in Baltimore—she was deeply prayerful and had talked of joining a cloistered order of nuns. Elizabeth had dissuaded her. "This is not a country, my dear one, for Solitude and Silence, but of warfare and crucifixion."

ELEVEN

~✼~

Elizabeth's sons had been just five and seven when she came back from Italy without their father. They'd lived with a confusing change in religion, with harassment and persecution, with never enough money in the house. They'd attended three boarding schools and had grown up in the strange, bewildering context of their mother's convent life. Now, as they neared the end of their school days, they were at a loss, unsure of what came next.

The boys were "as different as sun and moon." William was tall and fair, like his father; proud, quiet, and reserved to the point of coldness. Richard was boisterous, and, like his Seton grandfather, he was robust. Elizabeth described him to Julia as "an enormous young man" and called him "my giant."

The schoolteacher in Elizabeth wrote a candid assessment: "They are so far children of exemplary conduct as it relates to common behaviour, and the simple discharge of common duties, but they have no striking talents, no remarkable qualifications, nor are their dispositions even unfolded in many points." She wrote this to Antonio Filicchi in July 1814, her first letter to him in four years. "I hardly know where the thread of the story was broken." She thanked him for the money she was drawing from his account in New York, told him that Anna—his Anina—had died and that Rebecca was lame, and dropped a broad hint about her sons. "If they were near you all would be secure."

She had hoped that one of the boys would become a priest. When neither was interested, she considered a business career to be their best, if not their only, option. But Richard thought he'd be a farmer, and William wanted to go to war. President James Madison had signed a declaration of war against Britain in the summer of 1812, the first time the United States declared war on another nation. A major grievance involved sailors who had been born in Britain, then had become naturalized American citizens. The Royal Navy went after them, by intercepting and searching U.S. merchant ships to impress them into British service.

By the late summer of 1814, the British had invaded Washington, bent on burning the White House. President Madison and other government officials left town, while Dolley Madison stayed behind to oversee the saving of precious objects, including the Gilbert Stuart painting of George Washington. She left just before the British troops set fire to the house; the smoke could be seen in Baltimore, where Elizabeth's friends lived at the edge of danger.

In the Battle of Baltimore, the British attacked Fort McHenry. "It was an awful spectacle to behold," Carroll wrote. "Before us at least forty vessels great and small and for about twenty-five hours five bomb ketches, discharging shots on the fort, upward 200 pound weight each. You may suppose we did not sleep much." Francis Scott Key, an American lawyer and amateur poet, whose niece was a student at St. Joseph's, was spending the night on board a British ship, on a mission to arrange the release of an American prisoner. Rockets were glaring, bombs bursting in air. At dawn, he saw the American flag still flying over the fort and jotted down the famous verses on the back of a letter he was carrying.

William was so anxious to join the navy that Elizabeth gave in. She wrote to Carroll, whose nephew was a clerk in the Department of State, asking him to consider her son's application. The archbishop's response was not encouraging. "Truly since the misfortunes of the city of Washington and the deplorable condition to which the ignorance and perception of our leaders has brought our national affairs I see little prospect of Wm. proffiting by any appointment he might obtain—Yet every attention will be paid."

William was disappointed; his mother was not. She wanted him to remain among Catholics, so she wrote to Antonio again, more directly this time: "I take the final resolution with God to recommend to you my William as your own son—he has had a strong inclination to go to the Army or Navy and in sending him to either there is the greatest risque of his Salvation and loss of Faith—at 18 he must be doing something—no business can be done here in the distracted state of the country." When she learned that Simon Bruté was going to France early the next year, to visit his mother and to bring back more books, she decided to send William with him; from France the young man could go on to Leghorn.

She could not let him go without a letter of advice, its points carefully numbered.

My darling child, my William,

1st I recommend to you above every thing your Precious Soul dearer to me than my own life a thousand times . . .

2nd a kind attention to Mr. Bruté as your true friend and a devoted respect for his sacred character . . .

3— And to his family a grateful affection—you *will* I know my dear one

4— you will especially mind all his advices knowing your own inexperience—

5— You will mind oconomy in Every thing, as we have Nothing but what we receive from our friends . . .

6— When you are with the Filicchis take every opportunity to show them you remember their uncommon friendship to your father . . .

7. I beg you so much not to give way to national prejudices, but

to allow for many customs and manners you will see—why should not others have their peculiarities as well as we have ours . . .

8. be cautious and prudent, my son, with strangers till you know that they mean good to you . . .

9. again I recommend you the strictest oconomy . . . and on [no] account run into debt

10. And my William—my soul's darling the first object of every care and anxiety of my heart do do remember your own mother is your best friend.

Although she had not had a reply from Antonio, she wrote to him again, telling him that William was coming.

Rebecca had not been able to conceal her limp for long. When Elizabeth's sister and her husband had come to Emmitsburg, after Anna's death, Dr. Post had examined her and said there was nothing he could do. "My darling lovely gay little Beck is intirely lame and never leaves my room even with her crutch unless carried out of it," Elizabeth wrote to Julia. "One little fall neglected and thought of no consequence, now not to be remedied by the multiplied attentions of warm baths, alkalis . . . she is often in great pain but goes on at her perpetual delight the piano and says very gaily 'Oh this leg it will carry me to heaven.'" Mary Post wanted Rebecca to come to New York for treatment, but Elizabeth didn't think the child could bear the journey. She sent her daughter to Dr. Chatard in Baltimore, who said that the pain would lessen, but Rebecca would be permanently crippled.

Along with her concern for her children, she kept close watch on other people's children. She wrote to Archbishop Carroll that the guardian of Fanny Wheeler was so late in paying her tuition that he might have to be sued. Carroll had sent two young cousins, the Nelson sisters, to Elizabeth's academy; she reported to him that Ann found the school rules "extremely hard" and that Lotte was "wishing openly that she nor Ann had never entered the house." She told Robert Harper that his daughter Mary was so unruly that once she'd been given only bread and water at dinner. Elizabeth lamented Mary's "little proud heart which becomes really insupportable to her Teachers . . . she revolts openly and refuses all subjection, threatens to kill herself, declares she never will behave in so vile and bad a house . . . write her a few lines—that I have been obliged to complain to you of her bad example and the necessity of excluding her if she does not amend."

On August 28, 1814, Elizabeth turned forty. That year, Sisters of Charity left Emmitsburg for their first ministry outside the motherhouse.

The managers of an orphanage in Philadelphia, St. Joseph's Asylum, asked for three Sisters to come and take care of the children there. The women's salaries would total only six hundred dollars a year, but Elizabeth and her council met and discussed it: They "Unanimously agreed that no personal inconvenience should prevent Sisters of Charity from doing what duty and charity required."

Rose White was selected to be in charge. Once she had been prepared to take over as head of the community; now she felt herself so unworthy that she wrote to Archbishop Carroll, "I am as one stupid and all surprised; I know nothing, and can see nothing but my ignorance and weakness, which is ever before me . . . I know nothing but sin, and an unhappy disposition of impatience, which has caused myself and others much pain in this blessed family where I have often rendered myself an unworthy member of it."

That abject letter reflected Elizabeth's own rigorous concept of sin that dated back to her days as a Protestant. The lesson about the pervasiveness of sin was so ingrained that in the lazaretto, when Anna was eight, the child had thought "that God will call me soon and take me from this world where I am always offending him." Elizabeth's Catholicism, influenced by the Sulpicians, had reinforced that dark theology. In one of her reflections, she wrote, "Concieved in Sin—brought forth by *pain*—nursed by *misery*—consumed by *cares*—persuaded by *want*—carried off by *Death*—buried in *hell*." She underlined the word "hell" three times. When a Sister did not approach Communion one morning, Elizabeth asked why not. The

Sister replied that because she'd felt a little weak, she'd broken the prescribed fast before Communion and had taken a cup of coffee. "Ah, my dear child," Elizabeth said coldly, "how could you sell your God for a miserable cup of coffee?" In a letter to William in Italy, Elizabeth wrote, "You have been consecrated to God by me and I have never ceased to beg him to take you from this World rather than you should offend him." In another letter, she asked him to tell her how often he had gone to confession. Beginning in Emmitsburg, weekly confession was a rule Elizabeth laid down for her children—even Rebecca, who was then seven years old. The fear of sinning was so scrupulously embedded that Kit asked her mother whether biting the fingers and biting the nails was all the same sin.

Yet this looming sense of sin was leavened by the belief that repentance could bring forgiveness and mercy. Elizabeth lived with primary contradictions: God is an unrelenting judge, and, as the Epistle of John said, "God is love."

The Sisters set out for Philadelphia on September 29. They traveled light. "One trunk contained all our baggage," Rose wrote in her journal. And they traveled frugally, begging hospitality at the homes of Catholic families who would receive them kindly. When they reached Philadelphia, they immediately got lost. As they moved through the streets, the carriage driver would often ask them to hold the reins while he went to a house to get directions. No one could tell him the way, and it made him cross. "You might as well ask a pig about a holy day as to ask those people where St. Joseph's Asylum is."

The orphanage was five thousand dollars in debt. Children were lying three to four in one bed. The women were able to find separate beds for them, but their strict budget meant breakfasts of weak coffee made of corn, and dry bread. "We lived mostly on potatoes," Rose wrote, "and our fires were mostly of tar from the tar yard." One day there was only twelve and one-half cents left, just enough to buy a shin of beef at the market. As word of the Sisters' work spread, an old woman who kept a butcher's stall began sending meat; others left barrels of flour at the kitchen door, piles of greens and vegetables on the kitchen table.

What they could not accept was finer clothing. When a man saw them wearing thick, heavy flannel, he sent five gold pieces to one of the women who were helping to manage the place, to have gowns of bombazette★ made up for them. "We told her it would never be accepted by us," Rose wrote. From Emmitsburg, Elizabeth sent a note of thanks, confirming that their simple black gown with short black cape could not be altered. The white cap had changed to black, which led people to call the Sisters "black caps."

Snow fell thick and heavy on New Year's Day. Elizabeth trudged through deep drifts to St. Joseph's Church in the village, where Bruté was preaching. She stopped along the way to pick up a woman she knew, who needed help walking. Charlotte Melmoth was an actress who had decided to lead a penitential life. She'd followed Elizabeth to Emmitsburg, had made the first retreat with the Sisters, and now lived in the village. She clutched Elizabeth's hand all the way, as she kept murmuring broken thanks.

At recreation, Elizabeth wrote to him about his sermon that morning. "You take such a *hard* countenance when preaching of late G—not only when a son of thunder as to day, but as the angel of peace *last week*. What is the reason?—I wanted you to call the past year more to account and the threatnings of the *present*." Giving a critique of a sermon came easily to Elizabeth, who had been so attracted to Henry Hobart's eloquent preaching. When John Hickey, a newly ordained young priest, the first American to be educated for the priesthood at the seminary in Baltimore, gave a sermon that Elizabeth considered lazy, she confronted him. When he replied, "I did not trouble myself much about it Mam," she scolded. "O Sir that awakens my anger do you remember a priest holds the honor of God on his lips do you not trouble you to spread his fire he wishes so much en-

---

★ A thin plain or twill woven worsted cloth with a smooth finish.

kindled, if you will not study and prepare while you are young, what when you are old—there is a Mother's lesson."

Dr. Philip Syng Physick had studied in London with William Hunter, who had been Elizabeth's father's anatomy teacher. Now established in Philadelphia, Dr. Physick specialized in new methods of treating hip-joint diseases and was the first physician to prefer manipulation to traction. When a large, soft tumor developed on Rebecca's hip, Julia Scott insisted on taking her to see him. Elizabeth agreed that her daughter see the doctor but wanted her to stay with the Sisters at the orphanage, not with Julia. She worried that her friend's luxurious lifestyle might tempt the child away from the plain life at the convent. "Since we can have but a short life, let it be a merry one," Julia had once written to Elizabeth. "Dancing is the order of the day."

Elizabeth watched the carriage as it drove off. When it was hidden by dense woods, she went to the chapel, where she was interrupted by a Sister: "Mrs. Scott asks for you." Julia was standing in the hall, her coach-and-four ready to take Rebecca to Philadelphia. The women who had been best friends since they were young in New York, who remained best friends in spite of their opposite views on religion, who had not seen one another in eight years, who would never see one another again, were together for one hour.

"We hear Peace is declared," Elizabeth wrote to William. But even though the War of 1812 was over, normal trade on the sea had not resumed; Elizabeth's letter to the Filicchis, about William's coming, was delayed. When the young man arrived in Leghorn without notice, Antonio and his family were out of town, so William went to Filippo Filicchi, who sent Elizabeth a gently reprimanding letter. He said he had "almost a mind to scold you for having sent here your son without previous leave; but as that proves that you have had a great confidence in our goodness, I will not say anything, lest you should appeal from my sentence and that I should be condemned to give you thanks in lieu of reproaches . . . it will depend on him to get forward."

Because he had a nephew living with him, Filippo said, and because he had become "so fond of quiet and ease that the least trouble vexes me," he could not invite William to live with him; the young man would board with one of the Filicchis' clerks. He assured her that if William had "a mind to improve himself, if he renders himself capable of what I must do myself now, if he becomes useful, he will not have occasion to regret your resolution of sending him here. I hope he will, for he seems of a very good disposition and of model behavior. If he walks straight in the way shown to him, if he possesses . . . the principles of Christian morals in which he has been educated, you need not be anxious for him."

Elizabeth, of course, *was* anxious. She traced her son's European travels, from Bordeaux to Marseilles to Genoa to Pisa to Leghorn, on a globe that she studied in her room, by lamplight. She kept a basket of wood chips in her room, so that at night she could make a small fire to warm her fingers as she bombarded him with letters, sometimes three in one week. Bec and Kit often wrote notes to their brother on the other side of the paper, to keep the letter light—postage was expensive, and it was paid by the recipient.

"I long so to know if your American heart bends to your duties with a good grace," Elizabeth wrote, "if you are industrious and determined to show your good sense and *fortitude* in the position your God has placed you . . . do write us—it is all you can now do for us." She often wept as she wrote, and made sure he knew. "My child my own and dearest William I hold the handkerchief with one hand while writing with the other for my eyes are as streams till I know all about your situation and reception . . . O my child what would I not give to hear from you." In a letter to Antonio about William, she confided, "Why I love him so much I cannot account."

She was anxious about Richard, too. He was restless and took little interest in his studies at Mount St. Mary's. "Richard like all young people drags his chain," she told William. "He wants to be busy and getting on." She let Richard go to Baltimore with a classmate; meanwhile she wrote to Luke Tiernan, a Baltimore businessman whose sons were students at the Mount, asking him to take on Richard as a clerk in his countinghouse. Tiernan could not offer immediate employment. When Richard wrote that he might take a job with Basil Elder, a grocer, Elizabeth reacted like the New York aristocrat she once was. "I cannot be but sorry if he really goes to Mr. Elder," she told William. "I know too it will vex you . . . he shall not go to Mr. Elder if I can help it." At least, she said, Mr. Elder was a wholesale, not a retail, grocer.

Elizabeth wrote to Rebecca, too, mixing advice—"be good and obediant," the word "obediant" underlined three times—with gossip. She told Rebecca about a new student who was "so spoilt—She is fat and healthy and strong enough, but thinks herself so weakly you would have laughed enough to see her she began to tell me 'Mrs. Seton if any body speaks the least word hard or loud to me I begin to faint, just so' (and she began throwing herself back shutting her eyes and trembling) 'and if I go to learn anything I get such a headach, and I can hardly ever get out of bed before twelve oclock'—she could not eat our cooking *she was sure* . . . though she looked a little mad at me the first day, began to take it easy—and this morning she walked in my room with an orange in her hand for my Acceptance."

Elizabeth made sure to sound cheerful with her children, but she was honest with Julia. "Dearest friend," she wrote, "I have an ulcer in my breast (ugly word) which stops not night or day, and it being a consequence of Inflammation on the Lungs *I must go* in the common course of things—yet as I have an uncommon constitution . . . it may pass, or linger a long while."

She was being separated from people she loved. When Simon Bruté returned from Europe, he was reassigned—not to China, where he longed to go as a missionary, but to be president of the college in Baltimore. That job would severely limit his time in Emmitsburg. Dubourg had been sent to New Orleans, as administrator of the Diocese of Louisiana. And John Carroll was dying.

"It is harder on me than you would imagine," she wrote to a friend. The archbishop had been her dear friend for ten years. He was pleased when she took the confirmation name Mary, and he always addressed her in writing as "Mrs. M. E. A. Seton." He had helped guide her into the Catholic Church. He had helped pay her sons' tuition at Georgetown. He had been disappointed when Elizabeth and her tiny band left Baltimore for Emmitsburg; he was seventy-four then, growing frail, not easily able to make the rough journey to the country. He had last seen Elizabeth in Emmitsburg three years earlier, in 1812, when he came to administer confirmation. But two months before he died, although he could barely hold a pen, he had sent her fifty dollars, a gift from a friend. He had guided the American Catholic Church from its earliest days, before the Revolution, when Catholicism was illegal in most of the colonies, to a verified place on the American landscape. Because he had always believed strongly in the compatibility of the Roman Catholic Church with democratic ideals, he was a model of Enlightenment Catholicism. When he died, that model died, too, to be replaced by the monarchical Roman model, not to be resurrected until the middle of the twentieth century.

By Christmastime, both Rebecca and Richard were back home. Bec seemed improved. Richard, still a child at heart, played ball with her over the head of Elizabeth's bed. Simon Bruté, who had studied medicine in France before becoming a priest, said that there were instances of recovery in her situation, although she was extremely weak. "Rebecca is *just so*," Elizabeth wrote to Julia, by the last mail of the year, "wild and lively . . . making me laugh continually about her Philadelphia jaunt, especially her little conversations and the pleasure she had with you . . . say bless you friend this 1816."

William wrote that Filippo Filicchi had died suddenly, after a brief illness; Mrs. Filicchi was still in shock. William had visited his father's grave, and had met many of the people that Elizabeth had known there. He'd had tea with the Hall family—Rev. Thomas Hall had presided at Will's burial. William's letter brought back those desperate days—Will trembling with sweating fevers, Elizabeth kneeling by the mattress where he lay, praying and crying for him. "Write me if you ever see the old captain at the Lazaretto who was so kind to us," she asked William, "and our old loving hearted Loué must be dead . . . and a gentleman who lodged in the same house with us in Pisa and carried your dearest Father [in his arms from] the carriage to the chair—and then to his bed offering to assist . . . remember me affectionately to the Hall family—they were very kind to me and dearest Nina."

In the early spring, the tumor on Rebecca's hip broke, which brought some relief. She slept better. "It has been constantly drying," Elizabeth told Julia. "It may perhaps disappear entirely." Bec began attending classes again, reading all the books she could lay hands on. And Richard finally got the job with Luke Tiernan.

Four Sisters had gone out from the house, their second mission beyond the Emmitsburg community. This time, they stayed close to home. At the Mount, John Dubois had not been satisfied with the domestic help there. Americans, he said, did not like to lower themselves: "They prefer to eat bread and water and even beg to putting themselves in service." As a loyal friend, Elizabeth offered him Sisters to take charge of linen and clothing, the infirmary, and overall expenses. John Tessier, Dubois's superior in Baltimore, did not approve of the arrangement. "The only reason you might have for asking to keep the Sisters with you is the impossibility of finding other domestiques to replace them," he wrote. "As long as the impossibility lasts, it is necessary that you keep them, but it is my intention that you do all in your power to replace them."

The Sisters were never replaced. The practice of having nuns do a priest's housework took hold and continued into the twentieth century, as religious orders multiplied. When the head of a religious community in Texas protested that their Superior was making them cook and do laundry and therefore they could not concentrate on teaching, the priest declared that as long as that woman was head of her community, he would not administer the sacraments to any of the Sisters.

At an ecclesiastical hearing, she was found guilty; the priest ordered her to step down. At Emmitsburg, Simon Bruté was so pleased when he saw "with what perfect order all the ornaments, the linens, the folds, all arranged," that he wrote a meditation for the women: "Oh bless them, bless their happy work." He drew a pen-and-ink sketch of the Sisters making beds, sweeping the floor.

In the weeks before Rebecca's death, she could not lie down because of the inflammation of her leg and pain in her hip, where it was thought that tuberculosis had settled. Ulcers on her leg turned black. She was fourteen, but so frail and thin that she looked much younger. Elizabeth cradled her in her arms, sang songs to her, told her stories, and did anything she could think of to pass the time. She wrote to Julia, asking her to send Rebecca a doll, apologizing for requesting "so expensive a thing," explaining that Rebecca had "a particular delight" in dolls. Then for a moment, the deeply spiritual Mother Seton was back in her own childhood, a motherless little girl again. "I am extremely fond of them myself."

Bec's dying was dreadful, like Anna's, but much of the time calmer. When Rebecca asked, "Mother do I grow stronger or weaker?" Elizabeth spoke honestly. "Why my love *weaker* since your pain in side, sore breast and cough." "Well then," the child said, "I go to the land of the living sometimes how I long for it then again I lose sight of it." She told a joke about a country schoolmaster who asked a student, "What state do you live in my son?" And the boy replied, "In a state of sin and misery." "We too laughed like fools at the state we were in," Elizabeth wrote.

By September, Elizabeth needed the help of two Sisters to hold Bec as she quivered and shrieked with the tearing pains. Once, she writhed herself out of their hands till her lame knee touched the floor. Sweating and panting, she stared at them. "I am almost tempted to beg our Lord to ease me, *do you think that will displease him?*" Elizabeth made the sign of the cross over her—eyes, ears, and mouth—and pressed a little crucifix to her lips. "I think our Lord sent these sufferings for neglecting my little practices of piety," Rebecca said. She asked to go to confession. "I do try to be very sorry for all my sins." This child, who had lived in a convent since she was seven, was weighed down with the thought of sin. "If doctor . . . could say Rebecca you will get well I would not wish it—Oh no my dear Saviour I am convinced of the happiness of an early Death and to sin no more." She wrapped her arms tightly around Elizabeth. "There is the point, my Mother—I shall sin no more."

Near the end, "she is the liveliest little soul in her worst pains," Elizabeth wrote in her journal. When Bec saw Kit crying, she said playfully, "You may depend on it Kit if I do not pray you up when I get there it will be only in pity to dear Mother that she may not be quite alone." When she was offered paregoric to ease the pain, she was cheerful. "May be I shall get away in my sleep if I take it, so I will bid you all good bye, give my love to everybody." She told her mother that she hoped to live until Christmas, but she died in Elizabeth's arms on November 3, 1816. Rebecca Mary Seton was buried under the old oak, next to her sister.

Anna's death had shattered Elizabeth. But in the four years since, she had so grown in her spiritual life that she could now again focus on eternity. From the window in her room, she told Julia, she could look "direct on the little woods where my darlings sleep—it keeps up my heart to look over twenty times a day first thing in the morning and last at night, and think no more pain now—and up up up the beautiful joyous Souls." Early in the new year, she told Eliza Sadler, "I am well *and at Peace*."

John Connolly, a Dominican priest who had been named bishop of New York, knew of the Sisters in Philadelphia and wanted Elizabeth to send some to his city, to set up an orphanage. Three Catholic men in New York were behind the move: Robert Fox, whose three daughters were her students; Francis Cooper, the first Catholic elected to the state legislature; and Cornelius Heeney, Cooper's friend, who owned a fur shop on Water Street. The bishop wrote to Elizabeth. "I sincerely wish it may be in your power to immediately grant the laudable request of the said gentlemen, as the object of it would be productive of a great deal of good here."

Elizabeth was pleased at the idea of having her Sisters established in New York, but she felt that Sister Margaret George, whom the New Yorkers asked for, was too inexperienced to head the new mission.

Margaret Farrell George was "petite, graceful and charming, fluent in French, trained in bookkeeping and music," a description that fitted Elizabeth, except for the bookkeeping. Margaret had grown up in the Fells Point section of Baltimore. When she married Lucas George, a classics professor at Mount St. Mary's College, Dubourg presided at their wedding. They had been married for less than a year when Lucas was killed in a wrestling match with a young man from the college.

Margaret joined the community in 1812 and became a close friend to Elizabeth. After Elizabeth's death, Margaret was serving in Cincinnati as manager of a large orphanage and school. Known as hardworking and generous, "she rose at three o'clock in the morning to build the fires and have the rooms comfortable for the sisters . . . her cap was generally on one side, and her habit awry." When the Sisters were ordered to return to Emmitsburg as Daughters of Charity, their archbishop, John Purcell, like John Hughes in New York, wanted them to stay. Margaret stayed and became the Mother Superior of a new order, the Sisters of Charity of Cincinnati. Later she told Robert Seton, Elizabeth's grandson, that a strong factor in her decision was her loyalty to Elizabeth.

Elizabeth and Dubois wanted Rose White, who was doing such good work in Philadelphia, to take the new assignment. "I write her earnestly about New York," Elizabeth told Bruté. "The desire of my heart and soul for her going to New York has been long pressing for so much must depend, as says the good gentlemen who write about it, on who is sent to my 'native city' they say, not knowing that I am a citizen of the world." On behalf of the community, John Dubois wrote to Bishop Connolly, setting out the terms for the women's coming: that the management of the money be left in the hands of the trustees of the asylum, that an association of ladies be formed "with whom the Sisters will keep a freer intercourse than with the gentlemen," that the trustees allow thirty-six dollars a year for each Sister's clothing and other expenses, that traveling expenses to New York be paid, and that the head Sister be consulted when orphans were removed or admitted. In August 1817, Robert Fox came to Emmitsburg to escort the women on the seven-day trip to New York.

The house that had been bought for them, at Prince and Mott streets, was a disaster. The dilapidated frame structure, with entrance two steps below the street, had been used as a military hospital in the Revolutionary War and was known as "the Dead House." Darkened bloodstains covered the floor. The condition of the house, and the many hardships to be faced, brought into clear relief the question often asked about a woman who leaves all worldly comforts and joys behind to become a nun.

Why would a woman do such a thing? Is she running away from the world? People who take one look at what nuns do, from working—sometimes living—with the poor to running clinics for people with AIDS to sheltering abused women to going to prison for antiwar protests, know better. To say that a woman who makes this choice acts from deep faith, from the conviction that by devoting herself to the service of the people of God she is living a life of fulfillment and grace, is true, but too easy. There is no satisfactory answer, any more than there was when people had questioned Elizabeth's becoming a Catholic. As a modern writer says: "It is a mystery of the human spirit that cannot be completely explained or understood."

Until their house could be made habitable, the women stayed at the home of Elizabeth and Robert Fox. Elizabeth wrote to Mrs. Fox at once. "You receive three beings most dear to me in our God, in his name you will I know do all for them . . . remember your promise to think of me sometimes before God as I often do of you."

There was one orphanage already in New York, founded by Joanna Bethune, who had worked with Elizabeth in the Society for the
Relief of Poor Widows with Small Children, twenty years earlier.
The Sisters would staff the first Catholic orphanage for children who
had usually been sent to the almshouse on Chambers Street, which
housed criminals, the diseased, and the insane. When their house was
opened, they immediately took in five orphans, all boys. The Sisters
met older women who knew Elizabeth as the wife of Will Seton,
who had been a business associate of their husbands. Pierre Toussaint,
a black man who attended Mass at St. Peter's at six o'clock every morning, collected money for the nuns. Toussaint had come to America
from San Domingo as a slave. Now freed, he was a skilled hairstylist
who went to women's homes to do his work. Early on, he established
the reputation that would eventually apply to men and women who
work in beauty shops everywhere. "He was not only a meticulous
hairdresser, but a trusted friend and confidant, who mingled daily
with the great, yet never betrayed a secret."

With her sisters gone, and her brothers away, Catherine clung to her
mother. "Kit keeps so close to me it would really amuse you," Elizabeth wrote to Julia. "She is as it were jealous of my very writing or
any thing else that takes my mind from her." But Kit had the hacking
cough that worried her mother, so that when Mrs. Chatard suggested
that Kit come to Baltimore for a visit, Elizabeth agreed.

Kit did not. "Here is air exercise fresh milk every thing," she protested to Elizabeth, "and *My Mother* more than every thing how can I
leave you."

Elizabeth won. With her visit to Baltimore, Kit began a series of
trips away from home. When she visited Julia Scott in Philadelphia,
she was dazzled by the glitter. Invited to a military ball honoring
George Washington's birthday, however, she declined, because it was
the penitential season of Lent, and she thought her mother would not
want her to go. "But they persuaded me to go to the Washington Hall
to look at the decorations, which were splendid," Kit wrote. "We

were separate from the company that attended the ball. I saw two or three cotillions danced and came away. All was like a fairy scene to me. Such a collection of beauty and dress astonished me. I hope I was not wrong to go." She added that Mrs. Scott had dressed her with "a good many curls, a white velvet bonnet and a silk dress. She has procured me rather a stylish one, from material called poplin, but I will only wear it in company."

Kit liked the social climate of city life so much that she wanted to go further. As much as Elizabeth longed to have her daughter with her, she did not want to deprive her of a look at the wider world. "I can see plainly my Kit wishes much to go to New York, as I should in her place," Elizabeth wrote to Julia. "Perhaps the journey may be of use to her . . . I can only leave the whole decision respecting the affair to you . . . whatever is done I shall be contented."

When Julia said that Kit should go, Elizabeth gave her daughter a little red book with words of advice, much as she had done with William, only shorter; she was more sure of Kit's behaving well, and staying faithful to the Church, than she had been of her son. She set out a series of warnings. On gossip: "You can never be bound, my love, to speak on any occasion, or on any subject, unless you are sure of doing good by speaking." On avoiding talk of marriage: "Remember, darling, the uncertainty of life and how much you, in the motives I have told you before, should guard the purity of your heart." On dress: "Be sure that simplicity should be your only rule. It makes a lovely woman more lovely, and even an ugly one pleasing."

Kit had left New York, with her mother and her sisters, when she was eight years old. Now, at seventeen, she was entering a new aristocratic world, a world of luxury and fashion, where she was the center of attention. She had never known the warmth and excitement of a large family; even relatives who'd had no use for Elizabeth when she became a Catholic were kind to her daughter. Aunt Mary Post, Eliza Sadler, and Dué all wanted her to stay with them. She visited the widow of John Wilkes, the friend who had supported Elizabeth in those last troubled years in the city. She met John Henry Hobart, now a bishop, who seemed very glad to see her. She did not remember much of New York, but was so thrilled about being there now that she wanted to stay as long as possible.

In Elizabeth's valley, silent and secluded, where she was "Mother Seton," the strict supervisor of a houseful of women and girls, where she was calling herself "an old broken bit of furniture, enough to frighten the crows away," letters from Kit brought back the young, vivacious Betsey Bayley.

She had attended the Park Theatre, with its glass chandelier and red-cushioned box seats. She had thrilled to the first home of her own, on Wall Street, just down the block from Alexander Hamilton. She had played the piano, with Will at his violin, in their cozy parlor. She had strolled along Broadway, with its elegant shops, its bookstalls and flower stalls. She had danced with Will at George Washington's sixty-fifth birthday ball, wearing cream silk slippers, monogrammed.

TWELVE

·❦·

Mountain laurel swaying in summer storms. Black caps moving
purposefully through the house. Lilacs and white violets col-
oring the garden. Cats asleep in the sunshine. Gingerbread spicing
the kitchen air. Peace. "We talk now all day long of my Death and
how it will be Just like the rest of the housework."

William was as unhappy at the Filicchi firm as the Filicchis were unhappy with him. He didn't like the town, calling it "so so . . . the more
I see of Europe, the more I love America."

Antonio wrote to Elizabeth, saying that after watching her son
closely, he had concluded that William had "a moral indifference, if
not aversion, to trade in general." The young man had not tried to
adjust to Italian life; he preferred being with the Americans in Leghorn and still had his heart set on going to sea. When Antonio added
that William was unsuitable for commerce because of his bad handwriting, Elizabeth proved herself to be as protective, insecure, and
guilt-ridden as any mother anywhere, anytime: She blamed herself,
lamenting that when William was an infant, she had allowed him to
suck his fingers, which had made them weak.

William's return coincided with the ending of Richard's job at the

Baltimore countinghouse—Luke Tiernan was forming a partnership with his son. Richard had spent all the money he'd been given for his stay in Baltimore, including the money from Julia Scott and even from his sister, who'd given him what she'd earned from teaching piano to the girls at St. Joseph's. Bruté said that Richard had "a good heart, yet turned to pride and selfishness." And the young man reflected the racial attitude still prevalent in Maryland, where nearly one-third of the population were slaves. When Richard sent some crosses and medals from Baltimore to John Hickey at the Mount, he stipulated that they were "for your people, I mean blacks, for they are too ugly for any white man."

Again, Antonio proved his devoted friendship: he offered to take Richard in William's place, if Richard had "a good will and good handwriting." Elizabeth was relieved. Although Richard "took little interest in young women," she hoped that after an apprenticeship in Leghorn, he might be inclined to marry and settle down. "I have two little Harpers with me who are really like a part of ourselves, I often look with a loving eye on the eldest and think while her beautiful mind is daily unfolded by me that perhaps I am doing it for you."

She arranged for him to go to Italy at once, carrying a letter to Antonio. "Here is my Richard . . . your sending for him is a singular Providence . . . Richard's disposition is quite different from Williams if he does not fall into bad company I am sure he will do well, for all the turn of his mind is for business and activity, but with his quick temper and want of experience, he is in considerable dangers which his Brother escapes . . . we find William so improved, and with such excellent dispositions that we can have no uneasiness for him, he has set his heart on the sea life, and I can now put no more obstacles but trust it all to God."

Just as Elizabeth had admitted her sons' lack of brilliance, she admitted her "excessive indulgence" to them. "All I can say is, *that you will never want every nerve of my heart to exert itself for you in whatever path you enter,*" she wrote to William. "What more can your own Mother say, I would write, or even go to any one on earth I could reach, if I might help you." When she realized that the only way to help him was to get him a navy appointment, she began a letter-writing campaign, starting with Robert Fox in New York. Fox said he would ask Daniel Tompkins, the vice president of the United States, and John Quincy Adams, the secretary of state, for letters of recommendation. Very soon, William's name was moved to the head of a 1,400-man waiting list. In January 1818, he got his appointment to the United States Navy and was assigned to the *Independence,* out of Boston.

Almost immediately, he asked Elizabeth to help arrange a transfer. He preferred the *Macedonian,* a ship scheduled to make a two-year cruise around Cape Horn, with visits to all the western ports of North and South America. And he asked for money. The grocer was reminding her of unpaid bills, but when it was "My own Beloved" asking, Elizabeth could not refuse. "I write Mr. Barry pressingly to send you speedily as possible the 100, and if I am so happy as to get it, surely it will be your own, and not for return . . . I pray and trust that he will advance it, there is not so high as a 5 d[ollar] bill in the house . . . but cannot think Mr. Barry will hesitate, if *he* does I will surely get it *some where.*"

In August, William transferred to the *Macedonian,* which was to set off for the Pacific in October or November. There would be time, he wrote to his mother, for him to visit her before the sailing. Elizabeth immediately wrote to Bishop Cheverus, asking him not to tell William how sick she was.

She was very sick.

Her dark brown eyes were still luminous, but she was pale and thin, almost transparently fragile. Her feet were swollen—she could barely manage to walk to the chapel, so close to her room that when she left her door open, she could see the altar. An abscess in her breast was inflamed, and the doctor prescribed bloodletting, an ancient medical practice dating back to Hippocrates and used for conditions as varied as inflammation, pain, epilepsy, pneumonia, syphilis, and insanity. George Washington had been bled for a throat infection. Sometimes bloodletting meant the application of leeches. Sometimes it was cupping, which involved placing a heated glass cup on the skin, allowing it to cool so that a partial vacuum was formed; when the glass was pulled from the skin, the area would bleed. A more invasive technique made cuts in the skin, catching the blood in a bowl. In this early part of the nineteenth century, the procedure was beginning to be abandoned as not just useless but harmful, but not soon enough for Elizabeth. She was bled in both arms, which were then thickly bandaged.

Pierre Babade, her first priest friend and spiritual adviser in Baltimore, wrote to her, consoling yet straightforward. "Ten years are past; your work is consolidated . . . I would like very much to see you before you die, but I foresee that the Superior will not allow me to go to Emmitsburg . . . as soon as I hear of your death I will say Mass for the repose of your dear soul, as I have prayed during your sickness that you may have a happy death."

Julia Scott begged her to come to Philadelphia. Her sister urged New York. When Mary and her husband had made a second visit to Emmitsburg, after Bec died, Mary had been so taken with Elizabeth's way of life that she had written, "My dearest Sister, with all the difficulties & trials your life has been attended with, I still think you are blessed beyond the usual lot of mortals. I believe in a presiding providence, and that you have always been its peculiar care is to me most certain." But Elizabeth declined all loving offers. "I know your uneasiness for me," she wrote to Ellen Wiseman, who had been one of her students. "But that should not be . . . why uneasy at the fulfillment of the merciful designs of so dear a Providence that left me to take care of my *Bec,* to bring Jos★ to an age to take care of herself, and our dearest boys to enter the way of life they were to choose. St. Joseph's House well established wants not even my *Nominal* care." Still, knowing how deeply concerned everyone was, she added, "Yet my complaint may change." Either way, Elizabeth was determined to stay with her beloved community, although she was so indulged—buttered

---

★ Catherine's confirmation name was Josephine.

bread with sugar, currants and strawberries, a glass of port wine every day—that she worried it might be a source of scandal to her Sisters.

She yearned for her daughter to come home. Kit had left New York, but now she was visiting at Carrolton Manor, near Baltimore. She was having a grand time, she wrote. She had played the piano for guests; she was taking long walks in the fields. While Elizabeth was pleased at the welcome reception for Kit, she wrote her a pathetic letter. "My own little Darling . . . I do wish you so much to be again with your poor Mother at least for this summer . . . you will be able to return to New York . . . it will be better for you to go again next winter (we will not mind the expence) in comparison with being again together this summer . . . dearest child you know something of eternity Pity me—and never never be a Mother." Four days later, as though to reassure herself that asking Kit to come home was not selfish, she wrote to William, telling him what she had told his sister. "You must not blame your own Mother She can have here the best of summer produce which I will get on purpose for her . . . and in October or November there will be opportunities from New York again with which she can easily return . . . and to tell you all my weakness my William I cannot command myself to care for my poor life while you are all away . . . every thing around me wears the gloom of my own heart—look to it all, and you will excuse me though I should be ashamed to own it."

Word went around about Elizabeth's condition. "Perhaps you have conceived your situation more critical than it really is," her brother-in-law Wright Post wrote. "It may yet please God to restore you to that usefulness which has always marked the sphere in which you moved. That this may be his Will is my most fervent prayer."

Antonio Filicchi wrote. "Be perfectly at ease in the steadiness of my friendship . . . you are constantly in my mind."

Samuel Cooper, to whom Elizabeth had been attracted and who had donated the valley property, was ordained a priest in the summer of 1818. He was assigned to St. Joseph's Church in the town of

Emmitsburg and lived with Thomas Radford, a cobbler who was a parishioner at the church. Cooper came with a fiery zeal for turning people away from sin, and he thought he saw plenty of opportunity in a place where getting drunk was a popular pastime. Ott's Tavern, at the end of the narrow dirt road leading from St. Joseph's to the town, was one of four principal taverns. Seven or eight "tippling shops" were scattered around, under the sign LIQUORS AND FRUITS. Grocery stores and dry goods stores sold drams and whiskey.

Cooper himself had indulged in episodes of excessive drinking; now, with the zeal of a reformer, he decided to tackle the problem of drunkenness, which he said was "bringing disgrace on the Catholic Church," in a dramatic way. He asked Ambrose Marechal, the new archbishop of Baltimore, for permission to impose public penance. The archbishop referred the matter to John Dubois, who said that the plan seemed unwise. But Dubois did not forbid it, so on Palm Sunday 1819, when the church was filled, Cooper announced to his congregation that all those who were drunk in public would have to kneel or stand, or sit in a particular place in the church, while their names were read aloud from the pulpit.

The plan was not welcomed. Thomas Radford stalked out of the church. When Cooper then barred him from attending church at all, other parishioners protested so loudly that Cooper wrote to the archbishop: "I shall not continue in this congregation, and on Sunday last, I gave notice to the people that I should no longer be their Pastor." Bruté told Elizabeth, "Maybe providence and better—let him go."

William had proudly described his ship, the *Macedonian,* as "a most beautiful frigate, pierced for fifty (carrying forty-eight) guns, more completely and handsomely fitted out than any other ship that ever sailed." The ship left Boston in September, bound for Valparaiso, Chile. But one night, off the coast of Virginia, it was struck by a howling storm. William was asleep, dreaming that Elizabeth, dressed in white, was standing by him, asking sadly, "Are you prepared?" He jumped from his hammock into water up to his knees. The ship had to put in to Norfolk for repairs. When his request for leave was granted, he hurried to Emmitsburg.

William's visit so revitalized Elizabeth that by the early summer of 1819 her "complaint" had indeed changed. "I am so much better," she wrote to John Hickey, "cannot die one way it seems, so I try to DIE the other, and keep the straight path to GOD ALONE the little daily lesson to keep soberly and quietly in his presence, trying to turn every little action on his will, and to praise and love through cloud or sun shine, is all my care and study—*Sam*★ offers his battles from time to time, but our beloved stands behind the wall and keeps the wretch at his distance." She knew that tuberculosis would overtake her, but not yet, as she wrote to a friend. "I am sick, but not dying, troubled on every side, but not distressed; perplexed, but not despairing; afflicted, but not forsaken; cast down, but not destroyed; knowing the affliction of this life is but for a moment, while the glory in the life to come will be eternal."

The closer Elizabeth came to death, the closer she came to a spirituality that encompassed and reached to her core. Her spirituality was liberating, freeing her from the fear of death, which she called "this dear dearest thief who will come when least expected." Her spirituality was organic, an integrating dynamic in her life, based on unqualified trust in her God. Spirituality was her way of being in the world, a contemplative presence in the midst of everything that went on. Contrary to the assumption that people are human beings who may, from time to time, have a spiritual experience, she believed that people who are created by God and destined to go home to God are therefore spiritual beings having human experiences on earth. And so everything human is connected with the spiritual, including dealing with selfish children, money problems, and the despair that assailed Christ, who, as a human being, cried out from the cross, "My God, My God, why have you forsaken me?"

For Elizabeth, spirituality meant letting go—not only of life but

---

★ The devil.

of decisions, wishes, opinions. She lived as Bruté had counseled, by "the grace of the moment." Her inclusive spirituality meant coherent involvement in the world. When Kit was in Philadelphia, she had written to her mother, "Mrs. Scott says I am so extremely like you, only I do not laugh as much as you once did."

"I am laughing with God," Elizabeth said in her Italian journal. In the years since, she had come to know the peace that underlies laughter, the peace that comes from finding God everywhere, in everything, in everyone. As Gandhi would one day put it: "If you don't see God in the next person you meet, it's a waste of time to look further."

When it came time for the annual renewal of vows, Elizabeth was again elected the head of the thriving community. Nearly one hundred people, Sisters and students, lived at St. Joseph's House, and a new school building was planned. Elizabeth spent most of her time in her room; when she had to stop meeting everyone who came to the house, she told Julia wryly that it was "a loss I am quite willing to bear." She was no longer able to teach, but she continued to monitor the girls' progress and conduct. She wrote to Robert Harper that his daughter Elizabeth had drawn a map of England "quite correctly" on the blackboard, but that he would be "disappointed in her Musical Talent . . . she seems to forget from day to day what she learns." And she kept her edge: To John Hickey, who had written her just three lines on a whole sheet of paper, she replied, "Some politics of Eternity, I suppose. So with all due respect I will say also as little as possible."

She often wrote to Sister Cecilia O'Conway in New York with down-home news of St. Joseph's. She gave Cecilia the account of Sister Mary Elizabeth, who was so near death that she was anointed. When Dubois said to her, "Do you my dear child ask pardon of all your dear Sisters?" she interrupted him with a loud voice. "I asked their pardon *before I came from home.*"

"But my dear child, I mean your dear Sisters here around you, if you have given them any bad example, do you ask pardon?"

The nun looked around the room. "Oh, to be sure, *if I have*."

The priest then asked if she forgave her enemies. Mary Elizabeth was deaf; she shouted her reply. "I have not an enemy in the world that I know of!"

As another icy winter came to the valley, the mountains huddled under a slate sky. When Dubois came to say Mass, passing under pine branches rimmed with snow, his hair and his beard were often stiff with frost, his hands so cold and rigid that he could barely hold the reins of his horse.

On New Year's Day 1820, Elizabeth was strong enough to write to Robert Harper, greeting him and his wife "with every heart felt good wish of the Season," adding that their daughter Emily had called another girl "pig." As the winter wore on, and she seemed well enough, she kept writing.

She wrote to the parents of a new student, who had wanted to go home on her very first day at the school. "By little caresses and young companions she got over it so well that we have heard no more about it. Sweet child she has so affectionate a heart that I am sure she will soon love us—and you may be sure it will not be our fault if she does not."

She wrote to Eliza Sadler, who had gone off on another European jaunt. "I think I should have been a traveler too if I had had no Bairns to nail me."

She wrote to Julia, who wanted to have Kit come and live with her. Elizabeth did not tell Julia that she wanted her daughter to live with a Catholic family after her own death, but she explained how close they had become to the Harpers. "You know my own beloved friend I see all in the order of Providence . . . so put all together my Julia I think for the moment you need not be plagued with my darling, but her heart and soul with mine blesses and thanks you for the offer."

She wrote to Simon Bruté, who still had his heart set on going to China. "Again your restless thoughts strike me to the soul. You made the lesson of *the grace of the moment* so very plain to me . . . yet Physician you will not heal yourself . . . if God does indeed graciously destine you for China will he not seeing the overflowings of your boiling heart for it open an evident door."

She wrote to Antonio Filicchi. Her handwriting was getting shaky; it was a short letter, just half a sheet of paper. She talked of his wife, Amabilia, and his children; she told him that her room was next to the chapel, divided from it only by a partition. She said she went to sleep at night and wakened in the morning with a deep sense of the divine presence, for which "I try to make my very breathing a continual thanksgiving and no one can better understand my heart . . . than my dear Antonio who knows so well [what] I have been, and the long burning I deserve."

She kept up a stream of letters to her sons, and William wrote regularly. His uncle Wright Post had sent him fifty dollars, he said. A midshipman had died and was buried at sea, with fifes and drums, in a black coffin that sank into the ocean with such a hollow sound that it made William's heart sink, too. But at breakfast afterward, he joined a debate on how long it would take the dead man to reach the center of gravity. And he promised he'd be home in January. "I shall come like the prodigal son. I shall be ready for the newest fashions." To her former student, Elizabeth wrote more realistically: "*January* will come, my Ellen, but what it will bring he only knows who does all things well."

At first, Richard wrote, too. He had grown taller, he said, and was accustomed to enjoying a cigar and a little wine after dinner. He was working at the Filicchi countinghouse from nine thirty in the morning until seven in the evening. He was shipping a dozen urns for the churches at Mount St. Mary's and St. Joseph's in Emmitsburg and for the Sisters' chapel, and would send the bill, fifty-two dollars. He'd had his twentieth birthday. "Now that I'm growing older," he wrote, "I begin to think of the troubles you had on my account . . . my mother to whom I owe so much & to whom I have given so much pain—if you could feel the pleasure I did when you said your heart was at ease, and for me to think that I had soothed it, after so often, having planted in it the thorns of sorrow."

Then the letters stopped coming.

"My own love," Elizabeth wrote, "you can have no idea our anxiety to hear from you six, seven, eight months pass without one line . . . a thousand thousand blessings on you dearest only do write to a creature whose tears fall over you before God continually—I cannot think of you but my heart fills fearing something has happened [to] you."

Something *had* happened to Richard. He had been fired.

Antonio explained that Richard had not been willing or able to help in the countinghouse, and his moral conduct had not given full satisfaction either. Before Elizabeth received Antonio's letter, Richard was back. In a letter from Norfolk, Virginia, he told her he'd spent nearly all the $180 that Antonio had given him for his passage home. He was living in "a miserable place" where his rent took up most of the $30 he had left. Now he was in trouble over "a protested bill" in Alexandria.

Frantically, Elizabeth wrote to Robert Harper. "Who can I venture to address but you at this moment of real distress . . . it struck me he must be arrested . . . I thought you would have some friend in Alexandria who would kindly find out if he is there . . . Pardon this I cannot but be anxious." Richard sent a letter to Harper, too, a dishonest one. "To pretend, Sir, to give an account of my reasons for leaving Leghorn to you would be useless—suffice it to say that religious matters were the principal causes of it." Elizabeth never said whether Harper sent money, but she saw Richard one more time.

By late summer, construction had begun on the new brick building for the free school. In his enthusiasm, Dubois insisted that Elizabeth come out and see what progress the carpenters had made. Although the wind was sharp, he had her climb on a pile of boards to get a good look. She already had a fever; after the outdoor expedition, she was so much worse that Dubois came to anoint her.

On Sunday, September 24, two Sisters hurried to Emmitsburg to fetch Bruté. The priest was hearing a confession as a Sister knocked urgently on the door of the confessional: "Come, our Mother is dying." The priest grabbed the first horse at hand and rode to St. Joseph's in such a rush that on the road he passed the Sisters who had brought the message.

He found Elizabeth awake, serene, and, in his opinion, not about to die. He wrote that she was "so calm, so present, so recollected and wholly trusted to her blessed Lord; her eyes so expressive—the look that pierces heaven and the soul visible in it." He asked her to confess her sins, and she did, out loud. He asked her to renew her vows, and she did. Several Sisters, along with Kit, came to Elizabeth's room, and Bruté asked her, as the Mother of the community, to bless them. "Yes, I bless them and ask their prayers," Elizabeth said clearly. As he began the prayer "Depart Christian Soul," she fell asleep. Soon she was writing to Sister Elizabeth Boyle in Philadelphia, telling her all about it.

Betsy Boyle, one of the original members of the community, had been Elizabeth's assistant for six years; Elizabeth called her "dearest old partner of my cares and bearer of my burdens." Like Elizabeth, Betsy had become a Catholic against the violent objections of her family, especially her mother. Unlike Elizabeth, she had cried all the way from Baltimore to Emmitsburg, homesick already. Having grown up in a family with servants, she knew nothing about manual labor; at St. Joseph's, she was required to fetch water from the spring and to carry heavy buckets of mortar to workmen on the second floor of the house. "If the roads had not been so muddy," she liked to say, "I should have set out for Baltimore on foot."

But it had taken Elizabeth nearly a day to write that letter to Betsy Boyle, "blowing and puffing all the time." Five days later, she wrote to Robert Harper, telling him that his daughter Emily had "a singular talent for Geography, and it really [is] a pleasure to improve it." That letter of October 30, 1820, was the last dated letter she wrote.

In keeping with the religious vow of poverty, the mattresses in the house were thin and hard. Elizabeth needed hartshorn* to relieve the pain and help her sleep. When the Sisters brought in a featherbed,

---

* Ammonium carbonate, made from the antler of a hart, which had medicinal value.

Elizabeth burst into tears. She had not asked for it, she said, but it felt so much better that she feared the luxury of such comfort.

After that, Kit began writing letters for and about her mother. "My dear Mother is far from recovered," she wrote to Julia in November. "An abscess on her breast, as was the case two or three years ago, keeps her very, very weak. I have every hope that all will be well, though she may still for some time be kept suffering."

Cecilia O'Conway, who'd come back from New York, was one of Elizabeth's nurses. Cecilia had been the first young woman to join Elizabeth in Baltimore, one of the first little group that came to Emmitsburg more than ten years earlier to live in the old stone house where snow drifted through the roof onto the women sleeping on the floor. Cecilia still wanted to join a cloistered order, and later she did leave the community to join the Ursulines in Canada. Now she was spending much of her time with Elizabeth. One day, in her fervor, she asked Elizabeth whether she wanted a crucifix before her eyes, as Elizabeth had done for Anna. Elizabeth couldn't resist teasing: "No, dear . . . my eyes are generally closed." Cecilia was also a class mistress and had to make sure her students kept up with their studies. "Emmy," she said to Emily Harper, "you pain me enough, but my pain is for Mother when she calls for the books, what her disappointment and sorrow will be." She thus became one of the first nuns to instill in children an enduring sense of Catholic guilt.

Richard came back in December. Elizabeth was too sick to write about his visit. He did not stay for Christmas. William wrote that he would not be there in January, but sometime in the spring.

On the night that Bruté was so hastily summoned from the confessional, he sat by Elizabeth's bed and asked her for the names of people to whom he might write, thanking them for their affection and attention, when the time came. The list included Bishop Cheverus in Boston; Archbishop Marechal in Baltimore; Louis Sibourd, who once had been pastor at St. Peter's Church in New York; Benedict Flaget, who had brought the Rules of the Daughters of Charity from

France to the United States; John Hickey, whose sermon she had criti-cized; and William Dubourg, who was serving in New Orleans, since the Louisiana Purchase had doubled the size of the United States. When she came to John David—"obey in silence"—her voice broke. "Mr. David—to ask him pardon for all the pains I gave him."

Elizabeth signed her last will and testament on November 14, wit-nessed by Dr. Robert, the new physician at St. Joseph's, and Thomas Radford, who had stalked out of church when Cooper spoke.

She wrote that her sons could "with the assistance of God" and by their own prudence and exertions provide for themselves. "After grant-ing to my beloved boys William and Richard all the blessings which a most affectionate Mother can bestow and knowing that their broth-erly hearts will perfectly coincide with me in the distinction I make, I leave and bequeath unto my beloved Daughter Catherine Josephine all the real & personal property, either in my possession, or bequeathed or to be left to me, at the time of my decease, to her heirs and assigns for ever."

On the day after Christmas, Kit wrote to Julia: "If any change has taken place since you last heard from me, it is that my Mother is still weaker. The abscess discharges itself so slowly that she is reduced to almost a skeleton."

January 1, 1821: In the evening, Bruté found Elizabeth "extremely low." She asked for absolution. The priest repeated the words of Christ: "My peace I leave to you," and Elizabeth nodded.

January 2: Bruté came after Mass and found Elizabeth "like dy-ing." He said a petition that Elizabeth be granted heaven. Many Sisters came in. The priest had Elizabeth repeat the names Jesus, Mary, and Joseph. She joined in some prayers but seemed so fatigued that he stopped, asking her to pray for all. "Be sure," Elizabeth said. He told her that Dubois would come to anoint her again. "Very thank-ful," she said.

At one o'clock, Dubois came and anointed her. Bruté thought she looked easier, as though she were saying, "I feel a little better, whether for life or for death." Dubois summoned all the Sisters and said, "Mother, being too weak, gives me charge to recommend to you at this sacred moment in her place: first, to be united together as true Sisters of Charity; secondly, to stand firmly by your Rules; thirdly [to] ask your pardon for all the scandals she may have given you. I obey her desire. You know she gave none by the indulgences she was allowed. She means particularly in what she had to eat or other allowances for her situation, in which she did but follow my express prescriptions and those of the physician." As he began prayers, Elizabeth spoke in a faint voice. "I am thankful Sisters for your kindness to be present at this trial. Be children of the Church, be children of the Church." The Sisters were straining to hear, so Bruté repeated what Elizabeth had said. Both he and Dubois left then. Dubois returned at six o'clock and found Elizabeth the same as she had been in the morning.

January 3: The children in the house were preparing for their First Communion. When Bruté came to instruct them, he entered Elizabeth's room and asked her to pray for them. He told her what he would say to them, about the angels announcing to the shepherds the birth of Christ, about the Magi following the star. "God does more for us than we think or ask," he said to Elizabeth. "Ask and you shall receive. Ask Heaven, Mother!" When he had gone, Elizabeth asked Sister Xavier Clark, her assistant, whether the poor children at the school had enough for their dinner. Xavier said yes, with leftovers.

January 4: Sister Anastasia, Sister Susan, and Kit were sitting with Elizabeth. At one o'clock in the morning, Anastasia went to call Sister Xavier. "Come quickly. I think Mother is dying." When Xavier entered the room, Elizabeth said, "Well, Xavier, how do you do, dear?"

The Sisters had been told that Elizabeth suffered at the pit of her stomach. Xavier placed her hand there. "Nothing to be done," Elizabeth said. Xavier knelt at the side of the bed. Anastasia had promised Sister Cecilia that she would call her; Xavier told her to do that, but gently.

When Cecilia came, she brought Sisters Sally and Joanna with her.

"Dearest Mother, our Lord is going to take you to himself," Susan said. Cecilia thought she heard Elizabeth say, "I adore."

"Our dear Lord is going to take you to himself," Susan repeated. Kit began to cry loudly, convulsively, and was moved away from the bed. Elizabeth began the prayer, "May the most just, the most high, and the most amiable . . ." Susan finished for her: ". . . will of God be accomplished forever."

In their excitement and distress, no one had thought to call Dubois and Bruté. Then someone remembered, and asked Xavier whether they should be summoned. Xavier said yes. The Sisters left. It was close to two o'clock in the morning.

Knowing how much Elizabeth loved the French language, Xavier began to pray in French. Elizabeth seemed to smile. She was very tranquil. Kit was calmer now. Xavier said later that she felt the presence of Jesus more powerfully than she ever had.

The Sisters returned to say that Bruté was on his way. Elizabeth's breathing slowed. She did not gasp or struggle. Anastasia said that Elizabeth died very gently, "as to sleep." She was forty-six.

Elizabeth was buried in the little wood, next to her daughters. There was no epitaph for the woman who had been a Protestant, a Catholic, rich, poor, an aristocrat, an outcast, a wife, a mother (a *working* mother), a widow, a teacher, a social worker, a nurse, and the founder of the first order of active women religious in this country.

But there was a legacy.

Sometimes, when Sisters were talking at recreation, in a shady grove or on the bank of the stream that flowed by the house, they would speculate on the future of their order. "Here we are buried in the midst of woods and valleys," one lamented. "Nobody knows what we are doing, and truly the world forgets us."

Then a young Sister who had been listening in silence spoke playfully. "My dear children, don't grieve so much. Depend upon it, our valley, quiet as it is, will give such a roar one day that the noise will sound over all America."

EPILOGUE

E veryone in heaven, says the Catholic Church, is a saint. But the formal title, "Saint," is given to someone who lived a life of extraordinary holiness and is named in the canon, the Church's official list.

In the early Church, saint-making was easy. A person could be declared a saint by public acclamation: people knew a saint when they saw one, much as people view Mother Teresa today. A martyr—someone who had suffered a bloody death for God's sake—was automatically a saint. Then the mode of death spurred the symbols: St. Andrew with his X-shaped cross; St. Appolonia, whose teeth had been torn out, portrayed with a forceps gripping a tooth in her hands, clearly the patron saint of dentists.

In a Christian community struggling for a foothold in a pagan society, saints lived and died—mostly died—to edify the surviving population. Hagiography was often a collection of tall tales designed to make an inspirational point. Saints were admired for their endurance, their incredible feats, their record-breaking abilities. Did George slay the dragon? Did John get dumped into a kettle of boiling oil? Did Christopher ever live to ferry the Christ Child across the raging waters? Did Christopher ever live? Did it matter? Not when the moral was the message, as in the legend of St. Kevin, who stretched his arms out the window one morning to pray when lo! a blackbird nested in his arms. The bird stayed two, maybe three weeks, and Kevin waited, motionless, until the eggs hatched. "To the early Church, the lesson was patience, saintly patience," said a young theologian in Rome, at the time of Elizabeth's canonization. "For us, the lesson is, when you pray, don't stick your arms out the window."

The canonization process for Elizabeth followed, more or less, the formal procedure defined in 1634. An ecclesiastical court would examine the evidence, mostly writings, with a proponent of the cause and an adversary—a "devil's advocate"—sparring for years, usually decades. The first step was declaring the person "Venerable"—someone who had practiced the virtues of faith, hope, and charity to "an heroic degree." Next, she might be beatified—pronounced "Blessed"—before being canonized a Saint. Along with proof of profound virtue, miracles were needed: physical cures that could be credited to the intercession of the candidate for sainthood. Two miracles were required for beatification, two more for canonization.

The Decree of Introduction of the Seton Cause—the first Vatican document to be disseminated in English—was not issued by Rome until 1940, more than a century after Elizabeth's death, largely because of the bias against American Catholics within their own Church. Until 1908, the Vatican considered the United States to be "mission territory," and its Catholics prone to a heresy called "Americanism"—too pragmatic, too materialistic to be of saintly caliber. (The charge was squelched when it was decided that American Catholics were too anti-intellectual to be able to support such a sophisticated theological concept as a heresy.)

When Elizabeth died, Simon Bruté, who knew firsthand the depth of her holiness, told the Sisters, "Save everything." So the Church tribunal studying her cause was able to delve into her letters, hearing her tell Antonio that she deserved a long burning, hearing him say that for her he would fight men and devils. And had she attempted suicide, or just thought about it? What about her temper, her moodiness, her enthusiasm for Voltaire and Rousseau? "She had defects," acknowledged an Italian prelate who was involved in the proceedings. "We all have defects. But most of us treat our defects like guests at the dinner table. The saints try to put them out."

The process of investigating Elizabeth's writings took nearly twenty years. When all the writings had been studied and all the questions answered, or at least laid to rest, it was time for the miracles.

Of all the controversial aspects of a canonization—the time and money spent, the political considerations both inside and outside the Church—the requirement for miracles arouses the most debate. "To what extent is our asking for these jack-in-the-box signs the same kind of sin that Jesus condemned when he told the people, 'You're always asking for signs!'" said a young theologian in Rome. "The argument for Pope John XXIII is that he created such love around him, his whole life was a kind of miracle. Isn't it rather macabre now to ask him to start curing polio cases?" The counterargument came from a priest working for the Seton cause. "We don't want to force God's hand; we just want him to keep us from making a big mistake."

When word of the need for favors and miracles went out from Seton headquarters in Emmitsburg, tales of woe poured in, from gangrene to migraine, tumors, shingles, bones that wouldn't heal. Sometimes sick folks or their relatives just showed up in person at the Emmitsburg office. The Seton cause cut across class lines, reflecting the disparities in Elizabeth's own life: Somebody reported finding a job, another a suitable maid.

The first miracle attributed to Elizabeth's intercession involved, fittingly enough, a Sister of Charity. In New Orleans, a nun was found to have a cancerous tumor on the head of the pancreas, "as big as an orange," so matted to the surrounding organs that they just sewed her back up and waited for her to die. Some of the nuns prayed to Elizabeth; the Sister lived. When she died seven years later, of a pulmonary embolism, an autopsy showed a perfectly whole, normal, healthy pancreas, no sign of cancer.

At the Church tribunal, the interrogators asked every possible question, no matter how unlikely. Had the cancer shifted elsewhere? Had it disappeared, maybe, because when they cut her open, it was exposed to the air? Had the surgeon been coached how to answer? "If I had, I wouldn't be here," he snapped. "I'm not coachable." An Episcopalian psychiatrist was brought in. "Believing in mind over matter," he said, "I can perfectly well believe in miracles. A miracle is an unexplainable happening. I believe that saintly personalities have the power to accomplish things others cannot."

The case of a child diagnosed with acute lymphatic leukemia was harder to validate. The Daughter of Charity who took care of her in the hospital had placed her on the marble slab that covered Elizabeth's coffin, and prayed. The child recovered. For six years she'd been off all medication and had had bone-marrow tests done regularly. But had any of the drugs she'd been given, including a new one, aminopterin, caused a remarkably long remission? Had the violent case of chicken pox she'd had, concurrently, caused something good to happen? The hematologist who treated her, identifying himself as "a Jewish moderate," wouldn't say miracle. "I only know the behavior in this case is unique," he said, "and different from any I know of."

The Vatican accepted that cure as a miracle, too. Elizabeth was beatified in 1963, and immediately caused an argument between New York and Emmitsburg.

When Elizabeth died, she was buried in the little community cemetery at Emmitsburg. Her coffin was later placed under the marble slab in the chapel. Now that she was "Blessed," with sainthood looming, New York wanted her back. She'd been born in New York and had lived there most of her life. Her Sisters of Charity had begun a ministry there. New York wanted her interred in St. Patrick's Cathedral.

Emmitsburg wanted her to stay home. The exchanges between New York and Baltimore became so heated that the Vatican stepped in: She would stay in Emmitsburg. As in Elizabeth's lifetime, men decided where a woman belonged.

That year, 1963, was momentous, not only for Elizabeth but for the worldwide Catholic Church. The Second Vatican Council convened—the gathering of Church leaders that brought about earthshaking change. The Church was declared to be not just the pope and the bishops and the priests but "the whole people of God." Priests who had said Mass at the altar with their backs turned were now to face the people. The council decree that church services use the vernacular was at last the granting of the wish of Elizabeth's friend John Carroll that Latin be scrapped. ("Can there be anything more preposterous than an unknown tongue?") But the decree that most affected the many thousands of nuns who had followed Elizabeth, in some four hundred religious orders, was the mandate for reform and renewal. They were to reconsider their ministries and "look to the needs of the times." In Elizabeth's day, the need had been the education of girls. In the mid-twentieth century, nuns were needed in shelters for abused women, in clinics for people with AIDS, in professions ranging from psychotherapy to finance to lobbying for justice in the halls of Congress. They were told to adopt modern secular dress, in place of the medieval clothing—which one Sister called costumes—that set them apart from the people they served.

It was the matter of dress that brought up again the issue of male clerical control and caused a violent upheaval in the lives of some American nuns. In Los Angeles, the Sisters of the Immaculate Heart of Mary were ordered by the cardinal to keep their habits on, no matter what the council said. Much as Elizabeth had done when ordered to "obey in silence," the nuns stayed firm. "You will suffer for this," he warned them, as he insisted on ordering their lives: their bedtime, their prayer schedule, what books they could read. He wielded such control that one priest called it "comparable to the tactics of the Gestapo." When the Vatican backed him up, some three hundred Sisters withdrew from their schools, surrendered their vows, and formed a lay ecumenical community. Other nuns, other feminist impulses: Some Sisters of Loretto joined a public fast at the Illinois State Legislature in support of the Equal Rights Amendment. A Franciscan nun was one of the founders of the National Organization for Women.

In the fall of the year that Elizabeth was beatified, a sixty-one-year-old construction worker in New York, a Lutheran, was admitted to a Catholic hospital, nearly dead. His face was purplish-black, he had a temperature of 104, and before he lapsed into a coma, it took four people to hold him down. The doctor who diagnosed primary rubeola meningoencephalitis later wrote bluntly, "I thought he might survive an hour or two . . . he didn't seem to have a chance." The Sisters applied a relic of Mother Seton, and a novena of prayers was begun. The man got well, went back to work, became a Catholic, later retired to play golf in Florida.

The doctors and canon lawyers and theologians on both sides of the Atlantic argued the case incessantly. Was it primary rubeola, or only secondary? A bacterial or a viral infection? What about those antibiotics? And always the bottom-line question: Was it a miracle?

"It was a dramatic case," said a doctor. Others had no comment. One doctor said he had "scoured the medical literature" and had found only five such cases, in people from five to forty. All had died. Was this, then, a miracle? It was, he replied, "a most dramatic and complete recovery through no medical means that I can explain or understand."

"Doctors don't have to say 'miracle,'" said the priest who was heading the Seton cause. "They only have to say there's no natural explanation. And I don't blame the doctors. When you talk about miracles, you're getting close to the hand of God."

Twelve years went by. The Vatican, reminded of the generous financial support it received from American Catholics, and their need for a American saint of their own, waived the requirement for a fourth miracle. Elizabeth was on her way to Rome.

———

When Elizabeth was canonized, only 177 people had been canonized over three centuries. Pope John Paul II canonized nearly 500 in just three decades. One priest has called canonization "our favorite in-door sport."

But it's possible to be wry and somewhat skeptical about the tedious, expensive process of saint-making without losing sight of the person at the center. Without saints, sanctity might be considered only an abstraction. Saints help us see how a spiritual life can be lived in many different ways and under many different social and historical circumstances. Amid all the fuss over miracles, the fund-raising, and the Church politics, one thing stood out: Elizabeth's spirituality. Her deep awareness of, and profound connection with, her God. "Sorrow is the seed of holiness," said the Italian cardinal who acted as devil's advocate. Somehow the sorrows and trials of Elizabeth's life, and the grace with which she met them, nourished a spirituality within her that eventually stretched beyond ordinary limits. She went from having it all to losing it all to stretching to a core understanding of what "all" could mean—a bedrock human question, whether one thinks to ask it or not, within a religious context or not, at the safe distance of history or not.

A canonization ceremony at St. Peter's Basilica in Rome is a liturgical *Aida,* with triumphant music and stately entrances: prelates in scarlet and rose pink, ushers in white tie escorting members of the diplomatic corps and special guests. Plans for Elizabeth's ceremony were made months in advance. It would be telecast live around the world. It would be a thoroughly American affair: The Sistine Choir would be supplemented, for the first time ever, by a mixed chorus (really mixed: the Emmitsburg Community Chorus was made up of farmers, housewives, a librarian, and an undertaker, fewer than a quarter of them Catholic). Their director, a Daughter of Charity, would be the first woman ever to lead a choir at a papal function. Descendants of the saint would be there, along with descendants of Antonio Filicchi. They would come with a large group from Leghorn, renamed Livorno, where the cornerstone for the first church in the world to be named for Elizabeth had already been laid. Don Gino Franchi, the pastor, had argued with the Italian hierarchy, which wanted a traditional church awash with cherubs; Don Gino won out, with a modern, American-style church—no marble statues, just murals recalling Elizabeth's Italian journey. Gifts to the pope would include flowers and candles, a pair of parakeets recalling Elizabeth's love of birds, and two American flags.

On Sunday, September 14, 1975, Elizabeth Ann Bayley Seton was canonized, the first American-born saint in the Catholic Church.

"A woman born to love," says a Sister of Charity today. "No matter what happened, she could find God in her life. She could find God in *your* life."

❦

Catherine (Kit) Seton lived with the Harper family in Baltimore after Elizabeth's death, then with her brother William. In 1846 she entered religious life—not her mother's order, but the Sisters of Mercy in New York, working in prison ministry. One day, at the convent at Eighty-first Street and Madison Avenue, she received a trunk labeled "clothing for the poor." Inside was one suit of men's clothing and an assortment of "jimmies, pistols and other burglar's tools . . . all he had, sent to his only friend, Mother Catherine Seton, to remember him by."

William Seton served in the United States Navy from 1818 to 1834. He married Emily Prime, a wealthy Episcopalian, and had seven children. He wrote historical novels and *A Glimpse of Organic Life,* an attempt to reconcile Darwinism with Catholic doctrine.

Their oldest son, William III, was a captain in the 4th New York Infantry in the Civil War. He was wounded at Antietam. When a nun came to attend him, he asked, "Did you know my grandmother?" Another of Elizabeth's grandsons, Robert, became a priest, then an archbishop, and wrote a Seton family memoir.

Richard Seton became a navy clerk. He died at sea two years after his mother's death. He was twenty-five years old.

Dr. Richard Bayley, Elizabeth's father, is listed in several reference books, including *American National Biography* (Oxford University Press, 1999), vol. II.

Guy Carleton Bayley, Elizabeth's half brother, had a son, James Roosevelt Bayley, who became a Catholic, then a priest, then an archbishop who followed in John Carroll's footsteps in Baltimore. He founded Seton Hall College, now Seton Hall University.

Simon Gabriel Bruté never got to China. He was named the first bishop of Vincennes, in the Indiana Territory, in 1834, and died there five years later.

Rebecca Hobart, Henry Hobart's daughter, married an Episcopalian bishop. Both became Catholic.

Elizabeth's house in Baltimore on the Hookstown Road, renamed Paca Street, is open to visitors. Her house on State Street in New York City is now a shrine. The house in New Rochelle where she lived with her uncle William Bayley is still occupied. A plaque describing Elizabeth's time there is embedded in the ridged boulder, just right for a child to climb.

Two bronze busts stand in the garden of the Parrocchia Madre Seton in Livorno: Antonio Filicchi, stern, high-collared, and Will Seton, curly-haired, with a flowing scarf around his neck.

St. Andrew's Episcopal Church on Staten Island, New York, where Elizabeth's grandfather was rector for thirty years, remains a thriving parish. Elizabeth is celebrated there every January 4, her feast day. Several of her relatives are buried in its churchyard.

The painting of the Crucifixion by the Mexican artist José Maria Vallejo that scandalized Elizabeth's sister, Mary—"Our Saviour, ALL NAKED!"—still hangs above the altar at St. Peter's Church on Barclay Street in New York City.

The Graham Windham social agency in New York City traces its work back to the Society for the Relief of Poor Widows with Small Children, founded in 1797 by Isabella Graham, with Elizabeth as treasurer.

Notes pinned to babies left on church doorsteps by mothers who couldn't take care of them are preserved in the archives of the Sisters of Charity of New York, at the Foundling Hospital.

Mementos of Elizabeth kept in the archives of the Sisters of Charity and the Daughters of Charity include her wedding ring; the gold filigree brooch she wore on her wedding day; the christening dress she made for her daughter Catherine; her piano; her writing desk; her shawl, black belt, and black cap; her rosaries; and her cream silk dancing slippers, monogrammed.

The seventh-century Church of St. James in Livorno, whose bells Elizabeth heard every quarter hour, remains open, near a preserved section of the lazaretto, with the barred window from which she could look down on the foaming sea.

ACKNOWLEDGMENTS

❧

"Keep a grateful heart," Elizabeth wrote to Rebecca Seton in 1815. I begin with Irene Fugazy, Sister of Charity of New York, my lodestar and companion on this journey of discovery and delight.

Regina Bechtle, Sister of Charity of New York, who is writer and researcher at Mount St. Vincent, New York, and Judith Metz, Sister of Charity of Cincinnati, historian and archivist at Mount St. Joseph, Ohio, edited *Elizabeth Bayley Seton: Collected Writings*. Without their four volumes—nearly three thousand pages, representing thirteen years of work—I could never have written this book in narrative form.

Rita King, Sister of Charity of New York, was the first archivist to support my research at Mount St. Vincent, New York. Her successor, Constance Brennan, Sister of Charity of New York, has also welcomed me into their rich archives. Betty Ann McNeil, Daughter of Charity, Vincentian Scholar-in-Residence at DePaul University, who was provincial archivist at the Daughters of Charity in Emmitsburg when I was writing this book, made useful suggestions and responded patiently to queries. Bonnie Weatherly, archives manager of the Daughters of Charity, St. Louise Province at Emmitsburg, was particularly helpful with illustrations. Carole Prietto, former archivist of the West Central Province of the Daughters of Charity, was generous with her time, as was Kathleen Flanagan, Sister of Charity of Saint Elizabeth, New Jersey, who let me sit at Elizabeth Seton's cherrywood writing desk.

Among the archivists and librarians who could not have been more obliging are Tricia Pyne, Director of the Associated Archives at St. Mary's Seminary and University in Baltimore, and Alison Foley, associate archivist. Kathleen Sprows Cummings, associate professor of American Studies at the University of Notre Dame, arranged for me to work with archivists Kevin Cawley and Sharon Sumpter, who gave me Elizabeth's own prayer book to hold in my hands. Staff members at the New York Historical Society, the New York Society Library, the New York Public Library, and the St. Louis Public Library were untiring as they located just what I needed.

When I visited Livorno, Italy, where Elizabeth first encountered Catholicism, I was greeted warmly by Don Gino Franchi, pastor of the first church in the world to be named for St. Elizabeth Ann, and by Lara Bellagotti, who translated and took photographs and became a friend. Other folks made me feel most welcome, as Livorno's people had once done for Elizabeth.

Back home, Jane Dystel and Miriam Goderich at Dystel and Goderich Literary Management, and Marcia Markland, my editor at Thomas Dunne Books, believed in this book from day one. Associate editor Kat Brzozowski was always there for me at the other end of the phone.

Robert Burns, Eleanor Foa, Paul Gardner, and George Sullivan—writers and editors and close friends—read pieces of this book when I began working on it a decade ago and told me to keep going.

Matthew Gurlitz suggested the title.

My daughter, Anne Barthel, a developmental book editor with her own business, often took time from her work to help me get the manuscript in shape before it ever left my house. Some of the most auspicious passages in this book belong to her.

NOTES

❧

Elizabeth Bayley Seton, *Collected Writings* (cited as CW). Ed. Regina Bechtle, SC and Judith Metz,; SC mss. ed. Ellin M. Kelly. Vol. I, *Correspondence and Journals, 1793–1808*. Vol. II, *Correspondence and Journals, 1808–1820*. Vols. IIIa, IIIb, *Spiritual Writings, Notebooks, and Other Documents*. New City Press, 2000, 2002, 2006.

INTRODUCTION

1 Joseph Ratzinger quote: Herbert Vorgrimler, ed., *Commentary on the Documents of Vatican II,* (Herder and Herder, 1967), vol. V, p. 134.

1 radical feminist themes; corporate dissent: *Doctrinal Assessment of the Leadership Conference of Women Religious,* Congregatio pro Doctrina Fidei, 2012, pp. 2, 3.

1 a hostile takeover: The *The Diane Rehm Show,* National Public Radio, June 14, 2012.

2 editorial: *The New York Times,* April 19, 2012.

2 Sayyid Sayeed quote: *The Washington Post,* July 2, 2012.

2   Be truthful, but gentle and absolutely fearless: *National Catholic Reporter,* August 10, 2012.

2   the sins of patriarchy: Sandra M. Schneiders, *Beyond Patching: Faith and Feminism in the Catholic Church* (Paulist Press, 2004), p. 4.

2   open and honest dialogue: LCWR statement, August 13, 2012, https:// lcwr.org/media/lcwr-statement-meeting-archbishop-sartain.

2   respectful dialogue: United States Conference of Catholic Bishops, August 10, 2012, http://www.usccb.org/about/media-relations/archbishop -sartain-lcwr-august2012.cfm.

CHAPTER ONE

5   awoke in darkness: CW I, p. 254.

5   description of the lazaretto: CW I, p. 252.

5   prison: CW I, p. 251.

5   naked walls: CW I, p. 252.

6   bolted in: CW I, p. 251.

6   Matins Bells: CW I, p. 254.

6   next to madness: CW I, p. 221.

6   not the least disposition: CW I, p. 244.

7   At no loss to know the hours: CW I, p. 25.

7   Retrospections bring anguish; in the little closet: CW I, p. 254.

7   warm eggs and wine: CW I, p. 253.

8   My Seton is daily getting better: CW I, p. 245.

8   My Husband on the old bricks: CW I, p. 254.

8   My face was covered; opening my Prayer Books: CW I, p. 255.

8   We pray and cry together: CW I, p. 258.

8   His great cocked hat being off: CW I, p. 256.

8   le Bon Dieu: ibid.

9   It reminded me: CW I, p. 257.

9   Consider—my Husband: CW I, p. 259.

9   3,500 practicing physicians; quacks abound: William Frederick Norwood, *Medical Education in the United States Before the Civil War* (University of Pennsylvania Press, 1944), pp. 9, 22.

10   Keep the head cool: Rochester, *Medical Men and Medical Matters of 1776: Anniversary Address before the Medical Society of the State of New York* (Albany, 1876) (quoting Dr. Boerhaave).

10   The first medical school: Samuel Breck, *Recollections* New-York Historical Society.

10   Charlton family history: Rose Maria Laverty, *Loom of Many Threads* (Sisters of Charity, 1958), pp. 81, 82.

10   quite ready to parade himself: Annabelle M. Melville, *Elizabeth Bayley Seton* (Charles Scribner's Sons, 1951), p. 2.

10   the "court" section of town; "Turkey worked"; Wedgwood: Edwin G.

Burrows and Mike Wallace, *Gotham: A History of New York City to 1898* (Oxford University Press, 1999), p. 175.

11   Hanover Square shops; Mrs. Edwards: ibid., pp. 124, 125.

11   Twenty thousand people: David McCullough, *1776* (Simon & Schuster, 2005), p. 122.

11   Classes of society: Martha J. Lamb, *History of the City of New York* (Barnes, 1877), vol. II, p. 440.

11   foul with excrement: Burrows and Wallace, *Gotham,* p. 359.

11   more than four hundred men, women and children: ibid., p. 213.

11   smoky lamps; footpads: ibid.

11   two women hanged; the Holy Ground: ibid., p. 214.

11   silk stocking; big wig: ibid., p. 189.

12   Willem Kieft trying to tax the Indians: Milton M. Klein, ed., *The Empire State: A History of New York* (Cornell University Press with the New York State Historical Association, 2001), p. 41.

12   Boston Massacre: Howard Zinn, *A People's History of the United States* (1980; Harper Perennial Modern Classics, 2005), p. 67.

12   Battle of Golden Hill: Edward Robb Ellis, *The Epic of New York City* (1966; Carroll & Graf, 2005), pp. 152–54.

12   an irresistible impulse: Joseph Dirvin, *Mrs. Seton* (Farrar, Straus & Cudahy, 1962), p. 27.

12   the Mad Enthusiast: CW I, p. 334.

12   running away, over the seas: CW IIIa, p. 512.

12   Dr. John Bard's suits: Thomas E. V. Smith, *The City of New York in the Year of Washington's Inauguration* (A. D. F. Randolph, 1889), p. 93.

12   doctors' fees: Laverty, *Loom of Many Threads,* pp. 83, 228.

13   New York Tea Party: Ellis, *The Epic of New York City,* p. 155.

13   Samuel Adams's new coat: David McCullough, *John Adams* (Simon & Schuster, 2001), p. 24.

13   John Morin Scott and son: Melville, *Elizabeth Bayley Seton,* p. 1.

13   John Adams's opinion of New Yorkers: Burrows and Wallace, *Gotham,* p. 217.

13   The colonists must be reduced to absolute obedience: ibid., p. 215.

14   the city's population dropped: ibid., p. 227.

14   The tavern on the Post Road: Laverty, *Loom of Many Threads,* p. 62.

14   Bayley family history: ibid., pp. 67–74.

15   Bayleys they might be: ibid., p. 78.

15   Grandfather's will: ibid., p. 64.

16   William Bayley's advertisement: *New-York Gazette and Weekly Mercury,* June 13, 1774.

17   Sixteen religious houses: Gloria Deák, *Picturing New York* (Columbia University Press, 2000), p. 34.

17   unnecessary adornment: *Journal of Rev. Francis Asbury*, Wesley Chapel Museum, John Street Methodist Church, New York.

17   Lord Cornbury: B. Kim Taylor, *The Great New York City Trivia and Fact Book* (Cumberland House Press, 1999), p. 97.

17   The Protestant Episcopal Church, an American corporation: Sidney I. Pomerantz, *New York: An American City, 1783–1803* (Columbia University Press, 1938), p. 374.

17   penal laws; punishment of Catholics: John Tracy Ellis, *Catholics in Colonial America* (Helicon Press, 1965), p. 345.

18   a public nuisance; off-scourings: CW I, p. 373.

18   none but the first class of society: Eric Homberger, *The Historical Atlas of New York City* (Henry Holt, 1994), p. 64.

18   such pretty plain hats: CW IIIa, p. 512.

18   The first point of religion: CW I, p. 8.

CHAPTER TWO

19   dissolve the connection: McCullough, *1776*, p. 135.

20   pierced with the bayonet to trees: Burrows and Wallace, *Gotham*, p. 236.

20   choking smoke and fiery red wind-borne flakes, McCullough, *1776*, p. 221.

20   Providence, or some good honest fellow; Nathan Hale: Burrows and Wallace, *Gotham*, p. 242.

20   WM. BAYLEY, TINSMAN: Laverty, *Loom of Many Threads*, p. 102.

20 Goody Two-Shoes: ibid., p. 103.

21 At four years of age: CW IIIa, p. 510.

21 At six: ibid.

22 she learned to recite her lessons quickly: Robert Seton, *Memoir and Journals,* Archives, St. Joseph's Provincial House, Emmitsburg, MD.

22 Music and French: Charles I. White, *Mother Seton, Mother of Many Daughters* (Mother Seton Guild, 1953), p. 2.

22 in the occupied city, description: Burrows and Wallace, *Gotham,* p. 247.

22 a new bakery shop: I. N. Phelps Stokes, *The Iconography of Manhattan Island,* 6 vols. (Robert H. Dodd, 1915–28; rpt. Arno Press, 1967), vol. V, p. 1081.

22 Canvas Town: Burrows and Wallace, *Gotham,* p. 25.

23 in great affliction: CW IIIa, p. 510.

23 petition to the British commander: Laverty, *Loom of Many Threads,* p. 98.

23 William Bayley's property; description of the house: ibid., p. 118.

23 in theological disagreement: William Hague, *Life Notes* (Lee & Shepard, 1888).

24 delight to sit alone by the waterside: CW IIIa, p. 511.

25 Home again at my Father's: ibid.

25 The town now swarms with Americans: Stokes, *The Iconography of Manhattan Island,* vol. V, p. 1159.

25   Washington's letter to Carleton: ibid., p. 1180.

26   Oh where are all my dreams and Fancies fled: CW I, p. 18.

26   Never dwell on trifles: Melville, *Elizabeth Bayley Seton,* p. 16.

26   David Hosack: H. H. Sherk, "David Hosack, M.D., and Rutgers: The Politics of Medical Education in the Nineteenth Century," *New Jersey Medicine* 99 (July–August 2002): 18.

26   See, here is your mother's hand: Melville, *Elizabeth Bayley Seton,* p. 8.

27   found her coffin empty: Burrows and Wallace, *Gotham,* p. 386.

27   Doctors' Riot: Jules C. Ladenheim, "The Doctors' Mob of 1788," *Journal of History of Medicine and Allied Sciences* 5 (Winter 1950): 23–43.

27   two large holes in his forehead: Frank Monaghan and Marvin Lowenthal, *This Was New York* (Doubleday, Doran, 1943), p. 201.

27   a night passed in sweat of terror: CW IIIa, p. 511.

27   Dr. Bayley's affidavit: *New-York Journal and Patriotic Register,* April 15, 1788; *Daily Advertiser,* April 15, 1788; *New-York Packet,* April 18, 1788.

27   Dr. Bayley's will: Laverty, *Loom of Many Threads,* pp. 247, 248.

28   Walks among cedars: CW IIIa, p. 511.

28   Anna was beginning to cough: CW I, p. 260.

28   A large crowd of men: CW I, p. 261.

28   If I could forget my God: CW I, p. 258.

29 My heart has accompanied you: Letters, Archives, St. Joseph's Provincial House, Emmitsburg, MD.

29 oh the promises he makes: CW I, p. 262.

29 alone to all the world: CW I, p. 264.

29 In the year 1789: CW I, p. 265.

30 for him who would minister to his soul: CW I, p. 267.

30 I breathe out my Soul to you: CW I, p. 267.

30 Oh no, what had I to fear? CW I, p. 268.

CHAPTER THREE

31 descriptions of Elizabeth and Will; absorbed in one another: Marie Celeste, SC, *Elizabeth Ann Seton: A Self-Portrait* (Franciscan Marytown Press, 1986), p. 15.

31 Will's stories of Europe: *Letters,* Archives, Emmitsburg.

32 a reigning passion in my breast: CW I, p. 8.

32 Seton family history: Melville, *Elizabeth Bayley Seton,* pp. 16, 17.

32 one unlucky ancestor: Antonia Fraser, *Mary Queen of Scots* (Dell, 1971), pp. 508, 509.

32 I have heard, my dear William: *Letters,* Archives, Emmitsburg.

33 a sweet-tempered boy: ibid.

33 the shabbiest of the Lords: ibid.

33 Nothing could have been duller: ibid.

34 liked and esteemed by everyone: Letter of Captain Ralph Dundas, RN, March 1782.

34 a good idea of his integrity: J.-P. Brissot de Warville, *New Travels in the United States of America Performed in 1788* (1792), trans. M. S. Vamos and Durand Echeverria (Belknap Press, 1965), p. 151.

34 details of the currency: Herbert S. Parmet, *Commemorating the Bicentennial of the Founding of the Bank of New York, 1784–1984* (History Associates, 1984), p. 124.

34 She-Merchants: Burrows and Wallace, *Gotham*, p. 12.

35 description of Federal Hall: McCullough, *John Adams*, p. 401.

35 Washington's inauguration: ibid., p. 403.

35 many fine, well-dressed women; Holy Ground: Burrows and Wallace, *Gotham*, p. 214.

36 a most dangerous class of men—bachelors: Brissot de Warville, *New Travels in the United States of America Performed in 1788*, p. 142.

36 It is currently reported: Robert Seton, *Memoir, Letters, and Journals,* vol. I.

37 a family disagreement: CW III, p. 512.

37 footwalks: Pomerantz, *New York: an American City,* p. 287.

37 the gayest place in America: William Winterbotham, *An Historical, Geographical, Commercial and Philosophical View of the American United States* (London, 1795), vol. II, pp. 315–20.

37 the pride and bulwark of . . . the beauteous island: Washington Irving,

Knickerbocker's History of New York (1809; Doubleday, Doran, 1928), pp. 116, 117.

38   a little country home: CW IIIa, p. 512.

38   Folly, folly: ibid.

39   visit to Julia in Easton: Ellin M. Kelly, ed., *Numerous Choirs: A Chronicle of Elizabeth Bayley Seton and Her Spiritual Daughters,* vol. I (Mater Dei Provincialate, 1981), p. 36.

39   Elizabeth's friendships; cultural context: Judith Metz, "Elizabeth Bayley Seton of New York: A Woman's Life in the Early Republic" (doctoral dissertation, Union Institute, Cincinnati, OH, 2000), pp. 118–37.

39   There is not an hour of my Life: CW I, p. 18.

39   One of the pleasures of my attachment to you: CW I, p. 210.

39   What I most desire: CW I, p. 25.

39   Pray get her a husband: CW I, p. 194.

39   keep in your children's minds: Metz, "Elizabeth Bayley Seton of New York: A Woman's Life in the Early Republic," p. 143.

40   one of the great spiritual resources: Joan Chittister, *The Friendship of Women* (BlueBridge, 2006), p. 16.

40   to circumscribe my wishes: Dirvin, *Mrs. Seton,* p. 27.

40   population of New York City: Stokes, *The Iconography of Manhattan Island,* vol. V, p. 1259.

40   330 licensed drinking places: Pomerantz, *New York: An American City,* p. 80.

40 New York Society Library, fees and dues: Henry S. F. Cooper and Jenny Lawrence, eds., *The New York Society Library: 250 Years* (NYSL, 2004), p. 22.

40 No person has a right to insert any comments: ibid., p. 29.

41 a published essay: ibid., p. 46.

41 Alas alas alas: CW IIIa, pp. 512–13.

41 Calm that glowing of your soul: Letter, Archives, Emmitsburg.

42 She occasionally had her fits of melancholy: Robert Seton, *Memoir, Letters, and Journals,* vol. I.

42 the moment twenty years ago: CW II, p. 175.

42 lamentation and longing: David Dark, *The Gospel According to America* (Westminster John Knox Press, 2005), p. 85.

42 one of those agreeable creatures: Letters, Archives, Emmitsburg.

43 I congratulate you: ibid.

43 the first known Stradivarius: Robert Seton, *An Old Family* (Brentano's, 1899), p. 275.

44 Elizabeth's notes to Will: CW I, pp. 2–4.

45 wedding customs: Archives of the Merchant's House Museum, New York City.

45 wedding cake: Elizabeth Raffald, *The Experienced English Housekeeper* (J. Harrep, 1769).

45 Richard Bayley's letter: Archives, Emmitsburg.

46 the national debt; Hamilton's report; insider trading: Burrows and Wallace, *Gotham,* pp. 303–09.

46 Wall Street background: Homberger, *The Historical Atlas of New York City,* p. 30.

47 My own home at twenty: CW III, p. 513.

47 Calvinism: David N. Steele, Curtis C. Thomas, and S. Lance Quinn, *The Five Points of Calvinism: Defined, Defended, and Documented* (P&R Publishing, 2004), p. 25.

47 Common Council rules; the annihilation of taverns: Burrows and Wallace, *Gotham,* p. 269.

48 Hamilton's houses: Willard Sterne Randall, *Alexander Hamilton: A Life* (HarperCollins, 2003), p. 291.

48 one of the loveliest beings: CW I, p. 16.

48 Grandfather B: CW I, p. 9.

49 Dr. Bayley and public health: James J. Walsh, *History of Medicine in New York* (National Americana Society, 1919).

49 He proved yellow fever to be infectious: Jacobson, article, *The Medical Times,* 1923, from *New York Genealogical and Biological Record.* Quoted in Dirvin, *Mrs. Seton,* p. 49.

49 Jacob Roosevelt's will: W. W. Pasko, ed., *Old New York,* 2 vols. (Pasko, 1889–91), vol. I, p. 373.

49 Soap Boilers and Tallow Chandlers: CW I, p. 14.

50 all a mother's heart can wish: CW I, p. 19.

50   The world is so good: CW I, p. 29.

50   the first Commemoration Ball: Eric Homberger, *Mrs. Astor's New York* (Yale University Press, 2002), pp. 121, 122.

CHAPTER FOUR

51   a pot of incense: CW I, p. 257.

51   W. goes on *gently*: CW I, p. 269.

51   the most severe trials: CW I, p. 268.

51   days of retirement and abstraction: CW I, p. 270.

52   Oh well I know that God is above: CW I, p. 270.

52   you would find me a lioness: ibid.

52   Dear W: CW I, p. 262.

52   Must not touch, Signora: CW I, p. 266.

52   Why dear Mrs. Seton: CW I, p. 262.

52   several passages in Isaiah: CW I, p. 261.

53   no room for visions now: CW I, p. 269.

53   five or six times: CW I, p. 261.

53   the most truly amiable estimable young woman: CW I, p. 54.

53   Let all come to my strong box: CW II, p. 459.

53   You are the first of my children: Melville, *Elizabeth Bayley Seton*, p. 24.

54   letters from Will's grandmother: Archives, Emmitsburg.

54   my darling little wife: ibid.

54   my dearest treasure: CW I, p. 5.

54   These arms, heart and bed: CW I, p. 6.

54   Mr. Fisher: CW I, pp. 5, 6.

55   Thomas Jefferson's quote: Mary Beth Norton, *Liberty's Daughters: The Revolutionary Experience of American Women, 1750–1800* (Little, Brown, 1980), p. 61.

55   the true language of female determination: CW I, p. 116.

55   Olympe de Gouges: Jill Evans, essay, based in part on Joan B. Landes, *Visualizing the Nation: Gender, Representation and Revolution in Eighteenth-Century France* (Cornell University Press, 2001).

55   Mary Wollstonecraft: Wollstonecraft, *A Vindication of the Rights of Woman* (Dover Publications, 1996), 1792.

55   that weak elegancy of mind: ibid., p. 8.

55   a Disciple of Wollstonecraft: Lyndall Gordon, *Vindication: A Life of Mary Wollstonecraft* (HarperCollins, 2005), p. 153.

55   a work of genius: Ralph M. Wardle, *Mary Wollstonecraft: A Critical Biography* (University of Kansas Press, 1951), p. 158; Matthew L. Davis, *Memoirs of Aaron Burr* (Harper & Brothers, 1836), vol. I, p. 363.

56   Have courage to use your own reason: Immanuel Kant, *On History*, trans. Lewis White Beck (Bobbs-Merrill, 1963), p. 3.

56   Every hour I can catch: CW I, p. 95.

56   Elizabeth reading Rousseau: CW I, p. 76.

56   Mr. Olive: CW I, p. 63.

56   only overgrown children: Wardle, *Mary Wollstonecraft: A Critical Biography*, p. 21.

56   In the choice of a Husband: CW IIIa, p. 14.

57   Send me a kiss: CW I, 170.

57   companionate marriage; the word "friend": Metz, "Elizabeth Bayley Seton of New York: A Woman's Life in the Early Republic," p. 87.

57   Mrs. Sad: CW I, pp. 7–9.

58   free, white, male citizens: Gail Collins, *America's Women: 400 Years of Dolls, Drudges, Helpmates, and Heroines* (William Morrow, 2003), pp. 83, 84.

58   limited powers of reason: Burrows and Wallace, *Gotham,* p. 284.

58   more than a biological fact: Metz, "Elizabeth Bayley Seton of New York: A Woman's Life in the Early Republic," p. 100.

58   Isabella Graham's school: Smith, *The City of New York in the Year of Washington's Inauguration,* p. 196.

59   Isabella Graham and the Widows Society: *The Power of Faith: Exemplified in the Life and Writing of the Late Mrs. Isabella Graham of New York* (Kirk & Mercein, 1817).

59   Elizabeth Burgin: Burrows and Wallace, *Gotham,* p. 284.

59   Judith Sargent Murray's quote: Norton, *Liberty's Daughters,* p. 252.

60 beyond our most sanguine expectations: CW I, p. 27.

60 delicacy and decorum: Burrows and Wallace, *Gotham,* p. 382.

60 The poor increase fast: *The Unpublished Letters and Correspondence of Mrs. Isabella Graham, Selected and Arranged by Her Daughter, Mrs. Bethune.* (John S. Taylor, 1838), p. 224.

60 I am rocking the cradle: CW I, p. 16.

61 the inconveniences: CW I, p. 15.

61 I observed: CW I, p. 17.

61 my Father thought he could not recover: CW I, p. 18.

61 The privilege of being a mother: ibid.

61 In you I view the Friend: CW I, p. 57.

61 the great error: CW II, p. 83.

62 Fourteen Miles Round; Bloemen-dael: Homberger, *The Historical Atlas of New York City,* p. 30.

62 newspapers: Smith, *The City of New York in the Year of Washington's Inauguration,* pp. 95, 211.

62 Captain Thompson Baxter: Henry Collins Brown, *Old New York, Yesterday and Today* (Privately printed for *Valentine's Manual* and to be sold at the sign of the Dog and Duck, 1922), n.p.

63 Park Theatre, John Street Theatre: George C. D. Odell, *Annals of the New York Stage* (Columbia University Press, 1927).

63 a dangerous assault upon the Passions: *New York Mercury,* Dec. 7, 1767.

63 Washington laughed out loud: *Historic New York* (G. P. Putnam's Sons, 1899); *George Washington's Diaries,* Nov. 24, 1789.

64 exorbitant cost of a rental: CW I, p. 73.

64 the drinking and the quarreling: Melville, *Elizabeth Bayley Seton,* p. 12.

64 description of yellow fever: Jim Murphy, *An American Plague* (Clarion Books, 2003).

65 gifts to families without a provider: Walter Barrett, *The Old Merchants of New York City,* ch. VI (Carleton Publishers, 1863).

65 Persons carrying the dead: *Minutes of the Common Council of the City of New York, 1784–1831,* vol. II, pp. 468–69.

65 selling coffins from a wagon: C. E. Heaton, "Yellow Fever in New York City," *Bulletin of the Medical Library Association* 34 (1946): 67–78.

65 I was so terribly ill: CW I, p. 41.

65 Washington and tuberculosis: Donald N. Moran, "A Modern Medical Report on George Washington," 1999, *Revolutionary War Archives,* http://www.revolutionarywararchives.org/washhealth.html.

66 He has no friend or confidant now: CW I, p. 35.

66 What can I say to prepare your mind: CW I, p. 37.

67 Elizabeth's prayer: White, *Mother Seton, Mother of Many Daughters,* p. 8.

67 The will of God: Ray Stedman, *Finding the Will of God* (Discovery Publishing, 1995), pp. 1–5.

67 We have painted, Papered and White-washed: CW I, p. 52.

67   Elizabeth's early opinion of Rebecca: CW I, p. 54.

68   I never sweep the hall: CW I, p. 91.

68   Rebecca returned the love: Melville, *Elizabeth Bayley Seton*, pp. 30, 32.

69   Elizabeth was grateful: CW I, p. 268.

69   delighted with his change of situation: CW I, p. 272.

69   They talked about the past: ibid.

CHAPTER FIVE

70   throws handkerchiefs: CW I, p. 95.

70   looks everywhere: CW I, p. 86.

70   certain small contrivances: Norton, *Liberty's Daughters,* p. 233.

70   When Aaron Burr was born: ibid., p. 83.

71   New Year's Day: Burrows and Wallace, *Gotham,* p. 462.

71   great brilliancy of wit: Melville, *Elizabeth Bayley Seton,* p. 46.

71   Sunday after twelve: Letters, Archives, Emmitsburg.

71   If the news of our Misfortunes has reached you: CW I, p. 108.

72   Thank heaven we are not *all* sinking: CW I, p. 113.

72   in the stillness of despair: CW I, p. 33.

72   all the whys and wherefores: CW I, p. 119.

72   Shall we be compelled: Melville, *Elizabeth Bayley Seton,* p. 47.

72   I could not wish a pleasanter situation: CW I, p. 130.

72   I have the pleasure to inform you: CW I, p. 124.

73   eight days after her birth: CW I, p. 131.

73   we have had a scene of pleasure; 50 bowls of tea: CW I, pp. 133, 134.

73   last night at 8 o'clock: Melville, *Elizabeth Bayley Seton,* p. 49.

73   Come come Soul's Sister: CW I, p. 232.

73   Henry Hobart: Mary Kathleen Flanagan, "The Influence of John Henry Hobart on the Life of Elizabeth Ann Seton" (doctoral dissertation, Union Theological Seminary, New York City, 1978), pp. 159, 160.

74   zigzag mazes; he smiled often: John McVickar, *The Early Life and Professional Years of Bishop Hobart* (Talboys, 1838).

74   He appeared in the pulpit: Melville, *Elizabeth Bayley Seton,* p. 56.

74   The soother and comforter of the troubled soul: CW I, p. 201.

75   Elizabeth's reflection: White, *Mother Seton, Mother of Many Daughters,* p. 12.

75   something of a scold: CW I, p. 212.

75   The sweet creature: CW I, p. 139.

76   Are you well? CW I, p. 141.

76   Oh Julia, how happy must have been: CW I, p. 61.

76   my attentive friend: CW I, p. 70.

76   Slavery in New York, general: *New York Amsterdam News,* New-York
      Historical Society exhibit, 2005–6; Roi Ottley and William J. Weath-
      erby, eds., *The Negro in New York* (New York Public Library, 1967).

76   John Van Zandt whipping a slave to death: Burrows and Wallace, *Go-
      tham,* p. 149.

77   Reverend Charlton leaving a slave boy to Elizabeth: Arthur J. Burns,
      "New Light on Mother Seton," *America,* March 26, 1932.

77   leases expiring on May 1: Burrows and Wallace, *Gotham,* p. 392.

77   Elizabeth's schooling schedule: CW I, p. 150.

78   Noah Webster's *Spelling Book*: Noah Webster, *The American Spelling
      Book, Containing an Easy Standard of Pronunciation* (Young & Mc-
      Cullough, 1788); "A Reformed Mode of Spelling," in *The History of the
      United States*, ed. Neil Harris, David Rothman, and Stephan Thern-
      strom (Holt, Rinehart & Winston, 1969), pp. 237–45.

78   My Father cannot do more than he does: CW I, p. 137.

78   I cannot sleep: CW I, p. 181.

79   I never saw anything so beautiful: CW I, p. 185.

79   All the horrors are coming: Dirvin, *Mrs. Seton,* p. 96.

79   Elizabeth offering Kit: White, *Mother Seton, Mother of Many Daughters,*
      p. 23.

79   repugnant to Scriptures: E. Brooks Holifield, *Theology in America: Chris-
      tian Thought from the Age of the Puritans to the Civil War* (Yale University
      Press, 2003), p. 240.

79   we are miserable sinners: Leo Damrosch, *Jean-Jacques Rousseau: Restless Genius* (Houghton Mifflin, 2005), p. 121.

80   Abigail Adams to her son: Phyllis Lee Levin, *Abigail Adams* (St. Martin's Press, 2001), p. 120.

80   when the average life span was thirty-seven years: St. Louis Public Library Reference Desk.

80   Come sit by me: CW I, p. 182.

80   Cover me warm: CW I, p. 186.

80   My Christ Jesus have mercy on me: ibid.

80   taking him in his barge: CW I, p. 186.

80   Dr. Bayley's grave marker: CW IIIa, p. 22.

81   not the impulse of unrestrained sorrow: CW I, p. 184.

81   population had nearly doubled: Census Bureau data.

81   Elizabeth's toothache: CW I, p. 240.

82   I rise up early and late take rest: CW I, p. 197.

82   Is it possible that I am not to see you: CW I, p. 231.

82   It is needless to say: Letters, Archives, Mount St. Joseph, Cincinnati, Ohio.

82   A thousand thanks: CW I, p. 202.

83   My soul is very, very, very sick: CW I, p. 206.

83 all is well: ibid.

83 Thus far, my very amiable little friend: CW I, p. 211.

83 spiritual journal: CW I, p. 212.

83 I will tell you the plain truth: CW I, pp. 212, 213.

84 next to madness: CW I, p. 221.

84 My dear William: CW I, p. 223.

84 My own Richard: ibid.

84 My tears are dry: CW I, p. 240.

CHAPTER SIX

85 it made us cold: CW I, p. 273.

85 Christmas Day is begun: ibid.

85 Is she too in heaven: CW I, p. 279.

86 Tell all my dear friends: CW I, p. 277.

86 My Christ Jesus have mercy: CW I, p. 274.

86 his dear soul separated gently: CW I, p. 277.

86 to thank our Heavenly Father: CW I, p. 274.

86 Oh Oh Oh what a day: CW I, p. 275.

86 Will's grave marker: Dirvin, *Mrs. Seton,* p. 126.

87 Leghorn description and history: author's visit; city literature.

87 These three months has been a hard lesson: CW I, p. 282.

88 that they shall see their Father no more in this world: CW I, p. 281.

88 I am hard pushed by these charitable Romans: CW I, p. 279.

88 Elizabeth's dialogue with Filippo Filicchi: CW I, p. 290.

89 old Mr. Pope's words: ibid.

89 thronged with people and carriages: CW I, p. 283.

89 with a smiling look: CW I, p. 285.

89 being only an American: ibid.

89 she would not be known from any other woman: CW I, p. 284.

90 felt the void: CW I, p. 285.

90 I could not find the least gratification: CW I, p. 286.

90 Elizabeth's first visit to a Catholic church: CW I, p. 283.

90 sumptuous and splendid worship: Melville, *Elizabeth Bayley Seton,* p. 71.

91 engaged my whole soul: CW I, p. 293.

91 loaded with their blessings and presents: CW I, p. 291.

91 theological background on the Real Presence: author's interview with
Rev. David Fly, Episcopalian priest, St. Louis, Missouri.

92 Elizabeth's thoughts on the Real Presence: CW I, p. 292.

92 I am a *Mother:* CW I, p. 291.

92 a man would be ashamed to be seen kneeling: CW I, p. 297.

93 Elizabeth on the practice of fasting: CW I, p. 296.

93 the principles and passions of Luther: CW I, p. 315.

93 my whole heart, head, all are sick: CW I, p. 294.

93 We often receive blessings from the hand of God: CW I, p. 295.

94 As I approach to you, I tremble: CW I, p. 305.

94 Journal entries: CW I, pp. 300–303.

95 sexual desire; one cannot say more: Mary A. Donovan, SC, "The Woman Elizabeth Ann Seton: 1804–1812," *Vincentian Heritage* 14, no. 2 (1993): 267–85.

95 John Adams at a Catholic church: McCullough, *John Adams,* pp. 45–47.

95 the church that persecuted our ancestors: CW IIIa, p. 424.

95 Our Saviour, ALL NAKED! ibid.

96 A Quaker friend: ibid., p. 148.

96 Elizabeth and Rebecca prayed together: CW I, p. 309.

96 With her is gone all my interest: CW I, p. 313.

96 Hobart's lecture: Melville, *Elizabeth Bayley Seton,* pp. 85–86.

97   How can you believe there are as many gods: Dirvin, *Mrs. Seton,* p. 149.

98   your mind is over-influenced: ibid., pp. 149, 190.

98   the most unfit and dangerous man: Burrows and Wallace, *Gotham,* p. 329.

98   a melancholy event: CW I, p. 312.

98   Hamilton's funeral procession: *Thomas Jefferson.* Directed by Ken Burns. PBS, 1996.

99   I boil them in rice: CW I, p. 126.

99   Turn out at daylight in the coldest mornings: CW I, p. 336.

99   I will say nothing to you about your change of faith: Melville, *Elizabeth Bayley Seton,* p. 106.

100   If John Wilkes did not continue a faithful friend: CW I, p. 313.

100   those pretensions and indulgences: CW I, p. 314.

100   You know my heart you know my thoughts: CW I, p. 325.

100   I love, I esteem, I venerate you: Melville, *Elizabeth Bayley Seton,* p. 89.

101   like a Bird struggling in a net: CW I, p. 323.

101   a municipal market: Burrows and Wallace, *Gotham,* p. 46.

101   my prayers shall finally be answered: CW I, p. 319.

101   which turned my face to the Catholic church: Dirvin *Mrs. Seton,* p. 99.

101   My hard case is to have a head turned with instruction: CW I, p. 327.

102   a short and painful visit: Melville, *Elizabeth Bayley Seton*, p. 89.

102   O teach me teach me where to go: CW I, p. 338.

102   grace: Leonard Foley, "Grace, Our Love Relationship with God," *Catholic Update,* 1977.

102   Kierkegaard quote: J. J. Van der Leeuw, *The Conquest of Illusion* (Knopf, 1928), p. 9.

CHAPTER SEVEN

103   A crowd of Catholics: Joan Chittister, *Becoming Fully Human* (Sheed & Ward, 2005), p. 61.

103   who will rid me of the dreaded burthen: CW I, p. 344.

104   Should I again read those Books: CW I, p. 323.

104   My Soul is so intirely engrossed: CW I, p. 325.

104   Will you not return: CW I, p. 340.

104   I believe you are always a good Catholic: Melville, *Elizabeth Bayley Seton,* p. 96.

105   if he says you fools: CW I, p. 374.

105   Years ago I read in some old book: CW I, p. 370.

105   Why should we not say it: CW I, p. 369.

105   How often I argued to my fearful uncertain heart: CW II, 425.

105   I am between laughing and crying: CW I, p. 374.

106   exchange between Elizabeth and the Posts: CW II, p. 424.

106   I am forced to keep my eyes always on my Book: CW I, p. 350.

106   So much trouble has turned her brain: CW I, p. 401.

107   that you have bought me: CW II, p. 390.

107   The controversies on it: CW I, p. 374.

107   laughing with my heart: CW I, p. 375.

107   I came up light at heart and cool of head: ibid.

108   a connection with a Deist: CW I, p. 366.

108   indulgences: Alister McGrath, *In the Beginning: The Story of the King James Bible* (Doubleday, 2001), pp. 16–18.

108   As soon as the coin in the coffer rings: This couplet is popularly attributed to Johann Tetzel, but see James Swan, "Did Tetzel Really Say . . . ," *Beggars All*, January 7, 2012, http://beggarsallreformation.blogspot.com /2012/01/did-tetzel-really-say-as-soon-as-coin.html.

108   I could go almost mad: CW I, p. 345.

108   the good confession: CW I, p. 376.

109   a triumph of joy and gladness: CW I, p. 377.

109   You have led me: CW I, p. 349.

109   thirty pounds will buy winter cloths: CW I, p. 352.

109   the greatest luxury: CW I, p. 364.

109   the dangerous consequences: Melville, *Elizabeth Bayley Seton,* p. 107.

109   obtain Bread for her children: CW I, p. 362.

110   His cool and quiet judgment: CW I, p. 318.

110   Does your Sister and her husband: Melville, *Elizabeth Bayley Seton,* p. 113.

110   Some proposals have been made: CW I, p. 394.

110   a pleasant dwelling: CW I, p. 396.

110   Georgetown curriculum and uniforms: Annabelle M. Melville, *Louis William DuBourg* (Loyola University Press, 1986), vol. II, pp. 50, 51.

111   Mathew Carey: Jay P. Dolan, *In Search of an American Catholicism: A History of Religion and Culture in Tension* (Oxford University Press, 2002), pp. 19, 22, 25.

111   a bad habit which spoils books: Ellin M. Kelly, *Elizabeth Seton's Two Bibles* (Our Sunday Visitor, 1977), p. 20.

111   Eternity: CW II, p. 190.

112   if she persevered: Melville, *Elizabeth Bayley Seton,* p. 119.

113   Are you a Catholic? ibid.

113   My dear Charlotte: Dirvin, *Mrs. Seton,* p. 193.

113   In respect to your sister: Melville, *Elizabeth Bayley Seton,* p. 120.

113   Mrs. Startin has excused herself: CW II, p. 17.

113   the laughing stock: CW I, p. 423.

113   to pull down our church: CW I, p. 425.

114   the ally of tyranny: John T. McGreevy, *Catholicism and American Free-dom* (Norton, 2003), p. 34.

114   too many masters: Melville, *Louis William DuBourg*, p. 51.

114   both learned and pious. Melville, *Elizabeth Bayley Seton*, p. 113.

115   behaved like an Angel: CW I, p. 414.

115   my rigid, and severe friend: CW I, p. 431.

115   Carroll's joking letter: Annabelle M. Melville, *John Carroll of Baltimore* (Charles Scribner's Sons, 1955), p. 180.

115   Beefsteak and claret: CW I, p. 440.

116   James walked in my room: CW I, p. 469.

116   of flashing intellect and wit: Melville, *Louis William DuBourg*, p. 179.

116   Dialogue, Dubourg and the sea captain: ibid., p. 34.

116   Come to us, Mrs. Seton: CW II, p. 18.

116   We want example more than talents: ibid.

117   I believe you are destined: White, *Mother Seton, Mother of Many Daughters*, p. 143.

117   My own Cecil would scarcely believe: CW II, p. 2.

117   Friday, Saturday and *Sunday* are past: CW II, p. 3.

117   Do I go among strangers?—No!: CW II, p. 5.

CHAPTER EIGHT

118   Fells Point: Frank R. Shivers Jr. *Walking in Baltimore: An Intimate Guide to the Old City* (Johns Hopkins University Press, 1995), pp. 31, 42.

119   a little *bijou* of a thing: Frances Trollope, *Domestic Manners of Americans* (1832; Bell, 1904), p. 183.

119   Human nature could scarcely bear it: CW II, p. 7.

120   I was in the arms of the loveliest being: ibid.

120   If one year's experience persuades us: Melville, *Louis William DuBourg,* p. 162.

120   a neat, delightful mansion: CW II, p. 15.

120   Imagine twenty Priests: CW II, p. 65.

121   Jesus on the breast of Mary: CW IIIb, p. 19.

121   There is your rest: CW II, p. 7.

121   I find the difference of situation so great: CW II, p. 9.

122   To the Roman Catholics of the United States: Melville, *John Carroll of Baltimore,* p. 112.

122   a ridiculous and childish custom: Ray Allen Billington, *The Protestant Crusade* (Quadrangle, 1938), p. 19.

123   Maryland Society for Promoting Useful Knowledge: Francis F. Beirne, *The Amiable Baltimoreans* (E. P. Dutton, 1951), p. 129.

123   "An Address to the Roman Catholics of North America": ibid.

123   Mathew Carey; Enlightenment Catholicism: Dolan, *In Search of an American Catholicism*, pp. 19, 22, 25.

123   Can there be anything more preposterous: Stephen Klugewicz, *John Carroll and the Creation of the Catholic Church in America* (The Imaginative Conservative, July 5, 2011) vol. I, pp. 148, 149.

123   above all men: Melville, *John Carroll of Baltimore,* p. 220.

123   New York is a city of too much consequence: ibid.

124   If we had not devoted ourselves: CW II, p. 30.

124   I should not wish you to know him as I do: CW II, p. 24.

125   My fingers are almost frozen: Robert Seton, *Memoir, Letters, and Journals,* vol. 2, p. 41.

125   I am hard pushed by these charitable Romans: CW I, p. 129.

125   The gentlemen of the Seminary: CW II, p. 19.

125   *the scheme* of these revered gentlemen: CW II, p. 28.

126   It is expected I shall be the Mother of many daughters: CW II, p. 34.

126   ALONE WITH GOD: CW II, p. 22.

126   *My* Cecilia, you will *triumph*: CW II, p. 20.

127   Not one of them but anticipates the sorrow: CW II, p. 38.

127   Do not fail to send me five yards: CW II, p. 36.

127   What would amuse you: CW II, p. 41.

127   My Boys appear to be the most innocent: CW II, p. 38.

127   Now pray tell me Julia: CW II, p. 39.

128   Not to moralize or repine: CW I, p. 145.

128   folly, madness, bigotry and superstition: CW II, p. 492.

128   They are much more useful to us: CW II, p. 42.

128   From half past five in the morning: CW II, p. 41.

129   My dearest Antonio: CW II, pp. 44, 45.

130   This morning at communion: CW II, p. 52.

130   Bring only a black gown and flannels: CW II, p. 72.

130   I thought, 'He has money': White, *Mother Seton, Mother of Many Daughters,* p. 164.

131   she strangled herself: Jo Ann Kay McNamara, *Sisters in Arms: Catholic Nuns Through Two Millennia* (Harvard University Press, 1998), p. 546.

131   The dear ones have their first claim: CW II, p. 146.

132   Your friend is breathing the air of Peace: CW II, p. 48.

132   Mr. Cooper, even while protesting: Dirvin, *Mrs. Seton,* p. 229.

132   You are giving up a certainty: ibid., p. 233.

132   Baltimore Gin Party: Maryland Historical Society, J. Thomas Scharf Collection, 1730s–1892; Beirne, *The Amiable Baltimoreans,* pp. 145, 146.

133   so marked in her appearance and manner: CW II, p. 38.

133   an effectual means of extricating Anna: CW II, p. 60.

CHAPTER NINE

135   We are so far safe: CW II, p. 73.

135   History of Emmitsburg: James A. Helman, *History of Emmitsburg, Maryland* (1906) Emmitsburg Area Historical Society, available online at www.emmitsburg.net/history/.

136   Little Napoleon: CW II, p. 74.

136   excellent, superexcellent priest: CW II, p. 130.

136   half in the sky: CW II, p. 75.

136   If it were not for this engagement: CW II, p. 722.

137   Journey to Emmitsburg: *Mother Rose's Journal,* CW II, pp. 719, 720.

137   a beautiful country place in the mountains: CW II, p. 57.

137   as large as one's hand: Helene Bailey de Barbery, *Elizabeth Seton* (Macmillan, 1927), p. 262.

137   There is my place: ibid., p. 282.

138   We would carry our dinner in a sack: *Mother Rose's Journal,* CW II, p. 725.

139   I shall be at the head of a community: CW II, p. 62.

139   acting like a tyrant: CW II, p. 78.

140   the father and friend of her soul: *Mother Rose White* (St. Joseph's, Emmitsburg, 1936).

140   There has been some very busy persons: CW II, p. 78.

140   obey in silence: Melville, *Elizabeth Bayley Seton,* p. 171.

140   Sisters of Loretto: Margaret Susan Thompson, *History of Women Religious in the United States,* Now You Know Media, disc 3; McNamara, *Sisters in Arms,* p. 618.

141   Our Lord did not give him that place with us: CW II, p. 87.

141   When and how it will end: CW II, p. 149.

142   confusion and want of confidence: CW II, p. 87.

142   not withstanding all the uneasiness: Melville, *Elizabeth Bayley Seton,* p. 175.

142   be fairly obedient: Kelly, *Numerous Choirs,* p. 142.

142   female wolves: "Elizabeth Seton's Founding Community," Sisters of Charity of Cincinnati, www.srcharitycinti.org/about/founding.community.html.

143   dummy corporation, Howe and Bates: Robert P. Lockwood, "Maria Monk," *Catholic Heritage,* November–December 1996, pp. 19–21; Ruth Hughes, "The Awful Disclosures of Maria Monk," http://www.english.upenn.edu/~traister/hughes.html.

143   Sisters in the Civil War: Betty Ann McNeil, ed., *Charity Afire: Civil War Trilogy* (Daughters of Charity of St. Vincent de Paul, 2011), pp. 6–12.

144   no other monastery: CW IIIb, pp. 500, 501.

144   To my too worldly mind: Dirvin, *Mrs. Seton,* p. 222.

144   The thought of living out of our valley: CW II, p. 146.

145   Letter from the French nuns: de Barbery, *Elizabeth Seton,* pp. 295, 296.

145   What authority would the Mother they bring: CW II, p. 185.

145   God is like a looking glass: CW IIIb, p. 42.

145   novel things in the United States: Kelly, *Numerous Choirs,* p. 135.

146   I will love her, nurse her, and amuse her: Archives, Mount St. Joseph.

146   Indeed my Julia: CW II, p. 83.

146   schedule of the house: Kelly, *Numerous Choirs,* pp. 129, 130.

147   you will laugh: CW II, p. 89.

147   We might be a very large family: ibid.

148   All love and Peace: CW II, p. 102.

148   Our Harriet is gone: CW II, p. 93.

148   It seems to be the order of divine providence: Melville, *Elizabeth Bayley Seton,* p. 173.

148   a happy event: White, *Mother Seton, Mother of Many Daughters,* p. 182.

149   I can only offer a Mothers heart: CW II, p. 93.

149   I began to think we were all going: CW II, p. 102.

149   We have an elegant little Chapel: CW II, p. 105.

150 Mrs. Bonaparte, who being now an imperial princess: Dirvin, *Mrs. Seton,* p. 323.

150 Oh, the humiliation of it: Thompson, *History of Women Religious in the United States,* disc 3.

150 We have so few in the house: CW II, p. 318.

150 I remember when Anna was six months old: CW II, p. 116.

151 Sisters became sick several at a time: *Mother Rose's Journal,* CW II, p. 725.

151 Sister Ellen's bath: ibid., p. 724.

151 If you will accompany us: CW II, p. 118.

151 A more consoling departure: CW II, p. 123.

152 how hard to be good in Baltimore: White, *Mother Seton, Mother of Many Daughters,* p. 208.

152 The Bishop told me the other day: Melville, *Elizabeth Bayley Seton,* p. 176.

152 We must always rest contented: ibid., p. 178.

CHAPTER TEN

153 I dread the arrival: ibid., p. 164.

154 Certainly I have made no renewal of them: CW II, p. 184.

154 I am free: CW II, p. 172.

154 Everything here is again suspended: CW II, p. 155.

154   at any risk: Melville, *Elizabeth Bayley Seton,* p. 178.

154   a good deal altered: CW II, p. 168.

154   Rose's virtues are truly valued by me: CW II, p. 179.

155   If you should ever be permitted: Melville, *Elizabeth Bayley Seton,* p. 179.

155   Now, behave yourself: Judith Metz, "By What Authority? The Founding of the Sisters of Charity of Cincinnati," *Vincentian Heritage* 20, no. 1 (1999): 97.

155   let their names be heard no more: Mary McCormick, "New Beginnings," *Vision,* Sisters of Charity of New York, Winter 2006–7, p. 5.

156   My days ever the same: CW II, p. 161.

156   Anna you always refused me: Dirvin, *Mrs. Seton,* p. 283.

156   expressive of the romance of his age: CW II, p. 147.

156   as quiet as a puss in the corner: CW II, p. 162.

156   The young DuPavillon: CW II, p. 191.

157   Let me enjoy forever: Melville, *John Carroll of Baltimore,* p. 227.

157   if there must be a bishop in Boston: ibid.

157   What object can a retreat have? CW II, p. 159.

158   Verse: Trumbull, quoted in Linda Kerber, "Why Should Girls Be Learn'd and Wise?" in *Women and Higher Education in American History: Essays from the Mount Holyoke Sesquicentennial Symposia,* ed. John Mack Faragher and Florence Howe (Norton, 1988), pp. 32, 33.

158   Anna my sweet and precious comfort: CW II, p. 201.

159   like gold brocade: Melville, *Elizabeth Bayley Seton,* p. 188.

159   He will go ten times to visit the sick: ibid., p. 234.

159   I tell you a secret: CW II, p. 425.

160   *The Following of Christ*: CW I, p. 347.

160   On holiness: Joel Giallanza, "Be Saints," *Review for Religious* 70, no. 4 (2011): 391–97.

160   The very thought of your visiting: CW II, p. 172.

161   a change of air: Archives, Mount St. Joseph.

161   I cannot give up the hope: CW II, p. 177.

161   Since the weather is more mild and settled: CW II, p. 182.

162   The music did not answer my expectations: Robert Seton, *Memoir.*

162   Let all be hushed: CW II, p. 204.

163   If we sell our house to pay our debts: CW II, p. 206.

163   You must be in right earnest: Dirvin, *Mrs. Seton,* p. 339.

163   Your little Mother, my darlings: ibid., p. 327.

164   Do you know who I am? ibid., p. 326.

164   *In hearing the faults of their children*: Melville, *Elizabeth Bayley Seton,* p. 222.

165   We were at liberty to adopt these rules or not: *Mother Rose's Journal*, CW II, p. 731.

165   We are determined to form a society: Melville, *Elizabeth Bayley Seton*, p. 190.

165   I am very annoyed: ibid., p. 191.

165   I demand that we form all novices for Kentucky here: ibid., p. 192.

165   Journal of Anna's last illness: CW II, pp. 740–58.

167   You are *men*: Dirvin, *Mrs. Seton,* p. 319.

167   We part, nature groans: CW II, p. 117.

167   the Friend, the Companion, and Consolation: CW I, p. 57.

167   the grief of a mother: Judith Metz and Virginia Wiltse, *Sister Margaret Cecilia George: A Biography* (Sisters of Charity of Cincinnati, 1989), p. 6.

167   For three months after Nina was taken: CW II, p. 224.

168   I left you, dear Sister: Dirvin, *Mrs. Seton,* p. 322.

168   it seems that he is not there for me: CW II, p. 704.

168   the dark, tangled visceral aspect of Christianity: John Updike, *Rabbit Run* (Everyman's Library, 1995), p. 203.

168   uncertain of reunion: CW II, p. 228.

168   the companion of worms and reptiles: ibid., p. 229.

169   Tell her the front door: CW II, p. 252.

169   lovely little wood: Melville, *Elizabeth Bayley Seton,* p. 230.

169   vows: CW IIIb, pp. 563, 564.

169   poverty: CW IIIb, pp. 502–05.

170   chastity: CW IIIb, pp. 506–10.

170   Rules, prudence, subjections: CW II, p. 594.

170   obedience: CW IIIb, pp. 510–12.

170   Silence here at all times: CW II, p. 672.

171   This is not a country, my dear one: CW II, p. 499.

CHAPTER ELEVEN

172   as different as sun and moon: CW II, p. 132.

172   an enormous young man: CW II, p. 379.

172   my giant: CW II, p. 388.

172   They are so far children of exemplary conduct: CW II, p. 277.

172   the thread of the story; near you: ibid.

173   War of 1812: Jeremy Black, *America as a Military Power: From the American Revolution to the Civil War* (Praeger, 2002), pp. 44–69.

173   Dolley Madison: Willets, *Inside History of the White House* (Christian Herald, 1908), 218–25.

173   It was an awful spectacle to behold: Kelly, *Numerous Choirs,* vol. I, p. 170.

174   Truly since the misfortunes of the city of Washington: ibid., p. 175.

174   I take the final resolution with God: CW II, p. 289.

174   letter of advice: CW II, pp. 296–298.

175   My darling lovely gay little Beck: CW II, p. 238.

175   extremely hard; wishing openly: CW II, p. 349.

176   little proud heart: CW II, p. 282.

176   Unanimously agreed: Minutes, Sisters of Charity Council, Archives, Emmitsburg.

176   I am as one stupid and all surprised: Dirvin, *Mrs. Seton,* p. 352.

176   that God will call me soon: CW I, p. 260.

176   Conceived in sin: CW IIIb, p. 80.

177   how could you sell your God: Dirvin, *Mrs. Seton,* p. 342.

177   One trunk contained all our baggage: *Mother Rose's Journal,* CW II, p. 733.

177   You might as well ask a pig about a holy day: ibid.

177   We lived mostly on potatoes: ibid., p. 734.

178   We told her it would never be accepted by us: ibid., p. 736.

178   You take such a *hard* countenance: CW II, p. 293.

178   I did not trouble myself; Oh Sir that awakens my anger: CW II, p. 323.

179   Since we can have but a short life: Archives, Mount St. Joseph.

179   Mrs. Scott asks for you: CW II, p. 343.

179   We hear Peace is declared: CW II, p. 306.

179   almost a mind to scold you: Dirvin, *Mrs. Seton,* p. 365.

180   I long so to know: CW II, p. 337.

180   My child my own and dearest William: CW II, p. 334.

180   Why I love him so much: CW II, p. 356.

180   Richard like all young people drags his chain: CW II, p. 375.

181   I cannot be but sorry: CW II, p. 381.

181   be good and obediant; gossip: CW II, p. 353.

181   I have an ulcer in my breast: CW II, p. 585.

182   It is harder on me than you would imagine: CW II, p. 361.

182   instances of recovery: CW II, p. 416.

182   Rebecca is just so: CW II, p. 362.

183   Write me if you ever see the old captain: CW II, p. 370.

183   It has been constantly drying: CW II, p. 359.

183   They prefer to eat bread and water: Melville, *Elizabeth Bayley Seton,* p. 369.

183   nuns doing priests' housework: Thompson, *History of Women Religious in the United States,* disc 3.

183   The only reason you might have: *Elizabeth Bayley Seton,* p. 254.

184   with what perfect order: ibid., p. 255.

184   so expensive a thing; dolls: CW II, p. 372.

184   Mother do I grow stronger or weaker? CW II, p. 420.

184   Journal of Rebecca's last illness: CW II, pp. 432–45.

185   direct on the little woods: CW II, p. 449.

185   I am well *and at Peace*: CW II, p. 463.

185   I sincerely wish it may be in your power: Dirvin, *Mrs. Seton*, p. 398.

186   description of Margaret George: Metz and Wiltse, *Sister Margaret Cecilia George: A Biography*, p. 6.

186   I write her earnestly about New York: CW II, p. 494.

187   with whom the Sisters will keep a freer intercourse: Melville, *Elizabeth Bayley Seton*, p. 256.

187   It is a mystery of the human spirit: Barbara Misner, *Highly Respectable and Accomplished Ladies: Catholic Women Religious in America, 1790–1850* (Garland, 1988), p. 11, quoting Marcelle Bernstein, *The Nuns* (J. B. Lippincott, 1976).

187   You receive three beings most dear to me: CW II, p. 501.

188   He was not only a meticulous hairdresser: Marie de Lourdes Walsh, *The Sisters of Charity of New York, 1809–1959* (Fordham University Press, 1960), p. 66.

188   Kit keeps so close to me: CW II, p. 449.

188   Here is air exercise fresh milk: CW II, p. 478.

188   Kit's description of gaiety in Philadelphia: Dirvin, *Mrs. Seton,* p. 406.

189   I can see plainly my Kit wishes much to go to New York: CW II, p. 541.

189   advice to Kit: Melville, *Elizabeth Bayley Seton,* p. 262.

190   an old broken bit of furniture: CW II, p. 484.

CHAPTER TWELVE

191   We talk now all day long: CW II, p. 567.

191   so so . . . the more I see of Europe: Archives, Mount St. Joseph.

191   a moral indifference: Dirvin, *Mrs. Seton,* p. 400.

192   a good heart, yet turned to pride and selfishness: Melville, *Elizabeth Bayley Seton,* p. 271.

192   for your people, I mean blacks: ibid., p. 272.

192   a good will and good handwriting: CW II, p. 507.

192   took little interest in young women: Melville, *Elizabeth Bayley Seton,* p. 274.

192   I have two little Harpers with me: CW II, p. 651.

192   Here is my Richard: CW II, pp. 507, 508.

192   excessive indulgence: CW II, p. 556.

192   *you will never want every nerve of my heart*: CW II, p. 473.

193   I write Mr. Barry pressingly: CW II, p. 557.

193   bloodletting: Gilbert R. Seigworth, "Bloodletting over the Centuries," *New York State Journal of Medicine,* December 1980, 2022–28.

194   Ten years are past: Melville, *Elizabeth Bayley Seton,* p. 259.

194   My dearest Sister: Archives, Emmitsburg.

194   I know your uneasiness for me: CW II, p. 574.

195   My own little Darling: CW II, p. 553.

195   You must not blame your own Mother: CW II, p. 554.

195   Perhaps you have conceived your situation: Joseph I. Dirvin, *The Soul of Elizabeth Seton: A Spiritual Portrait* (Ignatius Press, 1990), p. 176.

195   Be perfectly at ease: Letters, Archives, Emmitsburg.

196   Emmitsburg taverns: Melville, *Elizabeth Bayley Seton,* p. 285.

196   bringing disgrace on the Catholic Church: Archives, Archdiocese of Baltimore.

196   I shall not continue in this congregation: ibid.

196   let him go: Melville, *Elizabeth Bayley Seton,* p. 287.

196   a most beautiful frigate: ibid., p. 270.

196   Are you prepared? CW II, p. 590.

197   I am so much better: CW II, p. 614.

198   I am sick, but not dying: CW II, p. 706.

198   this dear dearest thief: CW II, p. 573.

197   people as spiritual beings: Teilhard de Chardin, *The Phenomenon of Man*
       (Wm. Collins Sons Ltd., London; Harper & Row, 1959).

198   the grace of the moment: CW II, p. 402.

198   Mrs. Scott says I am so extremely like you: Dirvin, *Mrs. Seton*, p. 407.

198   I am laughing with God: CW I, p. 290.

198   If you don't see God in the next person you meet: Gandhi, *An Autobiog-
       raphy: The Story of My Experiments with Truth*, trans. Mahadev Desai
       (Beacon Press, 1957).

198   a loss I am quite willing to bear: CW II, p. 581.

198   letter to Robert Harper about Elizabeth: CW II, p. 648.

198   Some politics of Eternity: CW II, p. 637.

198   Anecdote about Sister Mary Elizabeth: CW II, p. 589.

199   with every heart felt good wish: CW II, p. 636.

199   By little caresses and young companions: CW IIIb, p. 646.

199   I think I should have been a traveler too: CW II, p. 632.

199   You know my own beloved friend: CW II, p. 642.

199   Again your restless thoughts: Melville, *Elizabeth Bayley Seton*, p. 289.

200   I try to make my very breathing: CW II, p. 643.

200   I shall come like the prodigal son: Archives, Mount St. Joseph.

200   Now that I'm growing older: ibid.

201   My own love, you can have no idea our anxiety: CW II, p. 650.

201   a miserable place; a protested bill: Melville, *Elizabeth Bayley Seton*, p. 277.

201   Who can I venture to address: CW II, p. 668.

201   To pretend, Sir: Melville, *Elizabeth Bayley Seton*, p. 277.

201   Come, our Mother is dying: ibid., p. 295.

202   so calm, so present, so recollected: ibid.

202   Yes, I bless them and ask their prayers: ibid.

202   dearest old partner of my cares: CW II, p. 671.

202   If the roads had not been so muddy: Marie de Lourdes Walsh, *Mother Elizabeth Boyle: Mother of Charity* (Paulist Press, 1955), p. 26.

202   blowing and puffing all the time: CW II, p. 673.

202   a singular talent for Geography: ibid.

203   My dear Mother is far from recovered: Letters, Archives, Mount St. Joseph.

203   No, dear . . . my eyes are generally closed: Dirvin, *Mrs. Seton,* p. 450.

203   my pain is for Mother: CW II, p. 673.

204   Mr. David, to ask him pardon: Melville, *Elizabeth Bayley Seton,* p. 296.

204   Last Will and Testament: CW II, pp. 770, 771.

204   If any change has taken place: Dirvin, *Mrs. Seton,* p. 452.

204   Elizabeth's last days: CW II, pp. 764–89.

206   Sometimes, when Sisters were talking at recreation: Charles I. White, *Life of Mrs. Eliza A. Seton, Foundress and First Superior of the Sisters of Charity in the United States of America* (Baltimore, 1853), book IX, p. 351.

EPILOGUE

213   Pope John Paul II canonized nearly five hundred saints: John Julius Norwich, *Absolute Monarchs* (Random House, 2011), p. 465.

213   sanctity might be considered only an abstraction: McBrien, *Catholicism,* (HarperCollins, 1994), p. 1114, from Karl Rahner, "Why and How Can We Venerate the Saints?" in *Theological Investigations,* vol. VIII (Seabury Press, 1977), p. 23.

All other material is from the author's research and interviews in Rome, Emmitsburg, Livorno, and New York.

BIBLIOGRAPHY

COLLECTIONS

Bechtle, Regina, SC, and Judith Metz, SC, eds. Elizabeth Bayley Seton: *Collected Writings*, Vols. I, II, IIIa, IIIb. Hyde Park, New York: New City Press, 2000, 2002, 2006.

BOOKS

Barrett, Walter. *The Old Merchants of New York City*. New York: Carleton Publishers, 1863.

Bass, Diana Butler. *A People's History of Christianity: The Other Side of the Story*. New York: HarperCollins, 2009.

Beirne, Francis F. *The Amiable Baltimoreans*. New York: E. P. Dutton, 1951.

Bethune, Joanna. *The Life of Mrs. Isabella Graham*. New York: privately printed, 1839.

Billington, Ray Allen. *The Protestant Crusade*. New York: Quadrangle Books, 1938.

Black, Jeremy. *America as a Military Power: From the American Revolution to the Civil War.* Westport, CT: Praeger, 2002.

Bliven, Bruce Jr. *New York: A History.* New York: W. W. Norton, 1981.

Brodie, Fawn M. *Thomas Jefferson: An Intimate History.* New York: W. W. Norton, 1974.

Brown, Henry Collins. *Old New York, Yesterday and Today.* New York: Valentine's Manual, 1922.

Burrows, Edwin G., and Mike Wallace, eds. *Gotham: A History of New York City to 1898.* New York: Oxford University Press, 1999.

Caspary, Anita M. *Witness to Integrity: The Crisis of the Immaculate Heart Community of California.* Collegeville, MN: The Liturgical Press, 2003.

Chernow, Ron. *Alexander Hamilton.* New York: Penguin Books, 2005.

Chittister, Joan. *The Friendship of Women.* Katonah, NY: BlueBridge, 2006.

———. *Becoming Fully Human.* Franklin, WI: Sheed & Ward, 2005.

Code, Msgr. Joseph B., ed. *Letters of Mother Seton to Mrs. Julianna Scott.* Baltimore: The Chandler Printing Company, 1960.

Collins, Gail. *America's Women: 400 Years of Dolls, Drudges, Helpmates, and Heroines.* New York: William Morrow, 2003.

Cooper, Henry S. F. and Jenny Lawrence, eds. *The New York Society Library: 250 Years.* New York: The New York Society Library, 2004.

Cummings, Kathleen Sprows. *New Women of the Old Faith: Gender and American Catholicism in the Progressive Era.* Chapel Hill: The University of North Carolina Press, 2009.

Damrosch, Leo. *Jean-Jacques Rousseau: Restless Genius*. New York: Houghton Mifflin, 2005.

Dark, James David. *The Gospel According to America*. Louisville, KY: Westminster John Knox Press, 2005.

Davis, Matthew L. *Memoirs of Aaron Burr*. New York: Harper & Brothers, 1836.

Deák, Gloria. *Picturing New York: The City From Its Beginnings to the Present*. New York: Columbia University Press, 2000.

de Barbery, Helen Bailey. *Elizabeth Seton*. Translated by Rev. Joseph B. Code. New York: Macmillan, 1927.

de Chardin, Teilhard. *The Divine Milieu*. Edited by Bernard Wall. New York: Harper and Row, 1960.

———. *The Phenomenon of Man*. London: Wm. Collins Sons Ltd. New York: Harper & Row, 1959.

de Sales, Saint Francis. *Introduction to the Devout Life*. New York: Vintage Spiritual Classics, 2002.

de Tocqueville, Alexis. *Democracy in America*. Translated by Gerald E. Bevan. New York: Penguin Books, 2003.

de Warville, J. Brissot. *New Travels in the United States of America, Performed in 1788*. Cambridge, MA: Belknap Press, 2007.

Dirvin, Rev. Joseph I., CM *Mrs. Seton*. New York: Farrar, Straus and Cudahy, 1962.

———. *The Soul of Elizabeth Seton: A Spiritual Portrait*. San Francisco: Ignatius Press, 1990.

Dolan, Jay P. *The American Catholic Experience: A History from Colonial Times to the Present*. Garden City, New York: Doubleday & Company, 1985.

———. *In Search of an American Catholicism: A History of Religion and Culture in Tension*. New York: Oxford University Press, 2002.

Ellis, Edward Robb. *The Epic of New York City*. New York: Carroll and Graf, 2005.

Ellis, John Tracy. *Catholics in Colonial America*. Benedictine Studies, Baltimore: Helicon Press, 1965.

Ellis, Joseph J. *Founding Brothers: The Revolutionary Generation*. New York: Vintage Books, 2002.

Fraser, Antonia. *Mary Queen of Scots*. New York: Dell, 1971.

Gandhi, Mahatma. *An Autobiography: The Story of My Experiments with Truth*. Translated by Mahadev Desai. Boston: Beacon Press, 1957.

Gelles, Edith B. *Abigail Adams: A Writing Life*. New York: Routledge, 2002.

Gordon, Lyndall. *Vindication: A Life of Mary Wollstonecraft*. New York: Harper-Collins, 2005.

Graham, Isabella. *The Power of Faith*. New York: Kirk & Mercein, 1817.

Greeley, Andrew M. *The Catholic Experience: An Interpretation of the History of American Catholicism*. New York: Doubleday and Company, 1967.

Harris, Neil, David Rothman, and Stephan Thernstrom, eds. "A Reformed Mode of Spelling," *The History of the United States*. New York: Holt, Rinehart & Winston, 1969.

Hague, William. *Life Notes*. Boston: Lee & Shepard, 1888.

Heilbrun, Carolyn G. *Writing a Woman's Life*. New York: W. W. Norton, 1988.

Holifield, E. Brooks. *Theology in America: Christian Thought from the Age of the Puritans to the Civil War*. New Haven, CT: Yale University Press, 2003.

Homberger, Eric. *The Historical Atlas of New York City*. New York: Henry Holt, 1994.

————. *Mrs. Astor's New York*. New Haven, CT: Yale University Press, 2002.

Hunt, Helen LaKelly. *Faith and Feminism: A Holy Alliance*. New York: Atria Books, 2004.

Irving, Washington. *Knickerbocker's History of New York*. 1809. Reprint, New York: Doubleday, Doran, 1928.

Kant, Immanuel. *On History*. Translated by Lewis White Beck. Indianapolis: Bobbs-Merrill, 1963.

Kelly, Ellin M. *Elizabeth Seton's Two Bibles*. Huntington, IN: Our Sunday Visitor, 1977.

————. *Numerous Choirs: A Chronicle of Elizabeth Bayley Seton and Her Spiritual Daughters,* Vol. I, *The Seton Years, 1774–1821*. Evansville, Indiana: Mater Dei Provincialate, 1981.

Kelly, Ellin M. and Annabelle Melville, eds. *Elizabeth Seton: Selected Writings*. New York: Paulist Press, 1987.

à Kempis, Thomas. *The Imitation of Christ*. Translated and edited by Joseph N. Tylenda, SJ. New York: Vintage Books, 1998.

Klein, Milton M., ed. *The Empire State: A History of New York*. Ithaca, NY: Cornell University Press with the New York State Historical Association, 2001.

Lamb, Martha J. *History of the City of New York: Its Origins, Rise and Progress.* New York, Barnes, 1877.

Laverty, Sister Rose Maria, SC. *Loom of Many Threads.* New York: The Sisters of Charity, Mount Saint-Vincent-on-Hudson, 1958.

Levin, Phyllis Lee. *Abigail Adams: A Biography.* New York: Thomas Dunne Books/St. Martin's Press, 2001.

Marie Celeste, SC. *Elizabeth Ann Seton—A Self-Portrait. A Study of Her Spirituality in Her Own Words.* Libertyville, IL: Franciscan Marytown Press, 1986.

———. *The Intimate Friendships of Elizabeth Ann Bayley Seton.* Lanham, MD: University Press of America, 2000.

McBrien, Richard P. *Catholicism.* New York: HarperCollins, 1994.

McCullough, David. *John Adams.* New York: Simon & Schuster, 2001.

———. *1776.* New York: Simon & Schuster, 2005.

McGrath, Alister. *In the Beginning: The Story of the King James Bible and How It Changed a Nation, a Language, and a Culture.* New York: Doubleday, 2001.

McGreevy, John T. *Catholicism and American Freedom.* New York: Norton, 2003.

McNamara, Jo Ann Kay. *Sisters in Arms: Catholic Nuns Through Two Millennia.* Cambridge, MA: Harvard University Press, 1996.

McVickar, John. *The Early Life and Professional Years of Bishop Hobart.* Oxford: Talboys, 1838.

Meacham, Jon. *American Gospel—God, the Founding Fathers, and the Making of a Nation.* New York: Random House, 2006.

Melville, Annabelle M. *Elizabeth Bayley Seton, 1774–1821*. New York: Charles Scribner's Sons, 1951.

————. *John Carroll of Baltimore: Founder of the American Catholic Hierarchy*. New York: Charles Scribner's Sons, 1955.

————. *Louis William DuBourg*. Vol. I, *Schoolman, 1766–1788*. Vol. II, *Bishop in Two Worlds, 1818–1833*. Chicago: Loyola University Press, 1986.

Metz, Judith, SC and Virginia Wiltse. *Sister Margaret Cecilia George: A Biography*. Sisters of Charity of Cincinnati, 1989.

Monaghan, Frank and Marvin Lowenthal. *This Was New York*. New York: Doubleday, Doran, 1943.

Morris, Charles R. *American Catholic: The Saints and Sinners Who Built America's Most Powerful Church*. New York: Vintage Books, 1998.

Murphy, Jim. *An American Plague*. New York: Clarion Books, 2003.

Norton, Mary Beth. *Liberty's Daughters: The Revolutionary Experience of American Women, 1750–1800*. Boston: Little, Brown and Company, 1980.

Norwich, John Julius. *Absolute Monarchs*. New York: Random House, 2011.

Norwood, William Frederick. *Medical Education in the United States Before the Civil War*. Philadelphia: University of Pennsylvania Press, 1944.

Odell, George C. D. *Annals of the New York Stage*. New York: Columbia University Press, 1927.

Pasko, W. W., ed. *Old New York*. New York: 1889–91.

Pomerantz, Sidney I. *New York: An American City, 1783–1803*. New York: Columbia University Press, 1938.

Raffald, Elizabeth. *The Experienced English Housekeeper.* East Sussex, England: Southover Press, 1997.

Randall, Willard Sterne. *Alexander Hamilton: A Life.* New York: HarperCollins, 2003.

Ravitch, Diane, ed. *The American Reader: Words That Moved a Nation.* New York: HarperCollins, 1990.

Roberts, Cokie. *Founding Mothers: The Women Who Raised Our Nation.* New York: HarperCollins, 2004.

———. *Ladies of Liberty: The Women Who Shaped Our Nation.* New York: William Morrow, 2008.

Schneiders, Sandra M. *Beyond Patching: Faith and Feminism in the Catholic Church.* Mahwah, NJ: Paulist Press, 2004.

Seton, Robert. *An Old Family: The Setons of Scotland and America.* New York: Brentano's, 1899.

Shivers, Frank R. Jr. *Walking in Baltimore: An Intimate Guide to the Old City.* Baltimore: The Johns Hopkins University Press, 1995.

Shorto, Russell. *The Island at the Center of the World: The Epic Story of Dutch Manhattan and the Forgotten Colony That Shaped America.* New York: Vintage Books, 2005.

Smith, Thomas E. V. *The City of New York in the Year of Washington's Inauguration.* A. D. F. Randolph, 1889.

Stedman, Ray. *Finding the Will of God.* Grand Rapids, MI: Discovery House Publishing, 1995.

Steele, David N., Curtis Thomas, S. Lance Quinn. *The Five Points of Calvinism: Defined, Defended, Documented.* Phillipsburg, NJ: P&R Publishing, 2004.

Stokes, I. N. Phelps. *The Iconography of Manhattan Island*. New York: Arno Press, Robert H. Dodd, 1915–28; Arno Press, 1967.

Van der Leeuw, J. J. *The Conquest of Illusion*. New York: Knopf, 1928.

Taylor, B. Kim. *The Great New York City Trivia and Fact Book*. Nashville: Cumberland House Publishing, 1999.

Updike, John. *Rabbit, Run*. New York: Everyman's Library, 1995.

Vedder, Henry Clay. *The Reformation in Germany*. New York: Macmillan, 1914.

Walsh, Sister Marie de Lourdes. *Mother Elizabeth Boyle: Mother of Charity*. New York: Paulist Press, 1955.

———. *The Sisters of Charity of New York*. New York: Fordham University Press, 1960.

Wardle, Ralph M. *Mary Wollstonecraft: A Critical Biography*. Lawrence, Kansas: University of Kansas Press, 1951.

Ware, Ann Patrick, ed. *Naming Our Truth: Stories of Loretto Women*. Oakland, CA: Chardon Press, 1995.

Webster, Noah. *The American Spelling Book Containing an Easy Standard of Pronunciation*. Philadelphia: Young & McCullough, 1788.

White, Rev. Charles I. *Mother Seton: Mother of Many Daughters*. Mother Seton Guild, Emmitsburg, MD, 1953.

———. *Life of Mrs. Eliza A. Seton, Foundress and First Superior of the Sisters of Charity in the United States of America*. Baltimore, 1853.

Willets, Gilson. *Inside History of the White House*. New York: The Christian Herald, 1908.

Wills, Garry. *Why I Am a Catholic.* New York: Houghton Mifflin Company, 2003.

Wilson, James Grant, ed. *The Memorial History of the City of New York: From Its First Settlement to the Year 1892.* New York History Company, 1893.

Winterbotham, William. *An Historical, Geographical, Commercial, and Philosophical View of the American United States.* London: Oxford University, 1795.

Wollstonecraft, Mary. *A Vindication of the Rights of Woman,* 1792. Mineola, NY: Dover Publications, 1996.

Wood, Gordon S. *The Radicalism of the American Revolution.* New York: Vintage Books, 1993.

Zinn, Howard A. *A People's History of the United States: 1492–Present.* New York: Harper Perennial Modern Classics, 2005.

MEMOIRS AND JOURNALS

Asbury, Francis. *Journal of Rev. Francis Asbury, 1787–1800.* Wesley Chapel Museum, John Street Methodist Church, New York.

Bethune, Joanna. *The Unpublished Letters and Correspondence of Mrs. Isabella Graham, Selected and Arranged by her Daughter, Mrs. Bethune.* New York, 1838.

Breck, Samuel. *Recollections.* New York Historical Society, 1877.

McCormick, Mary. *New Beginnings.* Vision, Sisters of Charity of New York, Winter 2006–2007.

Seton, Robert. *Memoir and Journals.* Archives, St. Joseph's Provincial House, Emmitsburg, MD.

Washington, George. *Diaries*.

White, Rose. *Mother Rose's Journal*. CW II, Hyde Park, NY: New City Press, 2002.

ARTICLES

From *Vincentian Heritage* 14, no. 2 (1993)

Bechtle, Regina, SC and Fay Trombley, SCIC. "Toward Eternity: Elizabeth's Experience of Suffering and Hope."

Donovan, Mary A., SC. "The Woman Elizabeth Ann Seton: 1804–1812."

Flanagan, Kathleen, SC. "Some Aspects of Elizabeth Seton's Spiritual/Theological World."

Foley, Gertrude, SC. "Elizabeth Seton: A Spirituality for Mission."

Harvey, Anne, SC. "Embracing Eternity in the Present: Elizabeth's Incarnational Spirituality."

Kelly, Ellin M. "Elizabeth Seton: Key Relationships in Her Life, 1774–1809."

Kelly, Margaret J., DC. "Her Doing Heart: Key Relationships in Elizabeth Seton's Life, 1809–1821."

Metz, Judith, SC. "Elizabeth Seton: Her World and Her Church."

Thei, Marilyn, SC. "The Woman Elizabeth Bayley Seton: 1793–1803."

From *Vincentian Heritage* 21 no. 2 (2000)

Bechtle, Regina, SC. "'In the Face of Adversity': The Response of the Vincentian and Charity Families to 9/11."

Clifford, Margaret Marie, DC. "Psalm 9/11."

Flannelly, Jean, SC. "Elizabeth Ann Seton: Model of Contemplative Presence for the 21st Century."

Foley, Gertrude, SC. "Saint Louise de Marillac: Woman of Substance, Woman of God."

Humphreys, Deborah L., SC. "be consoled."

———. "for john."

❧

Bechtle, Regina, SC. "The Impact of Women Religious on the Church of New York." *Review for Religious* 68, no. 3 (2009).

Giallanza, Joel, CSC. "Be Saints: Pathway to a Holy Life." *Review for Religious* 70, no. 4 (2011).

Heaton, Claude. "Yellow Fever in New York City." *Bull Medical Library Association,* 1946.

Hughes, Kathleen, RSCJ. "The Apostolic Visitation: An Invitation to Intercultural Dialogue." *Review for Religious* 69, no. 1 (2010).

Jacobson, Arthur C. *The Medical Times,* 1923.

Klugewicz, Steve. "John Carroll and the Creation of the Catholic Church in America." *The Imaginative Conservative,* July 5, 2011.

Ladenheim, Jules C. "The Doctors' Mob of 1788." *Journal of the History of Medicine and Allied Science* 5 (Winter 1950).

Metz, Judith, SC. "Elizabeth Seton's Spirituality of the Cross." *Review for Religious* 69, no. 3 (2010).

Sherk, Henry H. *New Jersey Medicine,* July–August 2002.

Seigworth, Gilbert R. "Bloodletting Over the Centuries." *New York State Journal of Medicine,* December 1980.

MANUSCRIPTS, ESSAYS, NEWSPAPERS

Evans, Jill. *Olympe de Gouges.* Personal reflection biography, 2007.

Helman, James. *History of Emmitsburg, Maryland.* Emmitsburg Historical Society, 1906.

Hughes, Ruth. "The Awful Disclosures of Maria Monk." http://www.english .upenn.edu/~traister/hughes.html.

Kerber, Linda. *Women and Higher Education in American History: Essays from the Mount Holyoke Sesquicentennial Symposia.* Edited by John Mack Faragher and Florence Howe. Norton, 1988.

McNeil, Betty Ann, DC, ed. *Charity Afire: Civil War Trilogy.* Daughters of Charity of St. Vincent de Paul, 2011.

Merchant's House Museum archives, New York.

Minutes of the Common Council of the City of New York, 1784–1831.

Minutes of the Sisters of Charity Council. Emmitsburg, MD.

New York *Daily Advertiser,* April 15, 1788.

New York Gazette and Weekly Mercury, June 13, 1774.

New York Historical Society. *Slavery,* "The New York Amsterdam News," exhibit, 2005–06.

New-York Journal and Patriotic Register, April 15, 1788.

New York Packet, April 18, 1788.

Parmet, Herbert S. *Commemorating the Bicentennial of the Founding of the Bank of New York, 1784–1984.* History Associates, 1984.

Rochester, Thomas F. *Medical Men and Medical Matters of 1776: Anniversary Address Before the Medical Society of the State of New York.* Albany, 1876.

Scharf, J. Thomas. Collection, 1730s–1892. Maryland Historical Society.

DOCTORAL DISSERTATIONS

Flanagan, Kathleen. "The Influence of John Henry Hobart on the Life of Elizabeth Seton." Union Theological Seminary, 1978.

Metz, Judith. "Elizabeth Bayley Seton of New York: A Woman's Life in the Early Republic." The Union Institute, 2000.

Misner, Barbara. "Highly Respectable and Accomplished Ladies: Catholic Women Religious in America, 1790–1850." The Catholic University of America, 1988.

AUDIO

Thompson, Margaret Susan. *History of Women Religious in the United States:* "Discovering Foremothers;" "From Enclosure to Apostolate;" "New World Initiatives;" "From New Orleans to Maryland;" "Patterns of Founding;" "Early Struggles and Sacrifices;" "Living the Life of a Pioneer American Nun;" "New Country, New Conditions, New Ministries;" "Ethnicity and Assimilation;" "Charism and Personality; Relations—and Tensions—with the Clergy, Parts I and II;" "Success and Standardization;" "Sisters on the Brink of Vatican II;" "Vatican II and Its Aftermath;" "Quantity or Quality?;" "Reaction and Response: Adjusting to New Circumstances." Now You Know Media, 2009. Compact disc.

INDEX